# CORPORATE GOVERNANCE OF
# NON-LISTED COMPANIES

# Corporate Governance of Non-listed Companies

JOSEPH A. McCAHERY
and
ERIK P. M. VERMEULEN

OXFORD
UNIVERSITY PRESS

# OXFORD
### UNIVERSITY PRESS

Great Clarendon Street, Oxford OX2 6DP

Oxford University Press is a department of the University of Oxford.
It furthers the University's objective of excellence in research, scholarship,
and education by publishing worldwide in

Oxford New York

Auckland Cape Town Dar es Salaam Hong Kong Karachi
Kuala Lumpur Madrid Melbourne Mexico City Nairobi
New Delhi Shanghai Taipei Toronto

With offices in

Argentina Austria Brazil Chile Czech Republic France Greece
Guatemala Hungary Italy Japan Poland Portugal Singapore
South Korea Switzerland Thailand Turkey Ukraine Vietnam

Oxford is a registered trade mark of Oxford University Press
in the UK and in certain other countries

Published in the United States
by Oxford University Press Inc., New York

First published 2008

British Library Cataloguing in Publication Data

Data available

Library of Congress Cataloging in Publication Data

Data available

Typeset by Newgen Imaging Systems (P) Ltd., Chennai, India
Printed in Great Britain
on acid-free paper by
Biddles Ltd., King's Lynn, Norfolk

ISBN 978–0–19–920340–6

1 3 5 7 9 10 8 6 4 2

# Preface

As the corporate governance scandals at the beginning of the twenty-first century focused the public debate on how publicly held corporations should be structured, it is hardly surprising that corporate governance has captured the legal and public imagination. Books, articles, and reports on the corporate governance of listed companies abound. Indeed, the focus of corporate governance reforms in developed countries as well as emerging markets has been on board structure, executive compensation, disclosure, the internal and external audit process, and sanctions on director misconduct. That's not all: we have also seen lawmakers create new standards of integrity for auditors, analysts, and rating agencies.

The numerous corporate governance reforms leave the non-listed company, such as family businesses, state-owned, private investor-owned, and joint ventures, as more of a backwater. As the impact of non-listed companies on society is significant, attending adequately to the quality of governance for these firms is not simply a matter of applying the same old legal rules to private firms: it is a matter of getting it right. Moreover, the absence of complete risk diversification and an active market for corporate control holds out the potential for greater risk and reinforces the demand for a separate set of corporate governance mechanisms. Our aim in this book is to contribute to a better understanding of the governance problems of non-listed companies and to provide a new perspective on how the legal rules, institutions, and other mechanisms can address firm-level conflicts as well as conflicts involving third parties and government actors.

In writing this book, we have benefited from the valuable comments and advice of many individuals. We would particularly like to thank John Armour, Marco Becht, Arnoud Boot, Louis Bouchez, William Bratton, William Callison, Douglas Cumming, Christoph van der Elst, Luca Enriques, Merritt Fox, Leo Goldschmidt, Gérard Hertig, Masato Histake, Grant Kirkpatrick, Reinier Kraakman, Florencio Lopez-de-Silanes, Wilhelm Niemeier, Enrico Perotti, Luc Renneboog, Larry Ribstein, Jun Saito, Armin Schwienbacher, Tom Smith, Allan Vestal, and Dirk Zetzsche. We also thank the many participants in seminars and workshops who received early drafts of some of the chapters in the book, and who provided helpful comments and suggestions. Among these were the participants at the OECD Russian Roundtable in Paris, March 2004 and Moscow, November 2004; participants in the RIETI Workshop in Tokyo, August 2005; participants in the RIETI-CARF Policy Symposium in Tokyo, February 2006, participants in the OECD/IFC Conference on Corporate Governance of Non-listed companies in Istanbul, April 2005; participants in the OECD experts meeting on Corporate Governance of Non-Listed Companies in Paris, December 2005;

participants at the Indian Ministry of Company Affairs/OECD Policy Dialogue on Corporate Governance in India in New Delhi, February 2006, participants in the OECD experts meeting on Private Equity in Paris, June 2007, and participants in the fifth European Company and Corporate Governance Conference in Berlin, June 2007.

We would also like to thank a number of students of the Tilburg University LLM programme in International Business Law who have provided very helpful research assistance to us: Gulkiz Bayrak (2005), Sandrine Dumont (2005), Aniek Hos (2007), Vladimir Kordos (2006), José Miguel Mendoza (2007), and Dominika Schweighoferova (2006). We are grateful to Wikke Hulsbosch for assisting us in analysing the use of the UK Limited in the Netherlands. We would like to thank James J Risser for his expert assistance in reviewing the final manuscript.

We would like also to acknowledge research support from a number of organizations: the Amsterdam Center for Corporate Finance (ACCF), the Amsterdam Center for Law and Economics (ACLE), the Center for Company Law at Tilburg University, the Tilburg Law and Economics Center (TILEC), the Organization for Economic Cooperation and Development (OECD), The Netherlands Ministry of Economic Affairs, The Netherlands Authority for the Financial Markets (AFM), and the Business Register Interoperability throughout Europe (BRITE) project.

We owe a large debt to our families. Joseph McCahery is immensely grateful to his wife, Coby, for her encouragement, understanding, and advice and to his daughter, Meagan, for her patience and good humour during the period which he worked on the book.

Finally, we would like to thank our editors at Oxford University Press, John Louth and Gwen Booth, for their support and professionalism.

Joseph A McCahery
Erik PM Vermeulen

# Summary Contents

# Contents

# List of Figures

# List of Tables

# Table of Cases

# Table of Legislation and Guidelines

EUROPEAN

*Regulations*

# INTERNATIONAL

# List of Abbreviations

| | |
|---|---|
| AETS | *Application Européene de Technologies et de Services* |
| AG | *Aktiengesellschaft* |
| AICPA | American Institute of Certified Public Accountants |
| AIM | Alternative Investment Market |
| ARB | Accounting Research Bulletin |
| BV | *Besloten Vennootschapmet beperkte Aansprakelijkheid* |
| CAD | Computer Aided Design |
| CAM | Computer Aided Manufacturing |
| CEO | chief executive officer |
| CFO | chief financial officer |
| CLRFC | Company Legislation and Regulatory Framework Committee |
| COO | chief operating officer |
| DG | Directorate General |
| DTI | Department of Trade and Industry |
| EC | European Community |
| ECGI | European Corporate Governance Institute |
| ECJ | European Court of Justice |
| ECU | European Currency Unit |
| EEIG | European Economic Interest Grouping |
| EPC | European Private Company |
| EU | European Union |
| EUV | extreme ultra-violet |
| EUVA | EUV Association |
| EVCA | European Venture Capital Association |
| FASB | Financial Accounting Standards Board |
| FATF | Financial Action Task Force |
| FDI | foreign direct investment |
| FT | *Financial Times* |
| FTA | free trade agreement |
| GAAP | generally accepted accounting principles |
| GmbH | *Gesellschaft mit beschränkter Haftung* |
| GNI | gross national income |
| GP | general partner |
| IAS | International Accounting Standard |
| IASB | International Accounting Standards Board |
| IFRS | International Financial Reporting Standard |
| IPO | initial public offering |
| IRC | Internal Revenue Code |
| IRS | Internal Revenue Services |
| IT | information technology |
| J-LLC | Japanese limited liability company |

| | |
|---|---|
| J-LLP | Japanese limited liability partnership |
| JPY | Japanese yen |
| KapCoRiLiG | *Kapitalgesellschaften- und Co-Richtlinie-Gesetzes* |
| KK | *Kabushiki Kaisha* |
| LBO | leveraged buyout |
| LLC | limited liability company |
| LLP | limited liability partnership |
| LP | limited partner |
| MBCA | Model Business Corporation Act |
| MBI | management buyin |
| MBO | management buyout |
| METI | Ministry of Economy, Trade, and Industry |
| MoMiG | *Gesetzes zur Modernisierung des GmbH-Rechts und zur Bekämpfung von Missbräuchen* |
| NASDAQ | National Association of Securities Dealers Automated Quotations |
| NAV | net asset value |
| OECD | Organization for Economic Cooperation and Development |
| OOO | Limited Liability Company (Russia) |
| R&D | research and development |
| RIA | Regulatory Impact Assessment |
| RULLCA | Revised Uniform Limited Liability Act |
| RULPA | Revised Uniform Limited Partnership Act |
| RUPA | Revised Uniform Partnership Act |
| SAS | *société par actions simplifiée* |
| SBA | Small Business Administration |
| SBIC | small business investment company |
| SCE | European Cooperative Society |
| SE | *societas Europaea* (European company) |
| SEA | Single European Act |
| SEC | Securities and Exchange Commission |
| SMEs | small and medium-sized enterprises |
| SORP | Statement of Recommended Practice |
| SPE | special purpose entity |
| ULLCA | Uniform Limited Liability Company Act |
| UNIZO | *Unie van Zelfstandige Ondernemers* |
| UPA | Uniform Partnership Act |
| VC | venture capital |
| VOC | *Vereenigde Oostindische Compagnie* |
| VPAG | *Vereinigung der Privaten Aktiengesellschaften* |
| WFBV | *Wet op de formeel buitenlandse vennootschappen* |
| YK | *Yugen Kaisha* |

# 1

# The Corporate Governance Framework of Non-listed Companies

## 1. Three Pillars of the Governance Framework

The new millennium is characterized and shaped by a dynamic and unparalleled change in corporate governance practices worldwide. Several finance-ridden scandals have provided new momentum for introducing important legal and regulatory reforms. Certainly the scandals were not only instrumental in moving corporate governance up the policy agenda, but also in making corporate governance an integral part of the day-to-day decision-making process of public firms. To be sure, managerial abuses have been around for as long as widely dispersed investors poured their money into risky ventures, such as the Dutch East India Company, and, as always, policy-makers and lawmakers have attempted to mitigate the underlying governance failures and errors (Ferrarini 2005). However, corporate governance discussions have never been of this magnitude in both an academic and geographic sense. It has become a common view that the current corporate governance movement has tended to overreact by creating too many and cumbersome rules which do not seem to prevent corporate failures (De Jong 2006). Unchecked, this trend could jeopardize entrepreneurship and long-term economic growth. For instance, corporate governance regulations have induced small firms to rethink their stock exchange listing (Kamar, Karaca-Mandic, and Talley 2006). More worryingly, the corporate governance pressure on top executives and the stiff penalties for violations make start-up companies reluctant to use an initial public offering (IPO) as a next financing stage, thereby hampering their performance and development.[1] This prompts questions about the 'one-size-fits-all' mentality of policy-makers, lawmakers, and gatekeeper institutions (Arcot and Bruno 2006) and the success of ready-made strategies that can be detrimental to the operation and development of non-listed companies.

Though corporate governance reforms specifically address publicly held companies, they arguably affect non-listed firms. Besides pressures from government

---

[1] *Wall Street Journal*, IPO Obstacles Hinder Start-Ups, 25 January 2006. The life cycle of a high-growth start-up will typically have three major financing stages: (1) early-stage financing; (2) expansion financing; and (3) IPO/acquisition/buyout financing.

agencies, external stakeholders (such as customers, lenders, insurance companies, and equity investors) increasingly require non-listed firms to abide by corporate governance rules and principles tailored to the requirements of listed companies. By doing so, these third party stakeholders endeavour to ascertain that the internal governance procedures meet the high reliability standards and deliver current and appropriate information about a firm's financial performance. This development would make non-listed companies 'losers' of the corporate governance reform. In most cases, however, the implementation of portions of the corporate governance reform measures seem to be self-imposed or recommended by auditors in the hope of reducing the cost of capital. Controlling shareholders or board members are often convinced that stronger internal controls and the appointment of independent directors help to improve the quality of the firm's decision-making. What is more, compliance with higher governance standards seems to increase opportunities to sell the company or even take it public.[2]

In this light, the question of the economic effect of the 'one-size-fits-all' approach to corporate governance regulation on the performance of non-listed companies has produced mixed results. On the one hand, it is widely acknowledged that corporate governance rules and principles promote efficiency, transparency, and accountability within firms, thereby improving a sustainable economic development and financial stability. On the other hand, if one takes the view that the corporate governance movement has gone too far, it could very well be argued that non-listed companies do not always benefit from the spillover effect of the application of disproportionate corporate governance rules and principles. Not only are the compliance costs exorbitantly high, but their typical organizational structures also demand an approach different from publicly held firms. Thus, it is altogether clear that a corporate governance framework that is not consistent with the social and economic requirement of non-listed companies will yield imperfections over time and would not achieve the legal strategies to control agency problems and reduce transaction costs.

Our main goal in this book is to provide a full account of non-listed companies and their business organizational needs and to suggest a corporate governance framework that will have a positive impact on the performance and development of these firms. The respective benefits and costs associated with the application of the corporate governance measures for publicly held firms to non-listed companies are explored. The aggressive corporate governance campaign and media attention have created awareness, but have also caused uncertainty among policy-makers and legal professionals as to the scope of the corporate governance regulation. Why? The case has never been stronger for policy-makers to focus their attention on the governance of non-listed companies. The traditional corporate governance discussion does not seek to understand the organization of closely held companies and the conflicts that arise within this type of firm, which is

---

[2] *Wall Street Journal* (J Badal and P Dvorak), 'Sarbanes–Oxley Gains Adherents', 14 August 2006.

evident from the mechanical application of legal strategies of public companies to non-listed firms. Moreover, most of the research on non-listed companies had been done on the economic dimension of private firms and hence the governance dimension to their analysis has been limited. Consequently, it is difficult to say that there is a corporate governance discussion that explicitly deals with the specific problems, mechanisms, and capabilities for addressing the needs of non-listed companies. However, as will be shown in the next chapters, we are beginning to see a trend, now that listed companies and their investors seem to have come to terms with the new and stricter corporate governance measures, toward policy-makers becoming more engaged in providing their non-listed counterparts with a governance framework that will foster strong decision-making, accountability, transparency, and ultimately firm performance.

It becomes even more pressing in the era where private equity funds and hedge funds, which largely have worked within the governance structure of close corporations and partnerships, play an increasingly important role in corporate governance and corporate control. The rapid transformation of activism by hedge funds and private equity funds, which has become so prevalent, is heralded by some as the next corporate governance revolution (Partnoy and Thomas 2007). This activism is characterized typically by mergers and corporate restructurings, increased leverage, dividend recapitalizations, and the replacement of management and board members. To a lesser extent, private equity funds provide a powerful incentive for managers to act in the interest of shareholders and to create firm value. The result has been if a firm is mismanaged, these funds use their capital in a focused and leveraged way so as to take over control and initiate different, more beneficial and effective business strategies. Yet even though they have the potential to impose immense discipline on boards and managers of firms, these equity funds are shrouded in nebulous mystery, obscurity, and complexity. Moreover, private equity funds and, in particular, hedge funds are being accused of neglecting long-term goals and pursuing short-term payoff. The risk involved in investing huge amounts of capital calls for corporate governance measures for investment funds. Hence by focusing on these other forms of non-listed firms, we seek to contribute a better understanding of the advantages and limitations of investor-owned firms, the contractual mechanism used to avoid opportunism by owners, and the market drivers that encourage fund managers to intervene in the governance of publicly listed firms.

A second, perhaps more important, reason to draw attention to non-listed companies is to see how the ongoing pressures of competitive global markets have brought to the fore different organizational arrangements, such as joint ventures, to cover a broad range of multinational firms' activities. The evidence suggests these organizations are important mechanisms for limiting risks, decreasing costs, and increasing economies of scale and scope. Multinational firms enter into worldwide joint ventures to obtain technological know-how. More importantly, globalization and consumerism increasingly push small and medium-sized enterprises to establish joint ventures, both among themselves and together with larger multinational enterprises, when access to manufacturing, distribution, and other assets is either too difficult or costly to create internally. It is therefore not surprising that joint ventures encourage the further development of new technologies and the reduction of international barriers. It is argued that a well-thought-out governance system can enhance the lifespan and success of joint ventures. The question is, however, which mechanisms joint venture partners usually employ to prevent opportunism and encourage value-maximizing outcomes. This book will identify the non-legal and legal mechanisms that facilitate cooperation and stress the positive aspects of introducing hybrid business forms that offer the parties limited liability, a flexible governance structure, and pass-through taxation.

Similar questions arise in relation to the governance of family-owned businesses in which a family has either significant influence or a controlling stake, and which is held either through a holding company, partnership, or other non-listed corporate entity. This form of indirect ownership implies that the effect of the organizational structures and control enhancing measures can often create tensions between different generations of families and between controlling and non-controlling shareholders. Family firms are the leading force in many sectors of the economy. Family-owned businesses promote growth and are generally viewed as job-creating companies (Villalonga and Amit 2006). Sometimes, too, they continue to be highly competitive, particularly in emerging markets, due to their informal structure that often provides effective decision-making procedures and a deep understanding of the market. Despite these built-up competitive advantages, family-owned businesses are often confronted with thorny governance and reorganization issues resulting from dynamic changes in both the family and business life cycle (Ward 2005). With each generation of succession or alteration in business development stage, i.e., start-up, expansion, and maturity, family-owned companies seem less able to draw on previous strengths, which can eventually lead to bankruptcy or dissolution of the firm if no more formal governance structure is adopted. Family-owned businesses with clear governance rules and guidelines, a strong brand, or access to leading-edge technologies are likely to survive and remain successful. While there are a number of successful strategies for family-owned businesses, it could be argued that policy-makers should concentrate their resources on developing solutions that enable families to embrace strategies that promote their long-term success irrespective of the stages of business development. This is especially important as recent empirical work shows large declines, for example, around family CEO appointments leading to significant long-term underperformance (Bennedsen, Pérez-Gonzáles, Nielsen, and Wolfenzen 2007). Not only will improved governance structures provide a more effective means to deal with family matters that affect the business, but also free up managerial resources that are necessary to run the business well, and thereby make it possible for capital-intensive work to remain in a country.[3]

---

[3] Indeed, it seems that there is a positive correlation between family firms' governance and innovation. Since involved family shareholders prioritize long-term growth over short-term profitability, more time is available to develop innovative products. See *Het Financieele Dagblad* (Hein Haenen), 'Innovatie gedijt in familie-bv', 4 October 2006.

In order to determine a policy approach for corporate governance of non-listed companies, this book provides an overview of the current practices and mechanisms for structuring and organizing closely held firms and attempts to explain the incentive structures for adopting an improved corporate governance regime. The corporate governance framework of non-listed companies can roughly be split in three separate pillars. The core pillar focuses on company law which provides rules and standards for registration and formation, organization and operation, distribution of powers and decision-making, exit and dissolution, information and disclosure, fiduciary duties, and liability protection. The second pillar includes contractual mechanisms, such as joint venture agreements and shareholder agreements, that enable parties to contract around irrelevant and inconvenient company law default rules and tailor rights and duties that are more consistent with the organizational requirements of non-listed companies. Due to information asymmetries and bounded rationality which limit the ability of firms to foresee and describe all future contingencies and, hence, hampers the parties to contract into the most optimal governance structure, best-practice principles or guidelines (the third pillar) could assist firms to organize and manage their business in the most effective manner.

As for this third pillar, closely held companies increasingly embrace parts of the corporate governance rules and principles that are tailored to the organization of their publicly held counterparts. Although internal control mechanisms and provisions regarding the composition of the board of management are not a 'must' for adoption, they seem to provide focal point solutions to corporate governance problems among business participants within non-listed companies. The chapters in this book will explore in more detail the reasons for voluntary compliance and evaluate which provisions are used in an attempt to make the organizational structure of non-listed firms more efficient. It is certainly reasonable to infer that best practice mechanisms that are imposed on listed companies contribute to the awareness creation of the importance of good governance and, at the same time, persuade non-listed companies across the board to opt into a well-tailored framework of legal mechanisms and norms. Indeed, examples from the organization of private equity funds, joint ventures, and family-owned businesses illustrate that parties themselves are in the best position to design good governance mechanisms. As we will see, business parties usually design contractually tailored arrangements, which, in combination with company law rules, serve to protect shareholders' and creditors' interests. The chapters suggest that non-listed companies have ample incentives to contract into effective information duties, stringent distribution procedures and participation rights, and minority protections. The recent company law developments in the United States, Europe, and Asia can be explained as a response to the demand for the reduction of regulation and improved legal vehicles that are better positioned to meet the contractual needs of different types of firms to facilitate the smooth running of the business. It is argued that the chances of success depend largely on how the business participants contractually address the economic issues underlying their business venture. The next section will discuss the core problems that business participants must take into account when designing a governance structure that may ultimately create value and boost firm performance.

## 2. The Economic Structure of Non-listed Companies

As noted, corporate governance in the last decade has become a top priority not only for international and national policy-makers and lawmakers, but also for performance-oriented companies wishing to attract investors. The corporate governance reform debate, jump-started by the Internet bubble and recent fraud and accounting scandals,[4] takes up the challenge to promote more effective incentive and monitoring structures that are crucial to designing and controlling the complex set of relationships among management, the board, shareholders, and other stakeholders within firms.[5] Recent corporate governance reforms have altered, among other things, the role of non-executive directors, executive pay, disclosure, the internal and external audit processes, and sanctions on managers' misconduct and self-dealing transactions. The objective of these corporate governance measures is to protect the primary stakeholders of the publicly held company, i.e., the shareholders, from managerial opportunism, thereby creating shareholder value. That is not to say that the interests of other stakeholders are neglected. A culture of honesty and responsibility towards employees, customers, and suppliers enhances business performance and financial growth.

The corporate governance movement, however, focuses mainly on creating mechanisms that are intended to curtail the agency problem between self-interested management and dispersed shareholders. Indeed, the core governance problem of the firm can be explained by the 'agency relationship' in a corporation in which the managers are the agents and the shareholders are the principals. It would be overly costly if shareholders, who are often small and numerous, were involved in the daily management of the firm. Since they are usually only interested in the company's dividend policy and share price levels, shareholders may lack the expertise and competency to take part in the strategic decision-making process.[6] The transfer of effective control to a team of specialists (i.e., the

---

[4] During the Internet bubble, important ingredients for market failure were present: (1) corporate malfeasance; (2) conflict of interests; (3) lack of oversight; and (4) inconsistent controls. Many financial crises followed—for instance, Enron, Adelphia, HealthSouth, Worldcom, Parmalat, Ahold, Shell, and Vivendi. New Internet opportunities combined with opportunism, abundant capital investments, and reduced transaction costs through online trading caused unrealistic investor expectations. The use of off-balance sheet transactions with special purpose vehicles made effective supervision almost impossible.

[5] Cf OECD 2004.

[6] Shareholders who are prepared to undertake the financial risk are not necessarily equally suited and talented to make the appropriate management decisions about the allocation of the firm's resources.

board of management) avoids the bureaucratic costs of collective decision-making. The delegation of control, however, leads to substantial monitoring costs, as opportunistic managers may be inclined to exploit collective action problems that bar effective monitoring by shareholders.[7]

It is generally recognized that this principal–agent problem is due to managers having superior information on investment policies and the firm's prospects. Managers tend to be better informed, which allows them to pursue their own goals without significant risk. Consequently, shareholders find it difficult, due to their own limitations and priorities, to prompt managers to pursue the objectives of the firm's owners. Information and collective action problems not only prevent close monitoring of management performance, but also enable directors and managers to develop a variety of techniques to extract profits and private benefits from the firm for their own interests. In addition to monitoring costs, the disparity between ownership and control leads to a number of other managerial transaction costs that are likely to frustrate firm performance: (1) exorbitant compensation and remuneration; (2) replacement resistance; (3) resistance to profitable liquidation or merger; (4) excessive risk taking; (5) self-dealing transfer pricing; (6) allocation of corporate opportunities; and (7) power struggles between managers.

The applicability of the traditional principal–agent theory to non-listed corporations is questionable. Problems that are related to publicly held firms are not necessarily present in their non-listed counterparts. To see this, we should distinguish between two extreme types of non-listed firms. On the one hand, there are so-called 'open', non-listed firms, such as companies with the potential to go public in the short term and unlisted mass-privatized companies with a relatively high number of shareholders.[8] On the other hand, there are contractual arrangements in which the firm-owners retain substantial autonomy and the small partnerships in which the owners are active managers themselves. A third category of firms includes the larger companies that have neither listed shares nor the direct intention to go public. This book will focus on the middle group of companies, in particular family-owned companies and joint ventures.[9] This type of company is often characterized by the three-way conflict between controlling shareholders, managers, and minority shareholders (Berglöf and Claessens 2004).

To be sure, since controlling shareholders dominate both listed and non-listed firms through their indirect and direct influence on board decisions, it might be

---

[7] Rational shareholders have incentives to free-ride on the costly monitoring efforts of other shareholders. Attempts to engage in collective monitoring will therefore fail if a few shareholders bear the entire cost, but receive only a portion of the benefits.

[8] In transition economies, many socially owned companies entered directly into mass privatization programmes through which shares were distributed freely to insiders, privatization and other funds, and citizens.

[9] This group of companies also contains group-owned companies, state-owned, and private-investor-owned companies.

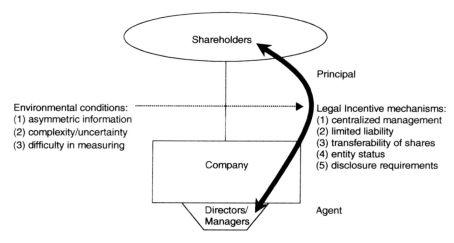

**Figure 1.1.** Principal–agent problem in listed companies
*Source*: Adapted from <www.encycogov.com>.

argued that these firms share many of the same governance problems (Bratton and McCahery 1999). However, the potential three-way conflict in publicly held companies is mitigated by gatekeepers' role in reducing information asymmetries between shareholders and in detecting fraud and other governance deficiencies. In contrast, the shareholders in non-listed companies have fewer market mechanisms to restrict opportunistic behaviour. These companies continue to rely on bank and internal financing and, in some cases, private equity sources for expansion and growth. It is suggested that the typical organizational structure of non-listed companies demand an approach different from listed firms. Indeed, a corporate governance framework for non-listed companies is highly contractual in nature. By drafting their agreement the business parties can choose among different sources of corporate governance mechanisms and techniques, thereby relying more or less on 'softer' mechanisms.

For instance, some characterize the relationship between an entrepreneur and a venture capitalist as a 'pure agency relationship' in which the entrepreneur is the agent and the venture capitalist is the principal.[10] From this perspective, the

---

[10] In this chapter, we use an example from the venture capital industry. Nowhere are the principal–agent problems more intense and proportionately more significant than in this area. Besides the agency relationship described in this section, another agency relationship exists in the venture capital market. As we will see in Chapter 6, venture capitalists act as agents for external investors, who invest in entrepreneurial venture through an intermediary rather than directly. This agency problem is furthermore likely to be particularly difficult. There is inevitably a high degree of information asymmetry between the venture capitalists, who play an active role in the portfolio companies, and their external investors, who are not able to closely monitor the prospects of each individual investment. Although the agency relationship is quite obvious in venture capital deals, it is comparable to the relationship between the shareholders and managers in a publicly held corporation or the relationship

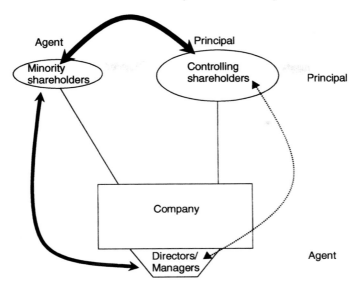

**Figure 1.2.** Principal–agent problem in non-listed companies

venture capitalist may encounter many complex and costly problems that need to be addressed contractually. Monitoring costs are substantial in high-growth start-ups. Venture capitalists invest large stakes in entrepreneurs about whose abilities they have less than perfect knowledge. They consequently need to monitor and bond the entrepreneur closely, as basic problems of shirking and opportunism exist from start-up and expansion until the financial buyout stage. The impossibility of complete risk diversification and the absence of an active market for shares emphasize the importance of monitoring. Empirical research shows that monitoring costs will increase 'as assets become less tangible, growth options increase, and asset specificity rises' (Gompers 1995).

Nevertheless, venture capitalists tend to monitor their investments through active participation, namely by due diligence, establishing a relationship with the start-up businesses' managers and by sitting on their board of directors. Whilst involvement in key corporate functions tends to limit moral hazard problems, information asymmetries are likely to persist and can potentially create significant value dilution for investors. Information asymmetries are likely to arise from two principal sources: (a) the entrepreneur has information unavailable to the venture capitalist; and (b) the entrepreneur's information is often distorted by overestimating his chances. The first kind of information concerns the actual

between the controlling and minority shareholders in family firms and joint ventures. However, as will be described in this book, various governance structures have been designed in practice to address similar problems in firms with different characteristics and preferences.

product, technology, and market, as well as the quality, ethics, and fortitude of the entrepreneurial team, whereas the second kind could diverge dramatically from reality due to the entrepreneur's personal attachment to the venture and the feeling that his bright idea will definitely yield the expected wealth. Nevertheless, to a certain extent the venture capitalists must contemplate the opposite interests of the business's founder in order not to destroy the incentive to the latter to be prepared to go to any lengths to make the venture a success.

Conflicting interests bear particularly on the control over the business and issues involving the venture capitalists' means of exit. Venture capitalists typically choose to exit the venture either through an IPO, transferring their shares piecemeal, or by trade sale. In the final stage, the venture capitalists reap the fruits of their investment, while the entrepreneur hopes to recoup control over 'his' firm. It comes as no surprise that the nature and costs of exit are also shaped by the venture's internal governance structures and *ex ante* contracts.

Whilst the literature on venture capital emphasizes the one-sided moral hazard issues that characterize the relationship between venture capitalists and start-up firms, this relationship cannot be explained exclusively in such terms. We now recognize that to a certain extent the relationship resembles a 'double-sided moral hazard problem', with each party contributing resources so as to maximize their joint wealth. In order for the venture to succeed, the (leading) venture capitalist must be willing to provide the entrepreneur with 'value-added' services, if the venture has the chance to raise its performance. The importance of these services has been demonstrated by the setback of the 'new economy' at the beginning of the twenty-first century, which showed that the provision of capital alone is usually not enough to fertilize promising ventures. Value-added services involve identifying and evaluating business opportunities, including management, entry, or growth strategies; negotiating further investments; tracking the portfolio firm and coaching the firm participants; providing technical and management assistance; and attracting additional capital, directors, management, suppliers, and other key stakeholders and resources. Since these non-financial contributions are a substantial element of the venture capital relationship, it might be argued that the entrepreneur, in obtaining these services from the venture capitalist, is also subject to shirking and opportunism. Entrepreneurs often believe that venture capitalists either fail to meet their obligation to provide value-added services, or try to renegotiate the contract, including their promise to add services, as soon as they obtain more leverage.

Nevertheless, the documentation for venture capital investments is usually silent on the breach of venture capitalists. It is argued that the fear of damage to their reputation gives venture capitalists sufficient incentives to refrain from opportunistic behaviour. The market for reputation may serve as a solution to agency problems or conflicts of interest between the entrepreneur and venture capitalists, if it is both quickly and accurately accessible to entrepreneurs. This appears to be the case when both sides of the market are relatively concentrated, both numerically and geographically, and venture capital funds specialize in portfolio firms geographically near to the fund's office.

Indeed, relationships within firms are largely governed by non-legal rather than legal norms and principles. In China, for instance, the so-called 'Guanxi'—which can be defined as a network of relationships built on trust and reputation—is often considered as the most important factor in the success of foreign joint venture projects. However, the asymmetry between the shareholders of a company often give a party an incentive to engage in opportunistic behaviour and shirking which is not easily solved by non-legal mechanisms. In these instances, the business parties and their legal advisers may attempt to deal with the so-called 'moral hazard problem' contractually.[11] However, these contractual mechanisms are sometimes costly solutions due to private information, strategic behaviour, and inexperienced judges. Moreover, if the gains of opportunism are very large, implicit and explicit contracts may be insufficient to limit controlling shareholders from engaging in grabbing and stealing. In these cases, company law and soft law mechanisms, such as principles and best-practice provisions, help fill the gaps in the firm's contract by defining and setting forth techniques and strategies that parties would have reasonably contracted if there were no costs involved in drafting a governance arrangement.

Given that non-listed companies are widely regarded as job-creating engines of the modern economy, policy-makers and lawmakers must become more engaged in providing these firms with a governance framework that will foster strong decision-making, accountability, transparency, and ultimately firm performance. The rapid pace of technological change and the decreasing international barriers to trade over the past decade have not only created new strategic and organizational opportunities for firms, but have also made them more vulnerable to risks. This put a premium on lawmakers to devise both at the national and international level the most efficient rules and standards as part of their long-term strategy to foster innovation and entrepreneurship, to help these companies fully exploit the new opportunities and adjust more easily to immediate uncertainty they face. Indeed, a shift in the focus from publicly held companies to non-listed companies is important, because, as we have noted earlier, the majority of firms are not listed and ownership and control are usually not completely severed. Even though governance is only one of many determinants of investment and expansion decisions by firm owners and investors (there is little doubt that the core considerations affecting these decisions are operational and macroeconomic), the changed economic environment in which firms operate makes them increasingly sensitive to governance issues. It is therefore necessary to learn more about the design and content of the legal corporate governance framework of non-listed companies.

---

[11] Two types of opportunistic behaviour should be distinguished: moral hazard and hold-up. Moral hazard arises because contracts are inherently incomplete and imperfectly specified. When a party's actions are not verifiable and contracted for directly, and information about his behaviour is costly, that party has an opportunity to bias his actions in his own interest.

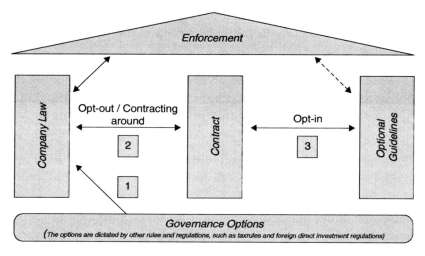

**Figure 1.3.** The legal corporate governance framework

As noted above, the legal corporate governance framework of non-listed companies can roughly be split into three separate pillars (see Figure 1.3). The core pillar focuses on company law. The second pillar includes contractual mechanisms, such as articles of association, investors rights agreements, and shareholder agreements, that enable parties to contract around irrelevant and inconvenient company law default rules and tailor rights and duties that are more consistent with their organizational priorities. Due to information asymmetries and bounded rationality which limit the ability of firms to contract into the most optimal organizational structure,[12] soft-law measures could fill gaps in the first two pillars and allow firms to achieve a stronger governance structure.

Indeed, the final pillar includes best-practice principles to help participants to organize and manage their business in the most effective manner. Such measures should not enshrine principles and norms that are a 'must' for adoption. These principles should be viewed as a form of advice. In that respect, they serve several functions: (1) they provide the business participants with recommended solutions to complement the contractual flexibility of the company law rules; (2) they provide focal point solutions to corporate governance problems among business participants; and (3) they are meant to assist business participants in the interpretation and implementation of good governance practices.

---

[12] People intend to act rationally, but they are simply not able to foresee and describe all future contingencies in a contract. As a consequence, economists claim that people are 'boundedly rational' (Williamson 1985).

### 3. Overview

The chapters in this book are divided into three parts. The first part introduces and discusses the first pillar. It evaluates the role of company law in formulating effective solutions to the core agency problems that arise in non-listed companies. Our work focuses on the contractual theory of the firm, which provides that company law mostly comprises default rules, which has been disputed insofar as the public corporation is concerned. This book describes how the creation of clear and simple default rules, tailored with the features of non-listed companies in mind, will not only help to minimize transaction costs but provide benefits for participants in these firms and their relationships. Chapter 2 recounts the history of corporate law from the development of a joint venture business form (*commenda*) that facilitated the networking of entrepreneurs and investors with their opposing interests to the recent initiatives that help to foster the legal infrastructure needed to keep a modern economy in gear. This chapter suggests that the company and securities law framework that gradually emerged in the wake of earlier stock market bubbles and governance failures is not sufficient to the task of curbing abuses within non-listed companies and inadequate to fostering a competitive environment which assists business parties to write equilibrium contracts. We argue that policy-makers and lawmakers have drawn attention to other legal measures that serve to minimize the specific agency, adverse selection, and moral hazard problems inherent in the governance of non-listed companies. This resulted, we argue, in a 'one-size-fits-all' corporate form for non-listed companies. Chapter 3 addresses the manner in which European legislators have responded to increased corporate mobility, which set in train the transformation of the close corporation form into a more flexible, all-purpose vehicle. Rigid formalities and capital maintenance rules locked the evolution of company law in a certain path, and so thwarted the emergence of more flexible legislation. Company law was mandatory in nature and made firms highly immobile until the path-breaking decisions of the European Court of Justice, involving the freedom of establishment of foreign corporations by member states, which introduced the possibility for existing firms to move across borders. Because mobility increases pressure on national lawmakers, who are prone to defending various interest group preferences, they are inclined to identify legal reforms that have the potential to be more cost-effective and more closely aligned to the changing requirements of many types of firms. In Chapter 4, we illustrate how competitive pressures could open up further opportunities for reform-mined lawmakers, who were previously blocked in their efforts to undertake company law reforms. These pressures, along with the influence activities of interest groups, gave rise to a flexible menu of partnership-type structures in the United States, which thus resulted in the erosion of traditional restrictions on the internal structure of legal business forms. These chapters show the large benefits from the offering of company law techniques that are effective in dealing with internal decision-making procedures, the conflicts between majority and minority shareholders, and the relations between the firm and third parties.

In the next part, in contrast to the previous chapters, we examine the governance framework for non-listed companies that is largely based on private ordering. Chapter 5 shows that hybrid vehicles usually offer businesses the freedom to contractually establish the rights and obligations within their organizational structure, which accounts for the growing popularity of these forms for pooled investments and other risky ventures. While there is great demand to the utilization of these forms, the ever-changing nature of the business environment confirms the importance of flexible provisions giving parties not only the opportunity to contract around the company law default rules, but also permitting them to contract into additional protective measures that reflect their preferences. In Chapter 6, we take this argument further by looking closer at the contractual governance structure of private equity and hedge funds. This chapter shows that, while both fund types rely on similar features of the limited partnership form to manage the risks and monitor investment decisions, the trend toward contractual convergence nevertheless is incomplete due to investor and other market pressures.

Even though it is commonplace that business parties themselves are in the best position to bargain for the optimal governance structure of their venture, the next two chapters indicate that optional guidelines and more responsive regulation could assist the business parties in overcoming the costs and deficiencies of legal contracting. Furthermore, these chapters make clear that several soft law initiatives in this area have been heralded as a solution to corporate governance issues in non-listed companies. Chapter 7 deals explicitly with the gap-filling function that best practice guidelines play in improving the contractual relations between parties in closely held companies. We will see that besides the enhancing effect on businesses, industry guidelines can serve another important goal as a self-regulatory mechanism in response to political pressures. We show that optional guidelines can offer the public important information about how the industry operates. In Chapter 8, which is the only chapter that deals with external market regulation, we make clear that the flexible corporate and business forms, which serve a diverse range of needs for businesses, can under special circumstances be used to undertake illicit and illegal activities. The investigations into recent financial scandals revealed that the fraudulent activities of major European and American corporations were facilitated by the misuse of offshore subsidiaries and other special purpose vehicles. It turns out that the prevalence of illicit related party transactions, which served not only to assist in tunnelling out corporate assets, but also to provide the means to cover up losses and manipulate market disclosures, caused regulators to make important legislative changes and increased enforcement efforts. The analysis in this chapter shows that a range of mechanisms, including optional guidelines, is needed to provide proper financial market oversight and to address the abusive or illegal activities by company law forms. Since many of these techniques are designed by financial intermediaries and lawyers, reformers have naturally had to think about their role in stimulating the abuse of legal entities, and correspondingly giving them incentives to assist regulatory authorities in the disclosure and prevention of these transactions.

## 4. Conclusion

This initial chapter has presented the basic governance structure of non-listed companies within which the legal strategies available to curb the agency problems and organize the firm can be explained. How can these strategies, many of which were designed originally for public companies but later adapted for closely held firms, be used effectively to promote economic value of the firm while detecting and correcting problems that may occur? How can the new soft law measures, such as optional guidelines, provide a more effective approach for dealing with problems in the existing organizational structure of firms? How do the major three pillars, company law, contractual arrangements, and optional guidelines—which form a legal framework of non-listed business entities—function? To this end, this book will examine the channels in which these pillars, which are complementary and mutually reinforcing, operate.

The objective has been to examine the core problems of non-listed firms and set the stage for understanding how the legal pillars work to support the business environment in which firms operate and deal with problems resulting from the firms contractual structure and decision-making processes as well as external relations.

# 2

# The First Pillar: Company Law—A One-Size-Fits-All Vehicle for Non-listed Companies

## 1. The Emergence of the Corporation or Joint Stock Company

The managerial agency problem and the corresponding governance concerns, which were discussed in Chapter 1, have existed as long as investors have allowed others to use their money and act on their behalf in risky business arrangements. In this respect, reputation concerns have always played a pivotal role in structuring and managing the governance framework of the arrangements between investors and entrepreneurs. Business parties in medieval and early modern times relied heavily on the self-enforcing norms of kinship and family ties to align agents' and principals' interests. Yet the emergence and development of long-distance trade prevented long-term business relationships from operating spontaneously without a legal governance structure that prevented deviation from the contractual arrangements and norms. Since non-legal mechanisms offered only a partial solution set to the governance problems in risky ventures, disclosure and enforcement mechanisms were devised through a system of notaries, guilds, and mercantile courts (Milgrom, North, and Weingast 1990). The rise of legal gatekeepers and institutions resulted in a rapid expansion of the law merchant throughout the Western European regions which arguably helped to lessen the costs of writing and enforcing legal contracts, thereby giving an important impetus to commerce in the Middle Ages.

In fact, when trade started to revive in the Middle Ages, after a long economic slowdown, medieval merchants needed a legal business form that could bring together scarce capital and adventurous entrepreneurs willing to undertake difficult and perilous overseas voyages. In response to the influence of powerful interest groups such as the nobles and the clergy, the mercantile system began to acknowledge the commenda with its Jewish, Byzantine, and Muslim origins. The commenda, which evolved from a loan contract into a limited partnership-type business form, was intended to mobilize risk capital for short-term overseas commercial ventures (Berman 1983). This limited partnership-type business form offered investors limited liability and anonymity, and thus made it possible for investors to pour money into lucrative ventures without risking being condemned for usury or violating inhibitions against engaging in trade. Because the investors could not be involved in the decision-making process, the limited liability feature was viewed to be efficient as it introduced the prospect of limiting the managerial agency costs. The function of limited liability is to reduce investors' monitoring costs, increase liquidity, and promote diversification, which reduces the level of risk overall. In fact, by having access to limited liability they only risked losing their initial investment, which furthered the emergence of risk capital.

At the end of the sixteenth century, the Dutch employed variations of the commenda—so-called *voorcompagnieën* or precompanies—in order to reduce information asymmetries and agency problems that were characteristic of perilous Dutch Asian trade journeys. These precompanies consisted of a number of commendas, each with its own investors and active merchant. With wars and conflicts with the Portuguese and the English, there was an urgent need for an integrated approach. In this regard, the city-based precompanies, which faced fierce competition for market share, decided to coordinate their actions by conducting a kind of merger in 1602, which led to the inception of the Dutch East Indian Company (*Vereenigde Oostindische Compagnie* (VOC)). Gradually the VOC evolved into a peculiar form of the modern corporation.[1] With the transformation of the VOC came a change not only in organizational form, but also in the venture's investor base. At the same time, the cities, in order to coordinate and structure the collaboration between the independent precompanies, created a charter which dealt with potential collective action problems and conflicts of interests. Despite these governance reforms, investors continued to express their dissatisfaction and frustration with dividend policies, the murkiness of the company's accounts, and the lack of disclosure and transparency (De Jong and Röell 2004). Other problems for investors were the limited involvement of the the the main board of directors—the Board of Seventeen Lords (*De Heren* XVII)—which convened only a few times a year and directly reported to the Dutch governmental authority rather than to investors (see Figure 2.1).[2]

It appears that the design of the VOC, despite the key features of limited liability and readily transferability of shares, made this business arrangement prone to fraud and deception. In response to these shortcomings, the government mandated full and open disclosure of accounts in 1622. Subsequently, the committee of nine and audit committee, an early form of the supervisory board consisting of

---

[1] Initially, the VOC was to have a limited lifespan of twenty years—upon which the proceeds of the VOC would be distributed back to the shareholders. However, this proved impractical and its directors continued the duration of the venture until the end of the VOC in 1799.

[2] The seventeen seats of the Board were held by representatives of the six cities with a VOC Chamber: Amsterdam, Middelburg (Zeeland), Rotterdam, Delft, Enkhuizen, and Hoorn. As Amsterdam's Chamber held eight seats, it 'controlled' the agenda-setting and decision-making process in the meetings.

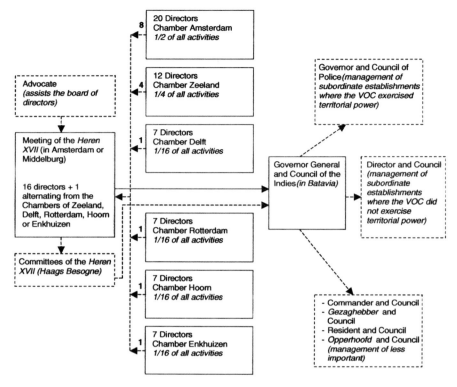

**Figure 2.1.** The organization of the VOC

*Source*: <www.tanap.net>.

'chief participants',[3] were introduced in 1623 to advise management and inspect the financial information of the VOC. With these major changes in the VOC structure, the corporate governance movement was initiated. Nevertheless, it could not solve effectively the problems surrounding the complex and cumbersome management structure inherent to the VOC arrangement.[4]

The precarious nature of the early corporate form was again perfectly exemplified by the collapse of the French Mississippi Scheme and the burst of British South Sea Bubble in 1720 (Loss 1998). The Mississippi Company and South Sea Company succeeded in attracting shareholders and creating a robust market for their shares by manipulating information and talking up share prices with

---

[3] 'Chief participants' were investors with a significant stake in the venture—more than 6,000 Dutch florins.

[4] Of course, the governance structure was exacerbated by the fact that long distance and limited communication means hampered the conveyance of decisions and information.

rumours and speculation about the companies' value and prospects.[5] In France, domestic and foreign investors were lured into the scheme by the sheer fact that the government granted the corporation monopoly control of Louisiana, which was conceived as the actual key to unlimited wealth creation. The government and the Mississippi Company kept the investors' imagination baffled with vague objectives to promote immigration and control the tobacco industry until confidence collapsed and the corporation ceased to exist, ruining the lives of many disappointed investors throughout Europe. For the same reason people rushed to invest in the British Company which was granted 'important' monopolies over English trade in South America. However, vital information about the Spanish being in control of these regions was concealed from the potential investors. The South Sea Company was in fact nothing more than an empty shell without any future cash flows and expectations.

Of course, the deflation of the bubbles fuelled the anti-corporate sentiment and chilled the investment interest by the public, but the corporate form never disappeared completely. Even though the corporate form was only available to certain types of businesses due to the formal concession of a sovereign person or government, its organizational and structural advantages—such as continuity of life, the possibility to sue outsiders and members in its own name, the distinction between corporation's assets and the personal assets of its shareholders, and the transferability of shares—prevailed over its susceptibility to fraud and abuse.

As the economies in the United States and Europe developed, numerous new corporations were chartered for the building of highways, canals, railroads, and telegraph lines. The improved transportation and communication systems led to many larger-scale firms which would also benefit from availing themselves of the management and finance structure of the corporation. In order to give effect to capital-intensive industrial and technological innovations, these larger-scale firms were compelled to amass substantial sums of equity capital from a relatively large number of investors. The use of the typical partnership form—in which investors share ownership, control, and profits—entailed shirking, opportunism, monitoring, and decision-making problems. Indeed, the integration of ownership and control often leads to a cumbersome, costly, and restricted decision-making process.[6] In order to circumvent the flaws of the partnership form—as well as the almost insuperable incorporation requirements—commercial businesses and their legal advisers started modifying and mixing legal structures so as to obtain free transferable financial participations and a differentiated management

[5] The Mississippi Company and South Sea Company were devised by financial geniuses and promoted by the British and French governments to buy the national debt of the respective countries. The governments granted a charter to the companies so as to facilitate the issuance of shares to the public in exchange for government bonds. The companies held all the debt with reduced interest rates (which the governments procured in exchange for generous monopoly grants).

[6] Economic theories show that integration of ownership and control limits the benefits of specialization in the firm's decision-making and induces free-riding behaviour among the business parties (Alchian and Demsetz 1972; Fama and Jensen 1983a).

decision-making process. However, the legality of these hybrid business forms was increasingly challenged by incorporated competitors.

With the growth of commercial and industrial activity, the pressures from politically influential industrialists to abandon the specific governmental approval of a corporate charter—and to introduce fully-fledged limited liability for corporations—grew steadily during the period of industrial revolution.[7] In the United States, the charter approval, which invited intensive lobbying, became increasingly standardized. By 1890, all states had adopted statutes providing for incorporation with limited liability by simple registration (Blumberg 1986). The introduction of a relatively simple incorporation procedure in France in 1867 resulted in the rapid proliferation of general incorporation statutes throughout continental Europe, which already embraced the corporate limited liability doctrine since the enactment of the *Napoleonic Code de Commerce* in 1807.

By embracing the new concept of incorporation by registration, policy-makers and lawmakers generally furnished industrial business firms with the corporate form with (1) full legal personality; (2) fully-fledged limited liability; (3) centralized management; (4) free transferability; and (5) continuity of life. These principles facilitated the separation of ownership and control, thereby reducing agency costs associated with the delegation of control rights. For instance, limited liability facilitates the diversification of the investors' investments, which obviously leads to low risk-bearing costs. Consequently, agency costs are reduced overall.

Centralized management is probably the most important—and precarious—feature of the corporate form (Rock and Wachter 2000). The delegation of control rights is not only necessary to facilitate management's participation in the firm, but also to attract specialized and competent managers and, more importantly, to give them sufficient incentives to encourage innovation and wealth creation. Although corporate law typically limits the shareholders' ability to intervene in management's decision-making power, it would be erroneous to conclude that shareholders are deprived of every control right within the firm. In order to mitigate shareholder hold-up by management, board members have a fiduciary obligation to the shareholders who, in turn, are given the right to elect and remove managers and to be involved in th decision-making process regarding 'major corporate actions' and 'fundamental' changes within the firm.[8]

---

[7] Limited liability was not an automatic consequence of the concept of the corporation as a separate legal person. Substantial industrial developments took place under a legal regime imposing liability on business parties for corporate debts and obligations. Limited liability emerged in the United States around 1825 and in England in 1855 and is a result of lobbying activities by high-powered industrial and political interest groups. Before that time firms attempted to obtain limited liability protection by employing a variety of devices, such as contractual clauses and insertion of the term 'limited' after the firm's name.

[8] Initially, shareholders could remove board members only for cause. Law has evolved since, and most corporate laws around the world permit the shareholders to remove a board member without cause (Cary and Eisenberg 1988).

As the ownership position of the shareholders evolved from that of a more active to that of a passive principal, the fundamental agency problem became more evident (Berle and Means 1933), thereby justifying the design and promulgation of more legal mechanisms to protect shareholders' rights and interests. Indeed, the individual shareholders' losing the ability to influence corporate decision-making and the subsequent stock market crash in the United States in 1929 served as a justification for the first corporate governance intervention by the US federal government. In order to maintain an orderly and fair stock market, Congress enacted the Securities Act in 1933, establishing the Securities and Exchange Commission (SEC). The Act, which has been modified extensively but is still in operation today, demands registration with the SEC of shares offered to the public and allows defrauded investors the possibility to bring an action against corporate wrongdoers in federal court. It also requires the disclosure of relevant transactions. As the stock exchange watchdog, the SEC investigates and imposes sanctions on violations of the Securities Act. In addition, the Securities Exchange Act of 1934 required the continuing disclosure of relevant information about the corporation.[9] For example, issuing corporations must file periodic information, such as financial statements and proxy statements containing details on such matters as remuneration of directors and officers, insider training, and conflict-of-interest transactions. Corporations are also obliged to report the occurrence of material events. Thus seen, disclosure has a prophylactic effect: it discourages managerial theft, fraud, and self-dealing transactions.

Other jurisdictions, like Germany and the Netherlands, introduced equivalent mechanisms in their corporation laws so as to minimize agency costs resulting from individual shareholders' losing the interest and ability to influence how corporations were managed. A mandatory supervisory board, for example, not only had to monitor management activities within large companies, but was also furnished with shareholder competencies, such as the election and removal of managing directors. By doing so, policy-makers and lawmakers attempted to prevent irrational and opportunistic decisions caused by voluntary shareholder absenteeism and strong corporate insiders.

Traditionally, corporate law serves thus a myriad of functions from encouraging the separation of ownership and control to curtailing managerial agency problems. It gives the general meeting of shareholders an *ex ante* incentive to make investments of financial capital, and delegates the control rights to management. In a publicly held corporation the shareholders are, as discussed in Chapter 1, usually unable to exercise the managerial rights of control. Corporate law sets the internal ground rules for each of the parties, their decision, information, and financial rights.

[9] The Securities Exchange Act of 1934 extended the disclosure requirements to securities listed and registered for public trading on the US securities exchanges. In 1964, the Securities Act Amendments extended disclosure and reporting provisions to equity securities in the over-the-counter market.

## 2. The Corporate Form as a Standard Contract

It is often said that economic concepts are fundamental to the analysis of corporate law. This approach casts a different light on the role and function of company
law than traditional theories of law and society. Understanding these concepts,
as adapted to corporate law, helps lawmakers to identify the needs and requirements of the participants in business firms, but also to define the role of the law in
offering an effective governance structure for business parties to pursue economic
objectives. The contractual theory of the firm, which dominates the thinking
of efficiency-minded lawmakers, can assist lawmakers in identifying the central
problems that business parties encounter, and the role that company law plays
in helping to resolve these problems. In a so-called Coasean world with complete and perfect information, and no transaction costs, we do not need to worry
about company law provisions (Coase 1988). The business parties will be able
to contract into the most efficient governance structure themselves. In the real
world, however, lawmakers could approximate the hypothetical world by offering
legal products, in the form of default and possibly mandatory rules that minimize transaction costs and remove impediments to private ordering arrangements
between the business parties.

Proponents of the contractual theory view company law as a nexus of contracts. The nexus-of-contracts theory treats business forms as products that serve
as a nexus for a set of relational contracts among its participants (Jensen and
Meckling 1976). From this perspective, the contractual theory of the firm is
arguably an appropriate and socially desirable concept, since it draws attention
to the variety of needs, i.e., rights and duties, of participants involved in different firms (Hart 1995). Nonetheless, the nexus-of-contracts theory of the firm
only partly explains why firms require a particular type of product. Moreover,
the theory's narrowly conceptualized assumptions—i.e., that (1) the firm is best
viewed as a set of incentive contracts; (2) the function of the legal system is to
supply rules and standards that are *ex ante* efficient; (3) rationally informed firm
participants will bargain themselves into efficient governance structures; and (4)
the firm's contracts are self-enforcing and do not require judicial enforcement—
are successfully challenged.

In general, the complaint against the nexus-of-contracts theory is not that relational contracts are irrelevant to understanding the internal organization of the
firm, but that it is difficult and costly to write *ex ante* complete contracts inside the
firm. For one thing, people intend to act rationally, but they are simply not able to
foresee and describe all future contingencies in a contract. As noted, economists
claim that people are 'boundedly rational' (Williamson 1985). More importantly, even if contingencies can be dealt with contractually, information asymmetries and strategic bargaining often prevent efficient and complete contracts
from emerging (Bolton and Dewatripont 2005). In short, relational contracts

are often incomplete due to the difficulties in (1) foreseeing some contingencies at the outset of the relationship; (2) specifying all contingencies in the contract; (3) monitoring the performance of the other participants; and (4) enforcing the relational contracts.

Viewing the firm as an incomplete contract thus provides a broader under-standing of the legal mechanisms required for the optimal production and design of corporate law and governance frameworks, and, more significantly, of the importance of having a variety of frameworks in general. Incomplete contract theories, which in many ways build on and formalize the concepts and ideas of transaction costs economics, attempt to explain how structuring as a particular type of firm helps to prevent opportunistic behaviour. Indeed, when parties can simply write a complete contract, they specify in full detail what each party must do in each state of the world and how the surplus should be shared. In practice, bounded rationality and private information inevitably entail contractual incom-pleteness. Consequently, firm participants may have to renegotiate the contract to react to unforeseen contingencies, which may lead to an opportunistic attempt by one of them to obtain more of the *ex post* return on investment.

In line with the incomplete contract paradigm, a company law framework could be viewed as a product, i.e., a 'standard set of governance rules', that rep-resents different points on the continuum of types of firms. This continuum ranges from an organization in which the owners themselves retain substantial autonomy to organizations that involve an increasing surrender of 'individual autonomy' in favour of reciprocity and 'firm autonomy'. On the scale of firm-ness, autonomy seems to shift from relational contracts with self-interested own-ers to organizations in which self-interest becomes more subordinate to the firm's collective interest. It is argued that organizational arrangements that have more firmness rank higher in terms of autonomy and, in traditional legal terms, are more easily perceived as entities (Lamoreaux 1998). In this view, corporations have relatively more firmness than general partnerships. In comparison with gen-eral partnerships, corporations have governance structures which are more based on hierarchy than consensus, 'lock in' firm-specific assets, and, hence, decrease an individual's ability to engage in opportunistic behaviour by threatening to break up the business relationship. At the same time, however, individuals may have information and skills to pursue their personal interest and to compete against the firm, whereas general partnership law contains provisions and duties prohib-iting individual partners from competition against the firm. It follows that legal business forms rate differently on the scale of firmness, thereby presenting differ-ent solutions to the failings of the parties to draft complete relational contracts.

However, in the second best world of incomplete contracts (Pistor and Xu 2003), lawmakers do not supply business forms that offer comprehensive and unambiguous guidance in all future contingencies, but determine, among other things, in company law statutes how control over the firm's resources is allocated, how hierarchy is created within the firm, and which implied fiduciary terms and principles will assist courts in filling possible future gaps in the relational business contract. Corporate law thus acts as a facilitator, enabling business participants to move towards the most optimal governance equilibrium within a firm. To see this, let us consider some of the key features of a corporation, which is the main choice of governance mechanisms for listed firms: (1) a corporation is a legal entity that holds the firm's assets; (2) a corporation creates centralized management, to which the shareholders delegate important control rights;[10] and (3) the limited liability feature allows shareholders, many of whom are wealth constrained and risk averse, to diversify their risks. These principles facilitate the separation of ownership and control, thereby reducing agency costs associated with the delegation of control rights. In a typical publicly held corporation the shareholders are too small and numerous to exercise the residual rights of control. It would be too costly if all of them were involved in decision management. Moreover, the shareholders, who are mainly interested in the company's share price, lack the expertise and competency to take part in the decision-making process. As a consequence, the incomplete contracts theory of the firm recognizes that delegating residual control rights is necessary to facilitate management's participation in the firm and to give management sufficient incentives to undertake relationship-specific investments as well as to fill possible gaps in the corporate contract.

## 3. The Rise of the Close Corporation

As we noted above, the corporation is best viewed as a particular standard form contract which offers limited liability, continuity, transferability of interests, and centralized management. Whilst the corporation may provide an effective nexus for implicit and explicit contracts and market relationships between shareholders, managers, creditors, and other stakeholders, it does not, correspondingly, offer a clear solution for the problems that occur in multi-owner closely held companies in which the identity of the shareholders is a much more important characteristic due to (1) the relatively small number of shareholders; (2) no ready market for the corporate stock; and (3) substantial (majority) shareholder participation in management, direction, and operation of the firm. First, the centralized management feature is poorly tailored to fit the governance needs of closely held firms. When ownership and control are typically not completely severed, as is the case in these firms, the delegation of control rights is not so important and precarious as in publicly held corporations. Second, the majority rule, which characterizes the corporate form and gives control to holders of a majority of the outstanding voting shares, creates an opportunity to oppress minority shareholders by, among

---

[10] The centralized management feature is not only necessary to facilitate management's participation in the firm, but also to attract specialized and competent managers and, more importantly, to give them sufficient incentives to encourage innovation and wealth creation.

other things, appropriating corporate opportunities and distributing cash and property to majority shareholders.[11]

From an efficiency standpoint, the business parties would always prefer to use a legal organizational form that defines and sets forth the ownership structure and provides important contractual provisions in advance.[12] This makes the law governing the organizational form key to the corporate governance framework for non-listed firms. The main question then is, if the general corporation does not offer an optimal governance framework to non-listed companies, which legal business form to focus on when analysing the persistent governance features that serve to protect business parties from the misconduct by fellow members? Publicly held firms are predominantly organized as joint stock companies or corporations. The close corporation (or private limited company) is, however, the prevalent business form around the world.[13] This type of company accounts for more than 55 per cent of registered businesses and 90 per cent of output in OECD countries (World Bank 2004). Figure 2.2 gives an overview of the total number of registered close corporations in the United Kingdom. The close corporation is also the preferred vehicle for non-listed firms in emerging and transition markets. Although the development has been quite different depending on the legal system, the close corporation has been adopted in almost all countries of the world.[14]

In the United Kingdom, the close corporation—the private limited company—has a single legislative base. It was initially developed in practice and later recognized by the legislature, which furnished it with certain distinct features (Lutter 1998). Most countries that once belonged to the British Empire included the close corporation form into their own corporate laws, as they were already familiar with basic legal principles of the donor jurisdiction. The second strand of development is the enactment of a separate statute for the limited liability company. Germany is renowned for its close corporation (*Gesellschaft mit beschränkter Haftung* (GmbH)), which was the precursor of separate close corporation legislations throughout the European continent, Latin American jurisdictions, Asia, and former Socialist countries. In Japan, for instance, a business

---

[11] In Chapter 8, we will see that even if shareholders, ostensibly, have no majority stake in a corporation's equity, dual class shares and pyramid structures often serve the purpose of remaining in control.

[12] Typically 'non-law-and-economics' scholars make the routine mistake of assuming that business parties are only influenced by distorted tax measures provided by rent-seeking jurisdictions. While this often occurs in practice, it nevertheless provides no basis for the efficient selection of corporate forms. Tax reforms aiming at the neutralization of legal business forms by pursuing equality of tax treatment, independent of the business form, may stimulate the creation and introduction of more efficient legislation. For instance, the federal 'check-the-box' tax regulations (Treas Reg §§ 301.7701-1 to 3, 61 Fed Reg 66,584 (1996)), under which unincorporated associations are taxed as partnerships unless they affirmatively elect to be taxed as corporations, appear to be responsible for the rapid development of more flexible and innovative legal business forms in the United States.

[13] See *Doing Business in 2004: Understanding Regulation*, a co-publication of the World Bank, the International Finance Corporation, and Oxford University Press.

[14] See for instance Abd Ghadas (2007) providing an overview of business forms in Asia.

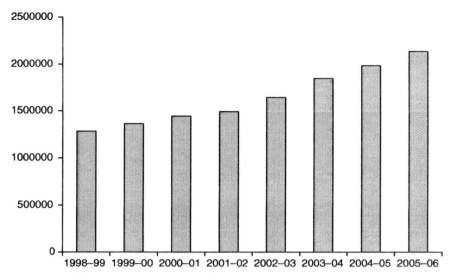

**Figure 2.2.** Effective number of private limited companies on register in the United Kingdom (at end of period)

*Source*: Companies House.

form (*Yugen Kaisha*) based on the *Gesellschaft mit beschränkter Haftung* emerged in 1940. The United States offers only a single corporate form which can be contractually tailored to the needs and wishes of closely held firms.

Generally the close corporation has developed in the image of the joint stock company with its capital-oriented structure. Since, as we have seen, the joint stock company is designed to attract substantial amounts of capital into the firm from passive investors and, consequently, to regulate the rich and intricate principal–agency problem between the shareholders and the managers, this structure is not sufficient for non-listed firms. Despite its perceived cumbersomeness and costly features, the close corporation has nevertheless become the preferred vehicle for closely held firms.

In order to meet the specialized needs that arise from the idiosyncratic relationships in non-listed firms, legislative and judicial adjustments have, over the years, been constructed in a piecemeal fashion across jurisdictions. Two sets of problems have arisen repeatedly due to the publicly held character of the close corporation forms. The first set of problems falls under the category of protection of minority shareholders' interests. Case law sometimes assumes that close corporations and partnerships are functionally equivalent business forms with similar organizational needs. This approach is based on the assumption that business participants choose the close corporation over the partnership form only to take advantage of limited liability and possible tax benefits. For instance, advocates often propose modifications of the exit rules so that business participants can enjoy the same exit options as partners in a partnership. The second problem arises out of contractual attempts by participants to modify and sidestep rigid legal rules intended primarily for publicly held corporations.

First, if we consider the application of traditional partnership principles to close corporations, we observe that in many jurisdictions, such as the United States and Germany, the judiciary has recognized that shareholders in a close corporation setting may owe each other a strict fiduciary duty of good faith and loyalty.[15] In the Netherlands, the Dutch Supreme Court articulated strict restrictions on interest transfer for shareholders of close corporations, based on enhanced good faith and fiduciary duties, where the articles of incorporation did not explicitly address these matters.[16] Likewise in *Ebrahami v Westbourne Galleries*,[17] the House of Lords decided that circumstances in which a UK private company is in essence a quasi-partnership (formed and continued by individuals who were essentially partners but who had chosen the legal mechanism of a corporate structure for its obvious advantages) justify the application of partnership just and equitable winding-up principles. In short, the application of strict precepts of fiduciary duty and good faith to protect shareholders to modify and sidestep rigid rules characterize the close corporation form as a 'quasi-partnership', 'incorporated partnership', or 'partnership corporation'.

Second, experimentation and subsequent innovations have given momentum to the search for more contractual flexibility. From a relatively early date lawmakers were, in response to the special wishes of larger firms that had little appetite for incurring the extra costs of the incorporation process, already undertaking to modify and mix legal structures so as to obtain the most cost-effective limited liability vehicle. Practitioners viewed the traditional limited partnership form as a product that could be traded in the market, as it could offer their clients a flexible limited liability tax shelter. They solved the problem of the general partner's unlimited liability by creating a hybrid business form between the limited partnership and a corporation, which played the role of general partner. The restrictions on the limited partners' rights to participate in management have occasionally turned out to be advantageous both to the founders, who want to retain control of the business in conjunction with limited liability protection, and to passive investors who covet the pass-through taxation and other favourable tax attributes. Despite the concerns about legal permissibility and the perverse influence of tax law on the limited partnership, this hybrid vehicle has been a success

---

[15] For instance, in the United States and Germany, the judiciary has viewed the close corporation as a 'quasi-partnership'. See *Donahue v Rodd Electrotype Co.* 328 NE2d 505 (Mass. 1975) and, to a lesser extent, *Wilkes v Springside Nursing Home, Inc.* 353 NE2d 657, 663 (Mass. 1976). In Germany, the German Supreme Court imposed a broad fiduciary duty on controlling shareholders of the German close corporation GmbH—in the *ITT* case (BGH 5 June 1975, BGHZ 65, 15 (ITT)).

[16] See Hoge Raad, 31 December 1993, (1994) NJ, 436.

[17] [1973] AC 360 (HL).

story in many jurisdictions. The German 'GmbH & Co KG', devised to combine the benefits of partnership taxation with the possibility of evading onerous corporate rules (such as the German co-determination act and other cumbersome statutory audit and disclosure rules) is a good example.[18] In other industrialized jurisdictions we also observe that the limited liability vehicle gained popularity due to its hoped-for tax advantages and flexibility. It has been most attractive not only to firms with small and dispersed passive investors, but also to closely held firms engaged in businesses of which the assets present valuation problems, or in which managers must make firm-specific human capital investments. In the fields of ship and film production or exploration, real estate developing and operation, venture capital funding, and family businesses, this variation on the limited partnership form is especially popular.

Notwithstanding the popularity of the limited partnership with a corporate partner, it is not always possible for closely held firms to use this form. Besides the fact that this hybrid form is not recognized or is prohibited from engaging in specific kinds of activities in some countries, the limited partnership and its statutory 'control rule' may not be optimal for firms in which the owners are unwilling to give up their control power. In addition, since this vehicle comprises two business entities that must be organized and administered separately, it is not a form that practitioners can always sell easily to their clients, who have to go through the extra expense and effort of setting up an intermediary corporation. Regardless, limited partnerships with a corporation as the sole general partner are suboptimal responses to the search for cheaply accessible limited liability vehicles.

This focus away from the corporate form is not accidental. In the USA, the rapid increase in partnership-type business forms has grown much faster than anticipated. Several factors contribute to the growth of new and more efficient partnership law structures. First, states have responded to the needs of a wide variety of firms for a more flexible set of forms, which has reduced reliance on or eliminated inefficient older forms. Second, the liberalization of partnership law has been accompanied by the virtual elimination of the distinctions between partnerships and corporations accompanied by a move toward the recognition of partnerships as entities. Third, the increase in the choice among business forms has resulted in the erosion of traditional restrictions of the internal structure of corporate law forms.

The emergence of new limited liability vehicles in Europe and Asia, which will be described in more detail in Chapter 4, has been influenced by both domestic and international factors. Undoubtedly, the US reforms have stimulated policy-makers' expectations that new legal business forms will create significant investment opportunities, increased employment, and higher growth rates. At

---

[18] Both the judiciary (already in 1912) and the legislature have acknowledged the German GmbH & Co KG. After the adoption of the *Kapitalgesellschaften- und Co-Richtlinie-Gesetzes* (KapCoRiLiG) the corporate statutory audit and disclosure rules also apply to limited partnerships with a corporation as the sole general partner.

the same time, legal innovation in the European Union has been encouraged by changes in European Court of Justice case law,[19] which, as we will see in Chapter 3, has triggered some jurisdictional competition in European business law and hence is responsible for the numerous reforms in the area of close corporation law designed to meet the needs of small and medium-sized firms (SMEs). Like the USA and Europe, Japan has recently embarked on the reform of its company law framework. This has resulted in the development of two new legal business forms, the Japanese Limited Liability Partnership (J-LLP) and the Japanese Limited Liability Company (J-LLC), as well as the modification of traditional corporate entities. This trend can be seen as a response to the demand for the reduction of regulation and improved legal vehicles that are better tailored to meet the governance needs of different types of firms.

Although new hybrid business forms hold out potential cost-savings for several classes of firms, their abrupt introduction would naturally tend to prelude candidate firms—either because they remain unaware or uncertain about their prospective inherent benefits—from taking up these new forms immediately. If we look to the US experience with the LLC, for instance, the practice appears to be more complex than predicted. For example, start-up firms in which venture capitalists invest are still more likely to be structured as corporations. The venture capital industry is characterized by uncertainty particularly at early stages of investment. Typically entrepreneurs who seek venture capital must contract into a legal business form that attenuates information problems (board structure and control) and incentive concerns (stock options), while retaining a flexible structure and providing tax advantages. In this context, entrepreneurs have a variety of legal business forms to choose from. Although the success of the US venture capital market has been attributed mainly to the combination of a vibrant and liquid capital market that facilitates IPOs, the critical use of financial instruments mitigate the double-sided moral hazard problem and support the efficient structuring of staged financing, and the sustained level of new entrepreneurs with a high capacity to realize their commercial aims. Yet the success of the venture capital market is arguably due to the availability of a corporate form that combines strong management and control characteristics with contractual flexibility.

As noted above, start-ups are predominantly structured as corporations. Contracting into this regular corporate form even seems to attract venture capitalists in their own decision-making about one-time legal decisions. From a fiscal perspective, this is surprising in that the choice to incorporate entails that the predictable tax savings arising from the pass-through tax treatment are not accessible. These alleged tax savings may provide them with a respectable sum of money. The usual losses from the start-up venture do not flow through to the 'partner-shareholders' in a corporation, while these tax-deductible losses could offset other sources of income at the parties' level. The use of other business forms,

---

[19] See Chapter 3.

such as a general partnership, limited partnership, or limited liability company (LLC), which couple internal flexibility with limited liability for all players and pass-through tax treatment, can yield more favourable benefits.

Naturally, a question arises as to why venture capital players forgo tax savings by selecting the corporate form. The factors prompting venture capitalists to prefer the corporate legal form to other vehicles are the subject of considerable controversy in the United States. Commentators have argued that the governance structure, rather than the lower tax rate, is the main consideration for entrepreneurs and venture capitalists selecting the corporate form (Bankman 1994). With respect to determining the optimal business arrangement, it is submitted that the general partnership is not a viable alternative, due to the excessive risks and agency costs in combination with personal liability for the partnership's debts. As for the limited partnership, it may be that taking part in the control of the business could render the limited partner personally liable. Consequently, even though venture capitalists try to avoid taking control of a start-up firm, the limited partnership is not a viable option due to the higher liability costs associated with downside risks. Furthermore, at least in Europe and increasingly in the United States entrepreneurs are unlikely to leave well-paid employment without *ex ante* liability protection.

The reluctance on the part of high-tech start-ups to select earlier versions of the LLC can be explained in terms of a preference to save on transaction costs and time in the course of the venture capital cycle.[20] By forming a public corporation, for instance, they avoid the costs of converting the LLC into the corporate form before an IPO. Underwriters in the United States rarely employ unincorporated business forms that can be utilized to issue equity interests.[21] Yet from an efficiency standpoint, the legal, accounting, and organizational costs of a conversion do not explain why venture capitalists and their legally literate advisers are reluctant to experiment with other business forms if tax savings exceed these costs. Paradoxically, venture capitalists and entrepreneurs, usually fond of innovations, are apparently not eager, in the absence of high-powered incentives, to experiment with other legal forms. This is especially true if these other legal forms fail to supply a comprehensive statutory template with regard to the governance structure, fiduciary duties, and possible waivability of default rules. The fact that parties in an LLC may be subject to broad fiduciary duties that may require a party to forgo

---

[20] Even though venture capitalists have continued to select the corporate form, we can expect that the LLC will gain wide acceptance. The underlying assumption is that both the LLC and the corporation have trade-offs that must be carefully considered for each situation or when determining the type of entity. But, the flexibility of the LLC operating agreement allows for different classes of membership interests and ultimately permits more creativity in structuring transactions. See Chapters 4 and 5.

[21] The recent spate of listings by US investment funds, such as the Blackstone Group LP and Kohlberg Kravis Roberts & Co, employing a limited partnership structure could spark a new trend in the direction toward some issuers relying on non-corporate vehicles for attracting external investment.

other interests appears to act as a deterrent to venture capitalists. If entrepreneurs are allowed to bring an action based on a venture capitalist's breach of fiduciary duty when their high-risk gamble does not pay off, thereby circumventing the contractual mechanisms put in place to overcome information problems, the transaction costs will increase significantly.

In this context, entrepreneurs tilt away from other business forms relative to the corporate form, because their investors and independent advisers prefer a vehicle that provides parties with a set of well-developed, standardized, and widely used contractual structures, in addition to a strong management and control structure. Thus, the learning and network effects arising from prior and future usage of corporate terms and/or statutes confer benefits such as existing and prospective judicial precedents, common business practices, cheaper legal services, and positive effects on the valuation of businesses.[22] Furthermore, the competition for corporate charters among states has broken down anachronistic mandatory state laws in the United States. As a consequence, commentators point to the success story of close corporations in the United States and view them as the only necessary link between partnerships on the one hand and publicly held corporations on the other (Lutter 1998). In this view, close corporations can take the form of a limited liability partnership as well as that of a public corporation, thereby covering the smallest start-up firms, joint ventures, and firms financed by debt and venture capital.

## 4. The Close Corporation as a One-Size-Fits-All Vehicle in the Twentieth Century

In the United States, as we have seen in Section 3, the general corporation laws have gradually transformed into an all-purpose vehicle, becoming more flexible and allowing non-listed businesses to modify its charters in accordance with their special needs. A review of European closely held business forms reveals the close corporation transformed into a one-size-fits-all vehicle is more costly and less flexible than its US counterpart.[23] While reforms are underway to streamline

---

[22] For instance, the use of stock options as a compensation system for entrepreneurs reflects the prevalence of standardized venture capital contracts. Stock options, as distinct from fixed cash salaries, function as a contingent compensation linked to the performance of the business. Ideally, stock options provide entrepreneurs with an incentive to benchmark their performance in accordance with the venture capitalists' expectations, and prevent overly risky actions and opportunism. Although the great flexibility of the LLC statutes warrants a similar compensation system, parties may prefer to use stock options, thereby forgoing alleged tax savings. Indeed, even though the US LLC allows for publicly traded 'units'—depository receipts for the owners' property interest—the efficiency of selling units is called into question because underwriters are probably unwilling to employ 'units' on a large scale.

[23] As will be explained below, there are substantial differences between 'one-size-fits-all vehicles' and 'all-purpose vehicles'. In the main, the former is characterized by a largely mandatory set

incorporation procedures, firms continue to suffer from a range of formation technicalities which restrict the ease of access to limited liability. The corporate law of the Netherlands is exemplary in this respect. Dutch corporate law currently requires a notarial deed which contains a comprehensive set of articles of incorporation that must be filed with the commercial registry.[24] A statement must also be issued by experts on the value of consideration in kind or the availability of the consideration in cash must also be submitted to the commercial registry. In addition, a certificate from the Minister of Justice that there have appeared to be no objections is required.[25] Dutch law moreover mandates that firms disclose essential information in their filed articles of incorporation, such as the capital structure, the company's objectives, and the deviations from the default rules supplied by the Code—among other things, the system of voting, supervision, and regulations concerning the conduct of the shareholders' general meeting.

Yet, the fact that we observe numerous multi-ownership structures employing the close corporation—more than 650,000 close corporations (*Besloten Vennootschap met beperkte Aansprakelijkheid* (BV)) were registered at the Dutch Chamber of Commerce in July 2007—suggests that corporate law rules may, in general, be trivial in the sense that in practice firms are able to bear the formation costs and adapt the corporate governance structure as they deem fit. As we have seen, the close corporation accounts for the majority of registered businesses in OECD countries. This is largely due to the positive externalities that arise as a consequence of firms having selected the closely held corporation for tax and liability reasons. Moreover, the widespread use of this structure reinforces and even strengthens the use of this form, arguably excluding the choice for other business forms. Nevertheless, the success story of the close corporation in many jurisdictions could give eloquent testimony to the fact that business participants often neutralize the law's detrimental effect by either relying on *ex post* gap filling by courts or by making contractual adjustments *ex ante* (Dixit 2004). Hence, the rules of corporate law appear not to matter.

In this view the close corporation form may function effectively and appropriately in an incomplete contracting setting. Legal entity status, for instance, is necessary to define the property rights over which participants within a firm can contract. In the absence of entity status, it would be practicably impossible to shield the assets of the firm from creditors of the firm's owners. First, the transaction costs of drafting and inserting provisions in all contracts between the participants inside the firm and the firm's creditors on the one hand and their personal creditors on the other will be prohibitively high. Second, the firm participants,

---

of organizational rules which apply to firms across the board, whereas an all-purpose vehicle is more contractual in nature and hence gives business parties more freedom in the design of legal provisions to suit their own preferences.

[24] Section 175(2) of Book 2 of the Dutch Civil Code. 'Formal use of lawyers as notaries seems to be a common trait' in Europe (see Thomas 1992: 4).

[25] Dutch Civil Code, ibid, section 179(2).

including the business creditors, would face a moral hazard problem, as it is virtually impossible to assure the business creditors of the existence of the necessary agreements with their personal creditors (Hansmann and Kraakman 2000).[26] The second (and secondary) purpose for choosing the close corporation is the limited liability feature. Its function is to protect owners by limiting creditors of the entity to pursue claims on the owners' individual and separate assets. Limited liability promotes inter-firm cooperation by limiting monitoring costs, externalizing risk, and facilitating the sectorial and geographical diversification of business projects.

Still, corporate law rules may be insufficient to provide an adequate basis to govern relations between the majority and minority and the firm itself in a closely held firm setting. Suppose, for example, that the majority shareholders take the decision to eliminate certain minority interests under the principle of majority rule thereby assuming complete control and squeezing out the minorities' views and wishes. Although this is a standard corporate transaction, no doubt many minority shareholders, who consider themselves partners in the enterprise with equal say and decision-making powers, will be unhappily surprised.

Similarly, while most closely held firms are governed by extra-legal mechanisms, corporate law rules could be used opportunistically encouraging disputes and litigation when the rules do not match expectations of investors. Indeed, the weight of economic evidence seems to confirm the view that business parties may be loath to bear the transaction costs of contracting around inadequate statutory terms.[27] Studies from the United States illustrate that even though business participants would theoretically be better off opting into specifically available close corporation rules, in practice these opt-in provisions have not been widely used. The standardization of the corporation statute due to network and learning effects suggested lower legal formation and operation costs than the not yet standardized 'innovations' with respect to close corporations. To be sure, judges and arbitrators could offer a solution to a puzzling and disturbing gap in the corporate contract, such as an easy buyout right for the dissatisfied partner, if the incomplete contract makes the minority vulnerable to opportunistic exploitation by the majority. However, judicial gap filling is not only costly and time consuming, but may also be prone to error. Judicial intervention can create a potential judicial wild card that creates costly uncertainty (Mahoney 1998). It is submitted that whilst intra-firm controversies are often observable to the exasperated

---

[26] Hansmann and Kraakman (2000) call the separation between the firm's assets and the personal assets of the participants inside the firm 'affirmative asset partitioning'. They view affirmative asset partitioning as the core defining characteristic of a legal entity. That is not to say that there are no other transaction cost advantages attached to the use of the corporate form that is bestowed with legal entity status. The entity status strengthens the firm's bargaining power *vis-à-vis* outsiders. Creditors and other outsiders can deal with the firm as a unit rather than with the individual members.

[27] An empirical survey in the United States found that deviations from state-supplied default settings are uncommon (Hochstetler and Svejda 1985).

parties, they may not be easily verified by a judge or arbitrator, and even less so when personal relationships in the family or between friends are involved.[28] As a consequence, many analysts think the judicial role should be limited, in the case of contractual incompleteness, to the selective enforcement of contracts according to their written terms. Indeed, the difficulty in predicting the judicial outcome explains why relatively few disputes seem to end up in court.[29]

   In light of the foregoing discussion, the absence of statutory guidance, which could be adopted *ex ante*, may have a detrimental effect on both the firm and its participants. As participants in a firm tend to react strategically to rules, the wrong rule could produce significant inefficiencies much greater than the nominal costs of contracting around a rule (Ayres 1998). For instance, the supply of the inefficient default rule could have a detrimental effect on relational arrangements in firms that are mainly governed by extra-legal and social norms. Even if the parties are completely unaware of the default rules *ex ante* and start their business on the basis of trust and reputation, midstream awareness of the legal rules might crowd out interpersonal trust and replace it with institutional trust in the legal system. Moreover, overconfidence, over-optimism, and excitement about the prospects of a new business venture prevent participants from engaging in business planning and contemplating methods for addressing future conflicts of interest. Because participants must either trust each other or forgo the deal, they often avoid tailoring their business arrangement, thereby intentionally leaving gaps in their relational contract. Furthermore, bargaining theory in law and economics recognizes that even if the contract parties are willing to accept the challenge of drafting an agreement and transaction costs are marginal, information asymmetries and strategic behaviour could prevent them from bargaining their way to the optimal governance structure.[30]

   The upshot is that governmental lawmakers (i.e., legislatures) should implement, administer, and enforce business form legislation. There are several advantages in putting the responsibility of business form design in governmental hands. In addition to economies of scale, the publicity of the legislative process reduces the information costs for potential users of the statutes. Moreover, new networks are arguably more likely to arise around legislative products. Arguably, the legislatures and courts should resolve the high costs of internal and external rules by adopting a deregulatory policy towards the laws relating to the governance

---

[28] O'Neill (1998) illustrates the artificiality of the family/market dichotomy with a US case, *United States v Chestman*, 947 F2d 551 (2d Cir 1991), in which the Second Circuit surprisingly ruled that marriage creates a confidential business relationship.

[29] Easterbrook and Fischel (1986) note that the available economic models of litigation indicate that the more trouble parties have in predicting how a judge will decide, the less likely they are to resolve their differences short of litigation, even when there are only two parties.

[30] It might be argued that the cost of drafting a customized agreement is minimal, because forms for special clauses abound in libraries and lawyers' files. However, the internal participants in many closely held firms seem, nevertheless, to be reluctant to deviate from statutory default rules.

of closely held business firms. To take the example of the close corporation, one is inclined to point to the troublesome nature of 'over-regulation' with respect to multi-ownership arrangements. The corporate form usually does not give unlimited freedom of contract in devising the ownership and governance structure of the firm. The mandatory and formal nature of provisions in the corporate statute could trump the terms set forth in the agreement between the participants, thereby making the enforceability of the contractual provisions a cumbersome process.

Central to this view is the claim that relaxing the provisions of investor and creditor protection will provide a clear set of benefits to the participants in closely held firms. As we can already observe, European economies, faced with growth challenges, are taking steps to modernize their corporate law arrangements and create the policies necessary to eliminate barriers to investment, with the emphasis on governance mechanisms that contribute to sustainable development.[31] There are a number of variables that affect the quality and development of an entrepreneurial environment. In Table 2.1, a common performance benchmark measures the corporate law policy environments of twenty-one European countries. The benchmark that focuses on both closely held and public corporations shows that, along three variables (time, administrative cost, and minimum capital requirements), the best jurisdictions have a positive score of 1, which indicates that the variables are below the overall average. Conversely, weaker jurisdictions have a score of 2 or 3, equal to the overall average or above respectively. The performance indicators, which focus on price, cost, and barriers to entry, is based on the methodology that was originally developed by Simeon Djankov et al (2002). As can be seen, in assessing the costs of alternative corporate law arrangements against the performance benchmark, the lowest score is to be preferred. For instance, the costs associated with setting up a company, meeting the minimum capital requirements, and time required to satisfy the legal formalities would be significant, lowering the competitiveness benefits of entry in a particular jurisdiction. The aim is to identify the least costly option consistent with meeting the needs for new firms and entrepreneurs.

In Chapter 3 we will see that recent empirical evidence from the EU suggests that the increased choice between different close corporation regimes provides the necessary impetus to help erode antiquated and burdensome entry regulations. To illustrate this point, let us return to Table 2.1. If we look at the minimum capital variable of the competitiveness measure, the survey shows that European member states should be responsive to demand pressures and consequently take steps slowly to abolish the requirement of minimum capital for the close corporation. In moving toward the provision of corporate law legislation that is both cost effective and lowers the administrative burden for firms, countries are able to set in place the conditions for renewed economic growth and expansion.

---

[31] See Chapter 3.

Table 2.1. Benchmarking time, administrative costs, and capital requirement in 'EU Company Law'

| | Score for private limited company | Typical elapsed business days | Typical administrative costs | Minimum issued capital | Score for public limited company | Typical elapsed business days | Typical administrative costs | Minimum issued capital | TOTAL SCORE |
|---|---|---|---|---|---|---|---|---|---|
| Austria | 2.3 | 1 | 3 | 3 | 2.3 | 1 | 3 | 3 | 2.3 |
| Belgium | 2.3 | 3 | 1 | 3 | 1.7 | 3 | 1 | 1 | 2.0 |
| Czech Republic | 1.7 | 3 | 1 | 1 | 1.7 | 3 | 1 | 1 | 1.7 |
| Denmark | 2.3 | 1 | 3 | 3 | 2.3 | 1 | 3 | 3 | 2.3 |
| Finland | 1.0 | 1 | 1 | 1 | 1.7 | 1 | 1 | 3 | 1.3 |
| France | 1.0 | 1 | 1 | 1 | 1.0 | 1 | 1 | 1 | 1.0 |
| Germany | 2.3 | 3 | 1 | 3 | 1.7 | 3 | 1 | 1 | 2.0 |
| Greece | 1.7 | 1 | 1 | 3 | 1.7 | 1 | 3 | 1 | 1.7 |
| Hungary | 1.7 | 3 | 1 | 1 | 3.0 | 3 | 3 | 3 | 2.3 |
| Ireland | 1.0 | 1 | 1 | 1 | 1.7 | 1 | 3 | 1 | 1.3 |
| Italy | 2.3 | 3 | 3 | 1 | 3.0 | 3 | 3 | 3 | 2.7 |
| Luxembourg | 1.7 | 1 | 3 | 1 | 1.0 | 1 | 1 | 1 | 2.3 |
| Netherlands | 2.3 | 1 | 3 | 3 | 1.0 | 1 | 1 | 1 | 1.7 |
| Norway | 1.0 | 1 | 1 | 1 | 1.7 | 1 | 1 | 3 | 1.3 |
| Poland | 1.0 | 1 | 1 | 1 | 1.7 | 1 | 1 | 3 | 1.3 |
| Portugal | 1.7 | 3 | 1 | 1 | 1.7 | 3 | 1 | 1 | 1.7 |
| Slovak Republic | 2.3 | 3 | 3 | 1 | 2.3 | 3 | 3 | 1 | 2.3 |
| Spain | 1.7 | 3 | 1 | 1 | 1.7 | 3 | 1 | 1 | 1.7 |
| Sweden | 1.7 | 1 | 3 | 1 | 1.0 | 1 | 1 | 1 | 1.3 |
| Switzerland | 1.7 | 1 | 1 | 3 | 1.7 | 1 | 1 | 3 | 1.7 |
| UK | 1.0 | 1 | 1 | 1 | 1.7 | 1 | 1 | 3 | 1.3 |

Source: Adapted from EVCA, Benchmarking European Tax and Legal Environments, May 2004.

An equally important component of the competitiveness benchmark, however, might be the operation requirements of the different statutory arrangements for the close corporation. As we have seen, the business participants in a non-listed firm have to deal with specific agency problems between the controlling shareholders and the minority shareholders. Remember that these firms are characterized by the relatively small number of shareholders which are not able to exit the firm through a market for the corporate stock and usually demand significant involvement in the corporation's decision-making process. Indeed, if we accept the view that a close corporation law regime helps to lower the formation costs while filling gaps in non-listed firms' contracts, by defining and setting forth techniques and strategies that parties would have reasonably opted into if there were no costs involved in drafting an effective governance arrangement, policy-makers and lawmakers must be engaged in providing corporate law provisions that efficiently serve to protect insiders' (shareholders and managers) and outsiders' (debt-investors and other creditors) interests. In the next sections, we will provide an overview of the three main areas of close corporation law: (1) information duties; (2) stringent distribution procedures and participation rights; and (3) minority shareholder protections. Figure 2.3 depicts the corporate law solutions to the typical agency problems that arise in non-listed business firms.

## 4.1 Disclosure and Transparency

While our focus is on non-listed companies, disclosure and transparency are important issues facing any business organization. Minority shareholders may gather public information. The main source of public information is the periodical publication of the company's annual reports. In Europe, corporations are obliged to publish audited annual reports under law. For instance, the Fourth European Companies Directive extended disclosure requirements in general to all close corporations.[32] It contains detailed requirements for the preparation of balance sheets, profit and loss statements, and annual reports. Moreover, the Directive requires the disclosure of transactions with related parties, such as key management members and spouses of board members, if these transactions are material and not carried out at arm's-length.[33] The objectives of the Directive are clear: (1) the annual accounts of corporations must give a true and fair view of the assets, liabilities, financial position, and results of the company; and (2) the information in the annual accounts must comply with a uniform set

---

[32] Some smaller enterprises are exempted from the publication of certain information.

[33] See Directive 2006/46/EC of the European Parliament and of the Council of 14 June 2006 amending Council Directives 78/660/EEC on the annual accounts of certain types of companies, 83/349/EEC on consolidated accounts, 86/635/EEC on the annual accounts and consolidated accounts of banks and other financial institutions, and 91/674/EEC on the annual accounts and consolidated accounts of insurance undertakings. This Directive entered into force on 5 September 2006 and should be transposed in the member states on 5 September 2008.

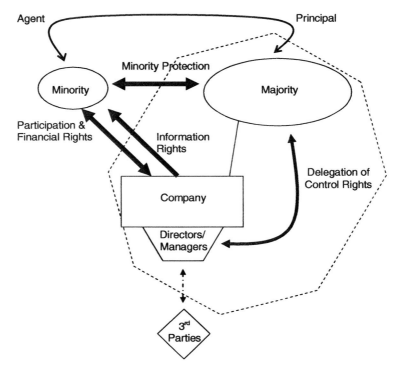

**Figure 2.3.** The principal–agent problem in non-listed firms

of minimum legal requirements in order to offer safeguards to shareholders and third parties who may be residents of different member states. Since the regulatory accounting burdens on particularly small and medium-sized firms are significant, the Directive creates the possibility for member states to alleviate their companies from costly disclosure requirements. The member states have several options to ease the reporting burden on small and medium-sized companies (see Table 2.2).

A closer look at the implementation of the thresholds by member states shows that the differences in the definition of small and medium-sized firms are substantial. This could arguably entail a negative impact on the competition strength between European firms if some of them experience less administrative burdens than others.[34] But even if companies prepare financial statements that conform to a required set of generally accepted accounting principles in a particular

---

[34] See DG Internal Market, Report on impacts of raised thresholds defining SMEs, Impact assessment on raising the thresholds in the 4th Company Law Directive (78/660/EEC) defining small and medium-sized companies, December 2005 (conducted by Ramboll Management).

**Table 2.2.** Fourth Company Law Directive (78/660/EEC) thresholds defining SMEs

'Small' companies that do not exceed two of the three following criteria for two consecutive years:

- balance sheet total: €4,400,000 (previously €3,650,000)
- net turnover: €8,800,000 (previously €7,300,000)
- average number of employees during the financial year: 50

are allowed to draw up abridged accounts and notes to the accounts and are exempt from (1) a statutory audit, (2) an audit opinion, and (3) drawing up an annual report

'Medium-sized' companies that do not exceed two of the three following criteria for two consecutive years:

- balance sheet total: €17,500,000 (previously €14,600,000)
- net turnover: €35,000,000 (previously €29,200,000)
- average number of employees during the financial year: 250

are allowed to adopt a different layout for the profit and loss account, aggregate balance sheet information, not to draw up consolidated accounts, and to leave out non-financial information from the annual account

*Source:* Directive 2006/46/EC of the European Parliament and of the Council of 14 June 2006 amending Council Directives 78/660/EEC on the annual accounts of certain types of companies, 83/349/EEC on consolidated accounts, 86/635/EEC on the annual accounts and consolidated accounts of banks and other financial institutions and 91/674/EEC on the annual accounts and consolidated accounts of insurance undertakings

member state (member state GAAP), the diversity among accounting regimes could hamper the usefulness and reliability of financial reports in a cross-border setting. It is for this reason that the International Accounting Standards Board (IASB) intended full compliance with the International Financial Reporting Standards (IFRSs) by both listed and non-listed companies. However, IFRSs are only mandatory for listed companies in the European Union. That is not to say the member states are not able to make IFRS a requirement for non-listed companies, but so far only three member states require all non-listed companies to comply with IFRS. As we can see in Table 2.3, most member states permit non-listed companies to follow IFRSs. Still, most firms, ranging from large groups of companies to one-person entities, elect to continue with their member state GAAP. They believe the benefits of adopting the 2,500-page rule book do not outweigh the compliance costs.

The IFRSs are considered burdensome in a small and medium-sized entity environment. For instance, for IAS 12, which deals with income taxes, there is a concern that accounting for current and deferred taxes may be too complicated for most SMEs. Furthermore, the accounting treatment (IAS 17) for leases, which is a very popular form of financing, creates costs for SMEs by requiring rental payments being written off the lease obligation and the interest expense. Moreover, employee benefits and pension accounting, which are dealt with under IAS 19, can give rise to complications particularly with regard to measuring post-employment benefits under defined benefit plans, where estimates are often required. Finally, if large multinational firms find it complicated to meet the requirements of IAS 39, we suspect that it is unlikely that small and medium-sized companies will have the resources, expertise, or the inclination needed to satisfy this requirement.[35] In response to the problems SMEs confront when complying with the original rule book, the IASB has drafted a slimmer version of IFRS taking a more principle-based approach.[36] In any event, it has yet to be seen whether the simplified 320-page draft IFRS for small and medium-sized enterprises will be widely adopted by non-listed firms.

No matter what standards companies decide to choose, the disclosed financial information is not always accurate. For instance, in the Netherlands, the annual accounts must be adopted by the shareholders within five months following the end of the financial year. But companies may, subject to shareholder approval, extend this period to thirteen months, which, obviously, will severely diminish the reliability of the disclosed information. Table 2.4 indicates that in practice a significant number of firms must make use of this extension period.

---

[35] IAS 39 provides a set of principles aimed to recognize and measure financial assets, financial liabilities, and some contracts to buy or sell non-financial items.

[36] IASB (2007), Exposure Draft of a Proposed IFRS for Small and Medium-sized Entities, February 2007. The EU, believing the IASB's proposed package of accounting principles for small and medium-sized enterprises are not simple enough, rejected the proposal for application in the EU. See Wolf 2007.

**Table 2.3.** Use of IFRS for reporting by non-listed companies

| | |
|---|---|
| Austria | IFRS permitted in consolidated statements, prohibited in separate statements |
| Belgium | IFRSs required in consolidated statements of unlisted banks and credit institutions, permitted for other companies. IFRSs not permitted in separate company statements. |
| Bulgaria | IFRSs required in both the consolidated and separate company financial statements of unlisted financial institutions and all large unlisted limited liability entities. Other unlisted companies are permitted to use IFRSs. |
| Cyprus | IFRS required for all. |
| Czech Republic | IFRSs permitted in consolidated statements, prohibited in separate company statements. |
| Denmark | IFRSs permitted in both consolidated and separate company statements. |
| Estonia | IFRSs required in both consolidated and separate financial statements of financial institutions. IFRSs permitted in both consolidated and separate statements of other companies. |
| Finland | IFRSs permitted in both consolidated and separate company statements. |
| France | IFRSs permitted in consolidated statements, prohibited in separate company statements. |
| Germany | IFRSs permitted in both consolidated and separate company statements. Statutory accounts that conform to national GAAP are also required. |
| Greece | IFRSs permitted in audited consolidated and separate company financial statements. |
| Hungary | IFRSs permitted in both consolidated and separate company statements. Statutory accounts that conform to national GAAP are also required. |
| Ireland | IFRSs permitted in both consolidated and separate company statements. |
| Italy | IFRSs permitted in consolidated financial statements except for very small companies. IFRSs permitted in separate company statements except for very small insurance companies, and some regulated companies |
| Latvia | IFRSs required for financial institutions, not permitted for others. |
| Lithuania | IFRSs required for financial institutions, not permitted for others. |
| Luxembourg | IFRSs permitted in both consolidated and separate company statements. |

**Table 2.3.** *(Cont.)*

| | |
|---|---|
| Malta | IFRSs required for all. |
| Netherlands | IFRSs permitted in both consolidated and separate company statements. |
| Poland | IFRSs required for consolidated financial statements of banks, permitted in consolidated financial statements of companies that have applied for stock exchange listing or whose parent uses IFRSs. IFRSs permitted in the separate financial statements of companies that have applied for stock exchange listing or whose parent uses IFRSs, prohibited in the separate financial statements of other companies. |
| Portugal | IFRSs required in consolidated financial statements of banks and financial institutions, permitted for others. IFRSs permitted in separate company statements of a company that is within the scope of a consolidated group that uses IFRSs, not permitted for other companies. |
| Romania | IFRSs required for consolidated financial statements of banks, permitted in consolidated financial statements of companies that have applied for stock exchange listing or whose parent uses IFRSs. IFRSs permitted in the separate financial statements of companies that have applied for stock exchange listing or whose parent uses IFRSs, prohibited in the separate financial statements of other companies. |
| Slovak Republic | IFRSs required for all. |
| Slovenia | IFRSs required for financial institutions, permitted for others. |
| Spain | IFRSs permitted in consolidated statements, prohibited in separate company statements. |
| Sweden | IFRSs permitted in consolidated statements, prohibited in separate company statements. |
| United Kingdom | IFRSs permitted in both consolidated and separate company statements |

*Source:* Data from <www.iasplus.com> (updated on 1 August 2007).

**Table 2.4.** Percentage of Dutch firms that disclose the annual account within five months of the financial year

|                                                   | %  |
| ------------------------------------------------- | -- |
| Annual account 2002 filed before 30 June 2003     | 14 |
| Annual account 2003 filed before 30 June 2004     | 16 |
| Annual account 2004 filed before 30 June 2005     | 19 |
| Annual account 2005 filed before 30 June 2006     | 14 |
| Annual account 2006 filed before 30 June 2007     | 26 |

*Source*: Adapted from Graydon (website of the *Financieele Dagblad*).

In fact, approximately 375,000 companies applied for the extension in 2006. It appears, however, that about 85,000 of these companies fail to disclose even after this period. This could be the result of Dutch regulators being lenient with these firms. Less than 1–2 per cent of them are fined.[37] This trend is also noticeable in other European member states, such as Germany.[38] It is not surprising, however, that in countries with a stricter enforcement regime more companies are willing to abide by the rules and timely disclose their financial information.[39]

This raises the question of why policy-makers in the European Union remain committed to full disclosure by medium-sized and larger non-listed companies. The purpose of mandatory disclosure is twofold. First, shareholders and other stakeholders will have access to financial and non-financial information about the company. Second, and perhaps more importantly, it encourages business parties, in particular, managers to analyse and understand the business. When they are used to communicate openly and clearly, the costs of mandatory disclosure will diminish significantly. To be sure, companies' shareholders may have other direct techniques, such as covenants and other contractual measures, to acquire information about the performance and financial situation of the company.[40]

In contrast, mandatory disclosure is restricted in the USA to publicly held firms.[41] Nevertheless, individual members of close corporations are entitled to substantial information. For example, Delaware corporation law provides:[42]

(b) Any stockholder, in person or by attorney or other agent, shall, upon written demand under oath stating the purpose thereof, have the right

[37] Empirical research shows that 17% of the firms do not disclose their annual accounts. See Graydon (*De Financieele Dagblad* (H Haenen), 'Liever in overtreding dan transparant', 15 August 2007).
[38] See Chapter 3.
[39] In Denmark and the United Kingdom, for instance, firms tend to disclose their financial statements on time (De Jong and Nieuwe Weme 2006).
[40] See Chapter 5.
[41] A US non-listed company which has total assets exceeding $10,000,000 and more than 500 shareholders must publish its accounts (Securities Exchange Act of 1934 §12(g)).
[42] Del Code Ann Tit 8, §220(b).

during the usual hours for business to inspect for any proper purpose, and to make copies and extracts from:

(1) The corporation's stock ledger, a list of its stockholders, and its other books and records; and

(2) A subsidiary's books and records, to the extent that:

    a. The corporation has actual possession and control of such records of such subsidiary; or

    b. The corporation could obtain such records through the exercise of control over such subsidiary, provided that as of the date of the making of the demand:

        1. The stockholder inspection of such books and records of the subsidiary would not constitute a breach of an agreement between the corporation or the subsidiary and a person or persons not affiliated with the corporation; and

        2. The subsidiary would not have the right under the law applicable to it to deny the corporation access to such books and records upon demand by the corporation.

In every instance where the stockholder is other than a record holder of stock in a stock corporation or a member of a non-stock corporation, the demand under oath shall state the person's status as a stockholder, be accompanied by documentary evidence of beneficial ownership of the stock, and state that such documentary evidence is a true and correct copy of what it purports to be. A proper purpose shall mean a purpose reasonably related to such person's interest as a stockholder. In every instance where an attorney or other agent shall be the person who seeks the right to inspection, the demand under oath shall be accompanied by a power of attorney or such other writing which authorizes the attorney or other agent to so act on behalf of the stockholder. The demand under oath shall be directed to the corporation at its registered office in this state or at its principal place of business.[43]

The Delaware approach is also followed in other non-EU countries, such as Brazil, China, India, and Russia. This is unsurprising if one endorses the view that the benefits of mandatory disclosure may be overstated. On this view, the costs outweigh the benefits due to loss of personal privacy, loss of competitive position, undermining of private property rights, direct compliance costs, and administrative costs. Naturally, business participants have an incentive to avoid mandatory disclosure because they are reluctant to disclose sensitive information. Another significant problem is that the information is not always timely and accurate and therefore few sophisticated parties would rely on such financial information alone. Even though the benefits and costs of disclosure do not impact all firms equally, mandatory disclosure is

---

[43] In addition, shareholders who have launched an action against a corporation can obtain information under the civil discovery rules (Rock and Wachter 1999).

nevertheless likely to promote a more effective, low-cost regulatory landscape that generates significant economic benefits by disciplining entrepreneurs, on the one hand, and offering enhanced protections for stakeholders, on the other hand.

Whilst private companies are not required to provide the same flow and rate of information as publicly held firms across the board, arguably they should have strong incentives for doing so. Indeed, the best-run companies, which are more attractive to investors, signal their accountability by supplying information about: (1) the company's objectives; (2) principal changes; (3) balance sheet and off-balance sheet items; (4) financial position of the firm and its capital needs; (5) board composition and company policy for appointments and remuneration; (6) forward-looking expectations; and (7) profits and dividends (Charkham 2005).

## 4.2 'Shareholder' Participation and Dividends

As discussed above, shareholders in close corporations often view themselves as partners with equal financial and managerial control rights. Arguably, this is true in a context of strong relational ties based on trust. Yet over-optimism regarding the success and trustworthiness of business parties at the time of formation sometimes leads them to underestimate the possibility of dissension when the venture matures. Naturally, the partners can amicably overcome possible problems ensuing from disagreement and disruption by working things out *ex post*, without reference to any legal rule or contractual provision. Yet sometimes this idea of a perfect relationship is just make-believe. Once the dissatisfaction or distrust disrupts the relationship, the exasperated participants are usually unable to negotiate their way out of the dispute.

Obviously, the problems that arise in endgame settings can have a particularly heavy impact on both the firm and its shareholders. For instance, internal strife often entails disagreement about the consequences of the dissolution of the relationship, thereby encouraging opportunistic behaviour. Moreover, given the limited market for and the restricted transferability of interests in a closely held firm, business partners could be locked into a very unpleasant investment in which hold-up problems abound. In fact, an intense dispute may lead to a serious deadlock in the event of business decisions being taken only by the unanimous consent of all the partners.

In close corporations, however, the deadlock problem is often avoided by the principle of majority rule and statutory norms of centralized management. These corporate principles may be conducive to minority oppression. Minority shareholders may face an indefinite future when there is, for instance, a falling-out between the controlling shareholder and the minority shareholders. In the event that all the shareholders work in the business, the controlling shareholder may fire the minority, who then can either hold on to their shares, which pay no dividend, or sell them back to the firm for whatever price the controlling shareholder is willing to offer (Rock and Wachter 1999).

That is not to say that in such a squeeze-out situation, minority shareholders are deprived from participation in any decision-making process. Shareholders are usually entitled to attend shareholders' meetings where they are able to participate in discussions and vote on agenda items. In most jurisdictions, shareholders are also allowed to convene a meeting when they hold at least a defined percentage (usually 10 per cent) of the issued share capital. However, in non-listed companies, which are characterized by 'the decision-making by majority' principle, controlling shareholders dominate the election of directors and influence directly the fundamental decisions, establish company policy, perform the main monitoring functions, and sometimes act as the firm's agents. That said, minority shareholders are particularly vulnerable to opportunistic acts by the controlling shareholders. Indeed, the majority shareholder has a range of strategies at its disposal to extract resources from firms they control. These include: (1) distributions of cash and property to confer benefits on shareholders; (2) dilutive share issues; (3) interested transactions; (4) allocation of corporate opportunities; (5) allocation of business activities; and (6) selective disclosure of non-public information.

To be sure, corporate law may allow charter provisions which provide minority shareholders with a right to veto important corporate resolutions. In this respect, three arrangements could be distinguished. Firstly, close corporation statutes sometimes require unanimity or a supermajority vote for particular shareholder actions, such as the alteration of the articles of association and mergers. Secondly, company law may allow for dual-class share arrangements which give some shares more votes than other shares on particular issues, such as the appointment of directors, or on all issues. Lastly, some company laws fix high quorum requirements for shareholders' meetings by default. A high quorum requirement in conjunction with a high supermajority vote requirement may even create double protection for minority shareholders. These protective devices could, however, create incentives for the minority to behave opportunistically toward the majority, thereby extracting disproportionate concessions.

In order to prevent opportunistic behaviour by the controlling shareholder, company law may also discourage divergence from the minority shareholders' interests by providing rules that limit the managers' power to act solely on the directions and instructions of the controlling shareholder. For instance, a legal rule could instruct director-managers to take into account the interest of minority shareholders and other stakeholders in exercising their powers. Moreover, shareholder approval may be required when weak management intends to enter into substantial property dealings on behalf of the company.

The safest way, however, to ensure that the interests of minority shareholders are represented on the board of directors is the use of different classes of shares that have identical financial rights but are entitled to vote separately as classes for the election of specified numbers of board members. Another option is

cumulative voting: a voting system found in a number of jurisdictions that gives
minority shareholders more power, by allowing them to cast all of their board
of director votes for a single candidate. Cumulative voting, however, may easily be eliminated or minimized by the controlling shareholder. For instance, a
controlling shareholder can simply alter the articles of association or remove the
minority shareholders' director without cause and replace him or her with a more
congenial person. Given the experience in East Asia and the USA, controlling
shareholders are reluctant to adopt cumulative voting.[44]

Unlike participation rights, it is much easier to protect the financial rights of
minorities. Corporate law plays an important role in solving problems involving
non *pro rata* distributions. First, it can provide the participants with a rule stating
that all shareholders share in the profit in proportion to their stake in the company, unless otherwise agreed upon. In the event of dissolution, the law can mandate that the residual assets of the firm—anything left after creditors are paid
and other obligations fulfilled—will be divided *pro rata* among the shareholders.
Moreover, shareholders in closely held companies can be bestowed with a legal
mechanism that gives them a statutory pre-emptive right to subscribe for newly
issued shares proportional to their existing shares in the capital of the company.[45]
Such measures tend to align the interests of the controlling and minority shareholders in close corporations.

## 4.3  Minority Shareholder Protection

Business parties can bargain to an efficient contract most of the time without resort
to legally enforceable norms. However, there are circumstances in which, due to
information asymmetries or other contracting infirmities, parties are unable to rely
upon contractual provisions that deal with dissension and deadlocks. This often
leaves minority shareholders unprotected and vulnerable to oppression. While
vague legal standards are often available in statutes, these provisions may be insufficient to cover the full range of contracting circumstances. In this case, courts must
play a central role in completing contracts *ex post*. Despite the beneficial effects of
such judgments, reliance on judicial gap-filling is not always an effective means of
conflict resolution. Not only could *ex post* gap filling be imprecise, but it also tends
to involve significant transaction costs and is time consuming. Moreover, some
commentators point to large variations in judicial decision-making, supporting

---

[44] See, for instance, Nam and Nam (2004) (noting that in Thailand, Indonesia, and
the Republic of Korea, only a few firms adopted this mechanism after it had been enacted).
Cumulative voting allows shareholders to multiply the number of shares owned by the number of board of director positions to be voted on, and then cast that number for one or more
directors.
[45] Dominant shareholders may use the issuance of new shares to expropriate private benefits from the minority shareholders. See Nam and Nam (2004) (stating that the pre-emptive
rights were not well protected in the East Asian countries until very recently).

the view that gap filling is often haphazard and costly in redistribution terms (Schwartz and Scott 2003). More significantly, whilst intra-firm conflicts may be observable to the contracting business parties, they may not be easily verifiable by judges and other conflict resolution bodies, and even less so when personal relationships in the family or between friends are involved.

Nevertheless, as we have seen, minority shareholders' interests can be protected by clear and simple rules that restrict managers' power to act in response to directions given by the controlling shareholders. At the same time, fiduciary duties can play a role in preventing oppression and supplementing the firms' organizational structure. But, open-ended fiduciary duties in markets with less experienced courts and legal systems may prove less effective. The duty of loyalty, for instance, provides an important safety mechanism to protect investors against the abusive tactics of controlling shareholders. From the perspective of continental Europe and emerging markets, however, these duties are not easily enforceable unless they are clearly enunciated as formal legal rules (Paredes 2004).

In this view, *ex post* enforcement can serve to protect minority investors in non-listed companies. Naturally, shareholders are expected to resort to this mechanism if other gatekeeper institutions are insufficient (clearly the case in non-listed companies). There is something to the *ex post* application of partnership law principles. As we have seen, equal distribution and managerial control rights are the preferred default rules in many close corporations. Still, the 'partnership law' analogy is full of perils and pitfalls.[46] For instance, it is not always possible to effectively draft around the statutory provisions of corporate statutes, in that the contractual variations may not always be fully enforced.[47] This is especially true when a contract between shareholders conflicts with the close corporation's articles of association and by-laws. The fact that many closely held firms are unlikely to adjust statutory corporate rules,[48] leaving dispute resolution to rest solely on judicial discretion in applying vague legal standards of good faith and fiduciary duties, reinforces critics' view of the partnership metaphor. The judicial discretion to meddle in the internal affairs of close corporations might entail deficiencies and inconsistencies, in that

---

[46] Cf DTI (2001: 33 and 163–4) (arguing that limiting the unfair prejudice claim under section 459 of the Companies Act 1985 (see *O'Neill v Phillips* [1999] 1 WLR 1092) will discourage the practice of making all manner of allegations which might conceivably sustain a case of unfairness).

[47] See eg Hochstetler and Svejda (1985: 918–19):

'[o]rganizing the close corporation as a partnership, however, runs counter to the idea expressed in some judicial opinions that a close corporation must be run like a publicly held corporation—not as a partnership. Corporations cannot revert to partnership practices in the management of the business whenever they so desire. Thus, courts' decisions have invalidated partnership arrangements in close corporations for being contrary to public policy. Specifically, courts have held that the parties cannot be partners as between themselves, and a corporation as to the rest of the world. A corporation cannot serve as the mere instrumentality of a partnership because a corporation is a distinct type of business organization and its characteristics cannot be mingled with those of a partnership.'

[48] It appears that departures from statutory rules raise procedural and psychological barriers. See DTI (1999: 56–7).

the firm's participants (e.g., the investors and creditors) might no longer be able to rely on the business form they deal with.[49] Judicial interpretation, especially when it stands apart from the statute itself, could limit the statute's certainty and its value for both public and closely held firms. Furthermore, it appears that, once partnership-type doctrines are accepted in the close corporation context, these doctrines are difficult to opt out of.[50] Finally, because these doctrines are vague and open-ended, they may create confusion, thereby preventing the formation of firms, international joint ventures in particular.[51]

Given the limitation of direct actions by individual shareholders, it is important to enforce the principle of non *pro rata* distribution on behalf of the company. In some jurisdictions (see Table 2.5), derivative suits provide minority investors with the possibility of clawing back their investment appropriated by managers or controlling shareholders.[52] Indeed, derivative suits are bought by one or more shareholders in the name of the company and for the benefit of the company as a whole, and are the exception to the usual rule that a company's board of directors manages the company's affairs. The success of these actions depends on investors' access to information, the financial incentives provided to lawyers and the sophistication of the court system. While these factors may vary across countries, the promulgation of clear and precise legal rules is, as we have seen, essential to the adequate protection of the minority's interests in non-listed companies. For instance, in order to produce guidelines for the duty of loyalty, lawmakers could define specific duties that comprise this fiduciary obligation. By providing more clarity, company law could reduce litigation costs since disputes could more easily be resolved at a preliminary stage before trial. However, these variations should not be exclusive.

Finally, it could be argued that minority shareholders should have identical exit options as partners in a partnership. Standard economic theory suggests that this could have some traction. Company law default rules traditionally lock in the participants by giving them only a very limited right to dissociate.[53] This is not

---

[49] See eg O'Kelley (1992a: 357) (arguing that efficiency-minded judges must weigh the potential gains from correcting for irrational form selection against the costs in form devaluation resulting from such erroneous second guessing). Cf Cheffins (1997: 333) (explaining that despite the approach English courts take to precedent and despite the division of labour within the High Court, the predictability of company law is undermined in some measures).

[50] See Oesterle (1995: 888) (discussing three doctrines that courts in the United States have used to protect the minority shareholder in close corporations).

[51] See Miller (1997: 427) (arguing that vague legal concepts regarding shareholder misconduct may increase rather than reduce the international shareholder's confusion regarding the scope of acceptable conduct).

[52] Derivative suits are brought by one or more shareholders in the name of the company and for the benefit of the company as a whole, and are an exception to the usual rule that a company's board of directors manages the company affairs.

[53] See eg sections 335–43 of Book 2 of the Dutch Civil Code (providing rules of disputes in close corporations); section 459 of the UK Companies Act (stating that a member of a company may file a petition for a buyout remedy on the ground that the company's affairs are being or have been conducted in a manner that is unfairly prejudicial to the interests of some part of the members

Table 2.5. Comparative overview of minority remedies

| Minority Rights in Close Corporations | United States | United Kingdom | France | Germany | The Netherlands |
|---|---|---|---|---|---|
| Right to request dissolution of the corporation | Action in oppression | Unfairly prejudicial remedy + Just and equitable remedy | Valid reasons remedy | Judicial substantial causes ('wichtige Grund') remedy | Yes in theory, but not illustrated by case law |
| Buyouts | Action in oppression (eg Section 14.34 of the Model Business Corporation Act (1984) | Unfairly prejudicial remedy | No | Judicial substantial causes ('wichtige Grund') remedy | A shareholder may institute proceedings against the co-shareholders if his or her rights or interests are prejudiced by the conduct of these shareholders |
| Derivative action | Yes | Restricted to certain conditions | 'Action sociale exercée ut singuli' | No—however, case law provides for a so-called action pro socio, which gives shareholders the right to bring a legal action against other shareholders | No |

| | | | | | |
|---|---|---|---|---|---|
| Inquiry proceedings | No but receivership or temporary receiver | Special audit | *'Expertise de gestion'*—minority shareholders holding at least 5% of the registered capital may request the court to appoint an expert to investigate the management of the company's affairs | No—but contractual mechanisms are allowed in the articles of association | Yes: main minority remedy—if there is a good reason to doubt the proper management of the company, shareholders representing 10% of the nominal capital or at least €225,000 may start inquiry proceedings. Parties can ask injunctive relief from the Enterprise Chamber. |
| Fiduciary duties of controlling shareholders | Yes, statutory and case law | Yes, case law | *'Abus de majorité'* | Duty of loyalty | Dictates of reasonableness and fairness |

surprising in view of the fact that company laws were originally designed to reflect the needs of publicly held corporations where the public market for shares provides shareholders with an escape route. The absence of a liquid market in non-listed companies' shares, however, deprives the business parties of an effective exit mechanism. To be sure, the lock-in effect of the corporate form may help to prevent an abusive use of an exit right, thereby furthering the stability of the firm. However, as indicated in Table 2.6, company laws increasingly introduce measures aimed at the protection of minority shareholders, such as the right of shareholders to demand a repurchase of their shares and the right to petition for the dissolution of the company. With respect to the involuntary dissolution measure, it should be noted that there is a trend towards the creation of explicit buyout remedies in deadlock situations (with, for instance, two 50 per cent shareholders) and oppression cases. These remedies provide for perpetual duration of the corporation and vary from dissociation at will provisions to limited and more restrictive exit rights.

The diversification of exit rights, as depicted in Table 2.6, shows the tension between the benefits and costs of easy exit rights. There is a trade-off between the disadvantage of being locked into a dissatisfying investment and the threat of shareholders using exit provisions opportunistically. Due to the significant costs of a member leaving the firm, 'for cause' exit rules prevail. Under the Russian 'at will' exit provision, for example, a company will surely not survive when an important shareholder decides to leave the company. It should therefore come as no surprise that investors often prefer to employ the joint stock company. 'For cause' provisions, under which a shareholder may only exit the company for a legitimate reason, attempt to balance the costs and benefits of disinvestment mechanisms. Still, complicated calculation issues, particularly the valuation of interests and whether payment should be deferred, abound in disassociations, since the fair value of interests is likely to be non-verifiable as majority shareholders will tend to low-ball departing investors (Feldman 2005).[54]

This is not to say that parties should be prevented from contracting around restrictive company law norms and rules. For example, joint venture partners usually bargain *ex ante* to provide exit provisions that assist in the resolution of any disputes or deadlocked issues. Currently, there is wide-spread consensus that company law legislation should allow shareholders greater flexibility in choosing how to operate their business. In the next section, we will briefly discuss the flexibility of the private limited company in the United Kingdom, which has

---

or that any actual or proposed act or omission of the company is or would be so prejudicial); Model Business Corporation Act §14.30(2) (stating that a court may dissolve a corporation in a proceeding by a shareholder in the event of a corporation being deadlocked in decision-making issues regarding the corporate affairs).

[54] Delaware provides, under Del Code Ann Tit 8, 604, that a resigning member is entitled to receive any distribution as provided for in the operating agreement. If the operating agreement is silent on this matter, the statute calls for a member to receive fair value, as of the date of resignation, based upon his right to share in distributions. Naturally, complications sometimes arise in practice making the fair value calculation difficult to resolve amicably between parties.

**Table 2.6.** A comparative overview of exit rights

| | Russia (Limited Liability Company—OOO) | Brazil (Limitada) | China (Limited Liability Company) | India (Private Limited Company) | Turkey (Private Limited Company) |
|---|---|---|---|---|---|
| Applicable Law | Civil Code Law on the Limited Liability Company | Civil Code, 10,404 Brazilian Corporations Law, No 6,404 | The PRC Company Law | Companies Act, 1956, amended by the Companies Amendment bill, 2006 | Commercial Code |
| Exit rights | Shareholders have the right to withdraw at any time with or without the consent of the other shareholders and receive the actual value of their interest in the Russian Limited Liability Company (under Article 26 of the LLC Law) | A partner who objects to an amendment to the articles of association or to a merger is entitled to withdraw from the *Limitada*. He/she is entitled to receive the book value of his/her interest based on balance sheet at the date of the action. | The revised company law grants shareholders the right to sell their shares to the company at a reasonable price if they oppose an acquisition or merger; if they oppose the disposal of major assets; if the company fails to distribute dividends for 5 consecutive years; if they oppose the renewal of the company's term | Sections 397 to 409 of the Act address 'oppression and mismanagement'. Minority shareholders can seek recourse to legal remedies if controlling shareholders cause oppression and mismanagement. | Right to petition for a withdrawal from the company on 'justifiable grounds' |

easy exit ⟶ more locked in

been updated under the Companies Act 2006. The new legal provisions will be brought into force in stages and be effective by October 2008.

## 5. The Close Corporation as an All-Purpose Vehicle in the Twenty-first Century

In the next chapter, we will see that non-listed companies within the European Union (EU) can choose from among the number of member states offering more optimal regulations and more favourable conditions to long-term relational contracting. As is reflected in Table 2.1, the absence of minimum share capital requirements is an attraction for many small, undercapitalized firms. As a consequence, the United Kingdom, which has signalled its commitment to regulatory responsiveness by offering varied and high-quality business organization laws, could be well placed to establish itself as the leading state for European business formations, like Delaware in the United States. To be sure, charter fees and franchise taxes, which provide a high-powered incentive for Delaware to enter the competition for business forms, do not encourage the United Kingdom. However, the United Kingdom could dominate firms' domicile choice as a side-effect of its aspiration to attract large volumes of business and risk capital. The United Kingdom has a substantial body of case law and a highly respected judiciary which could be an important advantage in this respect. The United Kingdom also has a responsive legislature that may be motivated to develop amendments to its business organization law regime in response to demands in the marketplace. Another attractive feature that could have a considerable effect on attracting migrating firms is that the UK's private limited company law was already significantly more flexible *vis-à-vis* other European jurisdictions. Furthermore, the popularity of the United Kingdom for closely held firms and financial intermediaries suggests that it is willing to offer legal rules that may be attractive for these firms. To the extent that the United Kingdom attracts a large number of new firms and is seen as a jurisdiction in which a firm might keep its statutory seat, UK lawmakers arguably have incentives to promulgate legislation capable of attracting firms located in other member states in the EU.

The new Companies Act 2006 must enable the law in the United Kingdom to continue to be attractive to both domestic and foreign firms. The new legislation not only allows non-listed companies greater flexibility to structure their organization and investment structure, but also makes it easier and cheaper to establish and operate a private limited company (see Table 2.7). Consequently, as national boundaries are of diminishing significance and the cross-fertilization of legal concepts is not so much a choice as a necessity, there is a revival of interest in company law reform projects in many European countries that presumptively could lead to formal convergence.

**Table 2.7.** Changes that simplify the formation and operation of UK private limited companies

| | |
|---|---|
| Formation | It is no longer mandatory to appoint a company secretary |
| | It is no longer required to state the objects of the company in the memorandum of association or articles of association |
| | Directors will only be required to file a service address on the public record of the Companies House. This may be the company's address |
| | Start-up (and existing) companies will be allowed to adopt new modern articles of association |
| | Most small companies are not required to have auditors |
| Decision-making | Annual general meetings are no longer required |
| | Written resolutions need not be signed by all shareholders |
| | Proposed written resolutions will no longer have to be notified by auditors |
| | It is allowed to circulate resolutions by email or other electronic means |
| Capital | Companies may reduce their share capital by a special resolution supported by a solvency statement by each of the directors |
| | Financial assistance to buy its own shares is no longer prohibited for a private limited company. Hence, the whitewash procedure does not apply under the Companies Act 2006 |

*Source*: Adapted from DTI, Companies Act 2006, A summary of what it means for private companies.

Due largely to the worldwide development of the Internet, it is relatively easy for lawmakers to take notice of foreign legal business forms that have already been tried and tested in a legal system with similar business, social, and political dimensions. If we take this a step further, the drive towards the modernization of company law could eventually lead to more efficiency, as countries adopt rules and institutions representing the best possible outcome. This theory is based on the premiss that unless a country's lawmakers consider foreign legislative approaches and solutions, the domestic economy will fall behind its competitors. The next chapter will analyse and discuss how improved corporate mobility has influenced company law in Europe and set a trend that converts the close corporation into an all-purpose entity.

# 3

# Company Law Developments in Europe

## 1. Introduction

This chapter seeks to understand the way we think about corporate law in the European Union (EU). It does so by tracing the developments in this area of the law back to the establishment of the EU in 1957. It appears that the member states have consistently attempted to block any intervention into their national corporate law legislation which in turn has limited cross-border mobility of firms. This immobility has, however, been challenged by the European Court of Justice's line of cases starting with *Centros*, which set in train the basis for cross-border movement of administrative headquarters and the migration of new firms to more favourable jurisdictions. In addition, the implementation of the *Societas Europaea* (European Company, SE) Statute in October 2004 created for the first time the possibility for reincorporation without liquidation of the old entity and the formation of an entirely new vehicle. Corporate mobility arguably invites a national legislature to update its company law products so as to ensure that they reflect modern needs and to enable them to compete effectively with foreign jurisdictions which will also feel strong pressures to overhaul their company laws.

Nevertheless, upon the inception of the European Union, most member states followed the real seat doctrine, which ties a firm's state of incorporation to its administrative seat. This limited choice of situs and foreclosed corporate mobility. On the one hand, national legal regimes created barriers to mobility to preserve national lawmakers' autonomy in the area of company law, while on the other hand preservation of national discretion reinforced the barriers. The member states looking toward preservation of national regulatory discretion have prevailed in the European corporate law setting for a long time, thereby setting the basis for a non-mobility equilibrium. Although we should emphasize that this was not intended with the creation of the EU,[1] founding member states, such as France and West Germany, feared the consequences of an outbreak of a so-called 'race to the bottom' in corporate lawmaking. This led to the introduction of top-down harmonization of national corporate law. Under this strategy,

---

[1] The Treaty of Rome (1957) provided for the right of establishment for foreign corporations to establish branches in another member state, without being subject to more restrictive corporate law provisions of the host state.

the member states entered into a cooperative game in which the parties agreed, in exchange for political benefits or rents, to desist from opportunism after attaining Community membership. The cooperative agreement among member states included another element: the member states would only agree to the harmonization of the national corporate laws if this could be achieved without the alteration of the core components of their laws.

The legislative autonomy was also confirmed by the reluctance of member states to adopt EU-level corporate law. While the EU continued to pursue its harmonization strategy, policy-makers within the Commission had set out to design a more independent agenda on the basis of Article 308 (ex 235).[2] The introduction of EU-level business forms, such as the *Societas Europaea*, was designed to stimulate cross-border mobility while, at the same time, covering the creation and conversion of undertakings. Despite the introduction of the European Economic Interest Grouping (EEIG) in 1985 and the SE in 2001, this strategy arguably failed to break down member states' continued preference for retaining legislative autonomy and control over core areas of corporate law.

Still, there is something to be said for the introduction of the SE. Although this EU-level business form, which entered into force in October 2004, is mainly viewed as a compromise legislation that offers a rigid and unattractive choice for firms to structure their internal affairs, the SE Statute at least allows these firms to merge across borders and transfer their seat from one member state to another. The internal governance structure of an SE continues to be governed largely by national legislation. It can be viewed as a first attempt to give firms a possibility to pursue the second type of corporate mobility. Since existing European firms may employ the SE to reincorporate in other member states, the Statute holds out a path around the obstacles surrounding the reincorporation process: a path which seems nevertheless too narrow to lead to undisturbed choice of situs of incorporation. For instance, start-up firms cannot establish an SE *ex novo* or *ex nihilo*.[3] What is more, the provisions set forth in the Directive on Involvement of Employees detail the level of employee involvement in the formation and operation of an SE and, as a result, decrease rather than increase the SE's attractiveness.[4]

In recent years, a series of path-breaking decisions by the European Court of Justice (ECJ) involving the freedom of establishment of foreign corporations and the mutual recognition of corporations by the member states have also disturbed

---

[2] Article 308 (ex 235) specifies two preconditions for unification: (1) action by the Community should prove necessary to attain; (2) the powers provided in the Treaty are insufficient (Buxbaum and Hopt 1988).

[3] The significant amount of minimum capital that is required to form an SE is yet another dissuasive element in the SE Statute. The minimum capital requirement of €120,000 would certainly prevent start-up firms from opting for this EU-level business form. See section 4 of the Council Regulation (EC) No 2157/2001 of 8 October 2001 on the Statute for a European company (SE), OJ 2001 L 294/1–21.

[4] See Council Directive 2001/86/EC [2001] OJ L294/22.

the EU non-mobility equilibrium. The rulings in *Centros, Überseeing,* and *Inspire Art* make it possible for new firms to migrate to more favourable corporate law jurisdictions.[5] However, these decisions do not explicitly introduce the possibility of free choice for existing firms that intend to migrate across borders. That is what they must mean if the EU is to approximate the freedom available to companies in the USA where both types of corporate mobility are possible and acknowledged. It could therefore be argued that so long as that zone of discretion remains in place, the real seat doctrine has only been eradicated in part. Residual barriers to reincorporation, such as tax barriers, continue to make European firms highly immobile. The main types of corporate mobility are thus partially achieved by the introduction of the SE Statute and the triad of ECJ judgments.

New legislation may be required to stimulate corporate mobility. However, rapid developments in ECJ case law suggest that member states can also embrace a judge-made mobility doctrine. For instance, the recent adoption of the Directive on Cross-Border Mergers certainly allows limited liability entities to merge and restructure themselves across borders within the EU.[6] In this respect, the implementation of the Directive will give an important impetus to the breakdown of the non-mobility equilibrium in the EU. It will help overcome some of the most important obstacles to cross-border mergers that still exist due to differences in national corporate laws. Particularly, it will give firms that are not able to seek incorporation under the SE Statute a legal instrument to merge with firms that operate in other member states. But here too the ECJ, forced to pre-empt defensive actions by member states in the *Sevic* case,[7] arguably filled in the gaps in the legislation even before the actual implementation of the Directive in the member states. This reinforces the question: what is the probability that member states are likely to accept fully-fledged corporate mobility without the promulgation of new EU legislation, such as Directives or EU-level regulations? Still, even if the member states endorse the ECJ case law, a puzzle surely remains: will the cooperative equilibrium break down and lead to more corporate mobility? Can we expect mobility where the critical tax barriers remain in place limiting corporate migration? To answer these questions, this chapter will critically assess the implications of the ECJ's statement in *Sevic* that EU-level legislation is not a precondition for corporate mobility. After all, harmonization Directives and ECJ case law could very well complement each other (Hopt 2007).

This chapter has five sections. In section 2, we analyse and assess the opportunities for increased mobility and corporate law reform imported by the EU-level

[5] See ECJ, Case C-212/97 *Centros Ltd and Erhvervs-og Selbskabsstyrelsen* [1999] ECR I-1459; Case C-208/00 *Überseering BV and Nordic Construction Company Baumanagement (NCC)* [2002] ECR I-9919; Case C-167/01 *Kamer van Koophandel en Fabrieken voor Amsterdam v Inspire Art Ltd* [2003] ECR I-10155.
[6] See Directive 2005/56/EC of the European Parliament and of the Council of 26 October 2005 on cross-border mergers of limited liability companies, OJ 2005 L 310/1–9.
[7] See Case C-411/03 *Sevic Systems AG* [2005] ECR I-10805.

initiatives, such as the Merger Directive and the SE. The level of cross-border mobility is measured and considerations about extending EU-level initiatives are analysed in respect of their effect on legal mobility. Section 3 surveys the evolution of recent ECJ case law that may disrupt the corporate law equilibrium and also accentuate pressure on national corporate law systems. It sets out a detailed map of current and potential paths of corporate law reform. We initially focus on the magnitude of mobility of start-ups and closely held firms that mainly consider the costs and time related to the formation of a company. Questions regarding the impact of the case law will be addressed. Section 4 considers the residual barriers to corporate mobility. We inquire into the possibility of free choice of corporate situs and tax residence while considering the question as to which additional routes—whether judge-made or through legislative action—could improve and stimulate cross-border mobility in the EU. Section 5 gives an example of how increased competitive pressures could induce lawmakers to adopt the company law rules that are value increasing. Under these circumstances, lawmakers, eager to please investors and other business parties, will identify practices seen as enhancing firms' economic performance, and introduce legal business forms that have the potential to be more cost-effective and suitably adapted to firms' changing business needs. In this respect, firms and their internal participants are viewed as consumers in a market for company law, in which lawmakers seek to design a predictable legal product that not only reduces firms' formation costs, but also the operational costs.

## 2. EU Legislation as the Foundation for Corporate Law Reform

### 2.1 The EU Corporate Law Directives

Under the historic pattern of corporate lawmaking at the EU level, national legislatures have had a virtual monopoly, supported by the twin pillars of the real seat doctrine in conflict of laws and national tax regimes. The real seat doctrine barred essential legal recognition to firms that attempt to relocate to another incorporation state. Moreover, firms that were termed 'pseudo-foreign corporations' had to apply to the core rules of the home member state. Some member states choose not to follow the real seat doctrine. But even in these jurisdictions, national regulators have for long attempted to restrain local entrepreneurs from incorporating elsewhere by restricting re-entry of their pseudo-foreign corporations. And even now there are substantial fiscal barriers that restrict an outbreak of corporate mobility. The real seat doctrine, restrictions on pseudo-foreign corporations, and exit taxes together constituted the foundations of a stable, long-run non-mobility equilibrium that effectively barred the need for substantial corporate law reform in the member states of the EU.

Recall, the equilibrium remained stable despite the appearance of the EC. Historically, Brussels has protected the member states' control of the corporate lawmaking agenda and respected their implicit cooperative approach. To look at the evolution of EU corporation law is to see that from the inception of the harmonization programme in 1957 through the modernization period of the High Level Group of Company Law Experts, the EU has not been able to stimulate the right of establishment of pseudo-foreign companies. The harmonization programme has not produced the coveted effect of limiting the barriers to corporate mobility. In fact, the emergence of a non-intervention approach in EU lawmaking reinforced the tendency by discouraging disruption of regulatory settlements concluded among interest groups in the member states. The EU, acting in accordance with a perceived public interest, has deterred member states both from dismantling costly legal barriers to reincorporation and from developing responsive measures aimed at encouraging corporate mobility. Let us look further into this to show how the harmonization programme contributed to the non-mobility equilibrium in the EU.

### 2.1.1 Corporate Law Harmonization: The Establishment of the EU Corporate Law Regime and the First Generation of Corporate Law Directives

Prior to the establishment of the EU, Europe amounted to a group of island jurisdictions, in which domestic lawmakers, each with different constituencies and political concerns, pursued their own policy agendas. Each jurisdictional island possessed an elite group of legislators, judges, regulatory agencies, professionals, and legal academics responsible for interpreting, preserving, and developing the law. They did so in conservative frameworks, undisturbed by and unresponsive to possible changes in the legal systems of surrounding islands. As jurisdictional islands, the states remained privileged to close their borders in response to exterior competitive threats. For example, in the nineteenth century, Belgium tried to play a non-cooperative corporate law game *vis-à-vis* France, encouraging French managers to change their jurisdictions of incorporation. France and other high-cost jurisdictions responded to this opportunistic initiative by introducing the real seat doctrine, in effect closing their borders. It gets of course more difficult to keep the border closed when an island jurisdiction becomes part of a common market and national barriers to trade gradually dissipate. In such a market, corporate mobility is more likely to surface. At the same time, actions by a federal lawmaking body can help stimulate cross-border activities.

The Treaty of Rome (1957) established the European common market. It was designed to encourage the creation of an integrated market by assuring the free movement of goods, services, people, and capital. The treaty provided foreign corporations the right to establish branches in another member state (host state) without being subject to more restrictive corporate law provisions. At that time, the real seat theory, which provides that the laws of the host state are applied if the actual centre of the corporation's activities lies in the host state, remained dominant. But, in 1957, many feared it was losing ground. The Netherlands had recently abandoned the doctrine. Furthermore, provision 293 (ex 220) of the Treaty invited member states to enter into negotiations regarding the 1968 Brussels Convention on Mutual Recognition of Companies and Legal Entities, which would have abandoned the real seat in favour of the incorporation doctrine. For a while it looked like the Treaty could usher in a new era of corporate mobility. But reaction was split. Some founding member states feared an outbreak of a so-called 'race to the bottom'. They had learned important lessons about the effects of charter competition from the US experience. Competition was seen to entail substantial losses for domestic interest groups. France in particular was concerned that the Netherlands, which had a more flexible corporation law code and was playing non-cooperatively on corporate tax matters (Bratton and McCahery 2001), would be able to attract a large number of pseudo-foreign companies.

Charter competition's opponents responded by using the lawmaking process, triggered by the Treaty and directed to elimination of disparities among the laws of EU member governments, to reduce potential benefits of competition. France and West Germany promoted top-down harmonization of national corporation laws as a EU agenda item. Existing members and new entrants went along, and the EU's mandatory corporate law Directives resulted. These sought to ensure compliance with a minimum level of regulation. With a common set of legal rules in each jurisdiction, no member state would have the zone of discretion needed to create law that attracted incorporations and hence no incentives to compete.

This first generation of corporate law Directives restated the existing content of the member states' national laws. Mandates resulted, such as minimum capital requirements and disclosure rules. At the same time, the Directives made no attempt to expand the zone of mutual recognition of firms. Even as EU lawmakers justified the harmonization Directives as measures to protect creditors and shareholders, their law-making scheme maintained special interest outcomes that had been reached in the respective member states prior to the elimination of trade barriers (Carney 1997). Incumbent management, for example, had every reason to support provisions that limit dividend payments and share repurchases so as to obtain more leeway to reinvest firm's profits.

To sum up, the early member states played a cooperative game respecting corporate law. They in effect agreed to desist from non-cooperative corporate law-making in exchange for membership in the Community. They negotiated and enforced a political agreement that protected their national stock markets and domestic labour settlements. Still small in number, they were concerned with political stability as well as economic integration. They valued political payoffs yielded by stable corporation law more highly than the chance for enhanced economic welfare held out by corporate mobility and competitive experimentation.

## 2.1.2 Later Harmonization and the Adoption of the Directive on Cross-border Mergers

The second wave of corporate law Directives was arguably more flexible, granting states options in respect of compliance. The change reflected added diversity of legal regimes due to the admission of the United Kingdom and other new member states. At the same time, an optional approach only ensured that the Directives did not interfere with core elements of given member states' national settlements. The move to flexibility thus followed from the cooperative agreement. Rigidity and top-down mandate remained the dominant theme, however.

The rigid approach eventually showed its limitations. Harmonization of core areas of corporate law, like the structure and responsibility of the board of directors and cross-border mergers, proved slow and ineffective (Woolcock 1996). This was no surprise: the member states valued the autonomy of their national legal regimes. They had fundamental disagreements regarding important issues, such as board structures and employee participation, and so proved reluctant to implement the harmonized rules. There being no politically acceptable consensus, regular vetoes of directive proposals under Article 100 of the EC Treaty (now Article 94) followed.

In 1985, the ECJ and the European Commission responded to calls for greater flexibility by adopting a 'new approach' to harmonization based on minimum harmonization and mutual recognition (Villiers 1998). The following year, the Single European Act (SEA) attempted to resolve possible veto blockages at Council level by providing for a consultation procedure and qualified majority voting. A number of corporate law Directives were promulgated between 1968 and 1989, removing a wide range of discrepancies between the European member states' rules with respect to the protection of stakeholders.[8]

The EU reached another stage in the evolution of the harmonization programme with the development of the subsidiarity principle, embraced by the member states in the 1992 Maastricht Treaty on the European Union.[9] The subsidiarity principle, embodied in Article 5 of the Treaty, concerns areas that are

---

[8] The European Community has adopted an array of directives (First, Second, Third, Fourth, Sixth, Seventh, Eight, Eleventh, Twelfth, and the Securities Directives), which regulate disclosure and *ultra vires*, capital requirements of public corporations, mergers, and divisions of public corporations, corporations' annual and consolidated accounts, the qualification of accountants, disclosure of branches, formation of single member corporations, admissions to stock exchange listing, public offers of listed and unlisted securities, acquisitions and sales of major holdings, and insider trading (Edwards 1999).

[9] Besides constraining the Commission's role through the subsidiarity principle, the Maastricht Treaty also introduced the co-decision procedure. As a consequence, the European Union's decision-making structure closely resembles the constitutional form of democratic federalism in which central government policies are agreed to by a simple majority of elected representatives from lower-tier governments (Inman and Rubinfeld 1997).

not within the exclusive competence of the European Union.[10] It commands the location of competence at the EU level or at the member state level, and, rather than listing the respective competencies, provides for an efficiency test to determine local decisions.[11]

The European Commission, building on the principles of subsidiarity and proportionality, has introduced a new, more flexible type of Directive. This moves away from the provision of minimum standards to a framework model. Despite the new approach, the EU has enjoyed only limited success in the area of corporate law. The 2003 passage of a significantly weakened Directive on Takeovers exemplifies the persistence of deeply rooted conflict among the member states over the direction and pace of the Directives.

The Commission's current efforts to reform the regulatory framework for corporate law are largely inspired by recommendations made by a group of experts commissioned by the EU.[12] These measures were designed to simplify existing rules and improve freedom of choice between alternative forms of organization. The programme looked toward reform at four levels. First, the Commission proposed to modernize corporate law by further harmonizing corporate disclosure, board structure, and director liability requirements, and by amending capital rules. Second, it planned to adopt rules facilitating corporate restructuring and mobility. Third, it proposed the establishment of a permanent coordination structure, the European Corporate Governance Forum, to work along with member state agencies to sanction unfit directors. Fourth, it proposed to strengthen the supervision of auditors and to adopt comprehensive rules on the conduct of audits. This initiative largely retraced the terrain covered by previous harmonization attempts and therefore its prospects for success were not too optimistic.

However, the High Level Group's call for an urgent submission of a revised Directive on cross-border mergers obviously bore fruit. On 15 December 2005, Directive 2005/56/EC entered into force. This Directive further facilitates the merger of corporations that have their statutory and business seat in one of the member states. Its provisions, which have implemented in national corporation law, apply to mergers where at least two corporations are governed by the laws of different member states. It took more than twenty years of negotiation before the EU legislature could obtain

[10] Areas within the exclusive competence of the Union are subject to the proportionality test of Article 5 § 3 of the Treaty, which provides that 'action by the Community shall not go beyond what is necessary to achieve objectives of the Treaty'; proportionality and subsidiarity both apply to non-exclusive areas.

[11] First of all, it has to be determined whether there is a power under the Treaty to take action. The subsidiarity principle then determines whether and how the Community may act. It must be shown that the objectives of the proposed action cannot be sufficiently achieved by the member states. The finding must then justify the further conclusion that in view of the measure the objective can be better achieved at Community level. The proportionality test as defined in § 3 of Article 5 still has to be satisfied.

[12] See Report of the High Level Group of Company Law Experts on a Modern Regulatory Framework for Company Law in Europe, Brussels, 4 November 2002.

approval for the adoption of this Directive.[13] Since a cross-border merger results in the ceasing of the acquired and absorbed companies, a member state's corporation law could lose its application to the protection of shareholders, creditors, employees, and other stakeholders. Indeed, the adoption of the Directive on cross-border mergers could be viewed as another disturbance of the EU's non-mobility equilibrium.

Still, the Directive does not allow merging firms to unlimitedly adopt a legal system that presents them with the most efficient governance structure and board composition. The strict principles and arrangements relating to employee participation—as set out in the Council Directive No 2001/86/EC of October 2001 with regard to the involvement of employees in the SE—apply when the corporation law of the absorbing company does not provide for at least the same employment participation regime as is applicable in one of the merging and disappearing companies. In order to ensure the working of the Directive on the involvement of employees, the merging companies must have an average of more than 500 employees in the six months preceding the publication of the draft terms of the merger. The Directive on cross-border mergers is largely based on the provisions of the SE Statute. It could be argued in this respect that EU-level business forms paved the way for more cross-border mobility. The next section will take a closer look at the emergence of the SE and its impact on corporate mobility in the EU.

## 2.2 EU-Level Business Forms as an Impetus for Corporate Law Reform[14]

First generation EU lawmakers were convinced that an SE statute could create an economic environment through which firms could reach their full development and more crucially to promote cooperation among firms located in different regions of the EU (Leleux 1968). In line with the first harmonization Directives, the Commission initially aimed to create a uniform and comprehensive legislative proposal that served as a basis for a truly genuine European business form.

---

[13] A first draft of the Directive on cross-border mergers was presented in 1984 [COM(1984) 727 final, OJ 1985 C 23/11].

[14] Because of the special nature of the European Economic Interest Grouping (EEIG) and the European Cooperative Society (SCE), sections 3.2 and 3.3 of this chapter only highlight the development and use of the SE. The EEIG was adopted in 1985 (Council Regulation (EEC) 2137/85 on the European Economic Interest Grouping (EEIG) [1985] OJ L199/1). The reason for the relatively early adoption of the EEIG was that this EU-level initiative was not detrimental to national doctrines and usages and hardly competed against national-oriented business forms. The EEIG is too limited in scope. Its activities must be related to the economic activities of its members. Unlike a corporation, which generally aspires to profits for itself, the nature of an EEIG is primarily aimed at facilitating or developing the economic activities and own results of its members. The SCE Regulation (Regulation (EC) No 1435/2003 OJ L 207 of 18 August 2003) entered into force on 21 August 2003 and aims to provide independent associations of individuals with a legal business form to satisfy their common economic, social, and cultural aspirations. On 2 May 2007, more than 1,500 EEIGs were established (see <www.libertas-institut.com>).

This led to a first proposal in 1970. Since its approach would threaten the member states' law-making autonomy, it came as no surprise that this proposal did not obtain the countries' approval. It took until 1989 before the Commission published a new draft Statute. In order to expedite its adoption, it was decided to address the employee participation in a different Directive. A report—produced by a group of experts chaired by former Commission President Étienne Davignon—outlining a compromise solution regarding labour participation, opened the door for a compromise legislation that resolved political difficulties by referring extensively to the national corporation law of the member state where the SE would have its administrative seat.[15] Only in December 2000 did the Council adopt the SE Statute, which entered into force in October 2004.

The SE Statute makes it possible for a firm to effect reincorporation from one member state to another by reorganizing as an SE and transferring the administrative seat. Under the Statute, legal persons may form an SE through (1) merger of two or more existing companies that are governed by the laws of at least two different member states (cross-border merger); (2) formation of a holding company promoted by public or private limited companies; (3) formation of a jointly held subsidiary; or (4) conversion of an existing public limited company.[16] Some governance matters are determined under the SE Statute. But most matters are determined by a *renvoi* to the national company law of the member state where the SE has its seat. However, the Statute explicitly allows firms to select a one-tier system in which the SE comprises a general meeting of shareholders and a board of directors. If the SE prefers to have a supervisory board that monitors the board of directors, the Statute provides for the implementation of a two-tier system.

Significantly, the Statute does open a door for a German AG to escape the strict German rules on labour codetermination, but does provide not a basis for doing so founded on a unilateral management decision. A special negotiation procedure for worker participation must be followed upon the creation of an SE.[17] The Directive distinguishes between information and consultation on the one hand and participation on the other hand. The employee representatives must in all cases be informed about material decisions and given the opportunity to influence the deliberation and decision-making process. In addition, where 25 per cent of the originating firm's employees have a right to participate in management, the employees' representatives must consent to the planned composition of the supervisory board (two-tier) or board of management (one-tier). Thus, a German AG whose unions agree to give up all or part of their supervisory board representation can reorganize as an SE with whatever governance structure agreed to by the unions. No movement of the administrative seat to another member state need occur.

---

[15] Council Regulation (EC) No 2157/2001 of 8 October 2001 on the Statute for a European company (SE) OJ L 294, 10/11/2001, 0001–21.

[16] See Art 2 and Title II of the Regulation.

[17] Section II of the Regulation.

The statute holds out three advantages. First, it is the first piece of European-level legislation that allows for cross-border mergers. It provides for a relatively easy possibility to alter the location of the administrative seat.[18] The Statute accordingly could stimulate some regulatory arbitrage across the EU (Enriques 2004), provided the firm in question otherwise moves its seat. Second, the Statute holds out cost advantages for a firm not seeking to change its seat but seeking to consolidate operations in multiple member states. A firm, even if it plans no change of seat, can merge its various subsidiaries into the SE. The SE emerges as a unitary entity organized in one member state and operating branches in other states across the EU. The difference is that all companies in the group now follow a single body of corporate law. The recent conversion of Alliance AG into an SE suggests that firms do see cost advantages in operating under a single set of rules. Third, the Statute makes it possible for a parent to merge out a minority share-holder interest in a subsidiary without having to take the potentially costly step of making a tender offer for the minority shares.[19]

Despite its advantages and possibilities for encouraging corporate mobility, the practical usage of the SE is often called into question. Many practitioners have expressed scepticism about whether the EU-level legislative measures would lead to significant changes in corporate practice. They point to the lack of statutory guidance to incorporate and operate as an SE. Moreover, they expect that firms would be deterred by the complexity of the process of setting up an SE. In particular, the need to enter into negotiations with employee representatives is believed to be a bottleneck. Lastly, the absence of a specific tax regime, particularly with regard to cross-border seat transfers, is likely to be a significant impediment to the use of the SE. Although to date (April 2007) fewer than eighty SEs have been incorporated—of which one is liquidated and two Dutch SEs have been converted into limited companies residing on the Cayman Islands—we can already draw some preliminary conclusions about the SE's role in stimulating corporate mobility.

## 2.3 The Practical Impact of the SE

When we look at the number of SEs that were formed in each quarter since its introduction in October 2004, it would seem that this EU-level initiative is still an unattractive alternative for firms seeking to pursue cross-border activities or migration strategies (see Figure 3.1). However, an average of almost eight SE

---

[18] The registered office of an SE may be transferred to another member state. Such a transfer shall not result in the winding up of the SE or in the creation of a new legal person. Council Regulation (EC) No 2157/2001 of 8 October 2001 on the Statute for a European company (SE) OJ L 294, 10/11/2001, 0001-21. Art 8 para 1.

[19] Allianz bought out minority shares of RAS, an Italian insurer, in connection with its conversion to SE status. See *Financial Times* (P Jenkins and T Buck), 'Corporate Governance: Why European Companies May See Benefits in a Company Statute with Fewer Limitations', 11 October 2005.

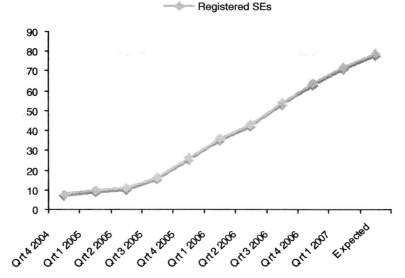

**Figure 3.1.** Total number of SEs registered (October 2004 to April 2007)

*Note:* This figure depicts the information available on 72 registered SEs.

*Source:* Adapted from information available at <www.seeurope-network.org>.

incorporations per quarter could indicate there is a demand for EU-level business forms to pursue cross-border movements. In particular, if we take the time-consuming formation procedures and legal advisers' unfamiliarity with this new business form into account,[20] it should come as no surprise that 'only' seventy-seven SEs have been incorporated so far. Indeed, in an environment where a non-mobility equilibrium prevails, the SE should already be considered successful if it not only enables more cross-border mergers and activities, but also offers firms across jurisdictions a cost-effective means of pursuing inter-jurisdictional strategies.

In order to give a more complete picture of the effect of the SE on corporate mobility, we will categorize the main determinants of SE formations. If we look at the available data at <www.seeurope-network.org>, we can draw some interesting, although not surprising, conclusions. First, it appears that mainly in jurisdictions with widespread participation rights, the benefits of establishing an SE outweigh its considerable formation costs. For instance, German BASF AG estimated an amount of €5,000,000 to convert to an SE. This amount includes

[20] A feasibility study of a European Statute for SMEs (financed by the European Commission) shows that business practice, especially in the area of small and medium-sized enterprises, is not familiar with the possibility of forming an SE. 91.3% were not familiar with this EU-level business form. See AETS, *Étude de faisabilité d'un statut européen de la PME*, July 2005.

**Table 3.1.** The relation between employee participation rights and number of registered SEs

| Countries with widespread participation rights at board level | |
| --- | --- |
| Germany | 29 SEs[a] registered |
| Finland | 1 SE registered |
| Hungary | 2 SEs registered |
| Luxembourg | 2 SEs registered |
| The Netherlands | 9 SEs[b] registered |
| Norway | 2 SEs registered |
| Austria | 8 SEs registered |
| Slovakia | 2 SEs registered |
| Sweden | 5 SEs registered |
| Countries with limited or no participation rights at board level | |
| Belgium | 7 SEs registered |
| Cyprus | 1 SE registered |
| Estonia | 1 SE registered |
| France | 2 SEs registered |
| Latvia | 2 SEs registered |
| Liechtenstein | 1 SE registered |
| The UK | 3 SEs registered |

*Source*: Adapted from information available at <www.seeurope-network.org>.

[a] One SEs is liquidated
[b] Two SEs are converted to private limited companies residing on the Cayman Islands.

the costs of compliance with the necessary legal and accounting requirements as well as registration and disclosure costs.[21] The fact that in April 2007, 78 per cent of the SEs were established in countries with strict regulations, particularly in the area of formation and employee participation (see Table 3.1), indicates that there are other important reasons that make it cost-effective to go through the cumbersome formation requirements than the importance of the adoption of a genuine European structure. Indeed, contrary to the incorporation mobility that merely involves the avoidance of formation costs, firms contemplating the establishment of an SE find the flexibility with respect to corporate governance and participation rights the main attraction of this EU-level business form.

However, while the SE allows firms to voluntarily adopt the corporation law of a more flexible and liberal jurisdiction, firms tend not to change the administrative seat for practical and psychological reasons. If we only take the 'normal' SEs

---

[21] See Conversion Documentation, Conversion of BASF *Aktiengesellschaft* into a European Company (Societas Europaea, SE) with the company name BASF SE (available on the company website).

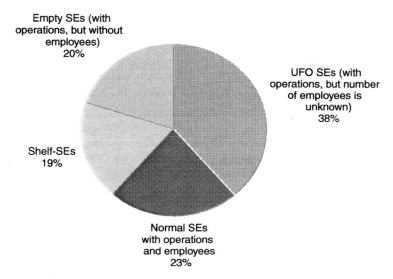

**Figure 3.2.** SEs per category

*Note*: Most of the so-called UFO SEs operate in the financial service sector.
*Source*: Adapted from information available at <www.seeurope-network.org>.

with operations and employees into account, we see that 65 per cent of the existing SEs are formed by the conversion of national corporations that had one or more subsidiaries in other member states (see Figure 3.2). Instead of stimulating reincorporation mobility, the SE competes with national business forms, such as for instance the *Aktiengesellschaft* in Germany. The following business cases exemplify the advantages of the SE.

In August 2006, MAN B&W Diesel AG, a German market leader in the world of two- and four-stroke engines,[22] converted to an SE. Significantly, it was the first German company that successfully concluded an agreement with the employee representatives of different European business divisions. Even though Augsburg remained the administrative and statutory seat of MAN Diesel SE, the conversion offered the possibility to deviate from the rigid co-determination provisions that apply to the *Aktiengesellschaft* by reducing the number of supervisory board members from twelve to ten as well as giving its board (*Aufsichtsrat*) a more international composition (through reducing the influence of German workers on the board).[23] The intended conversions by Fresenius AG, a German healthcare company, and BASF AG shows that this is the prime motivator for German

---

[22] <See www.manbw.com>.
[23] This explains the specificity of the SE and its virtual absence in jurisdiction without stringent participation rights. For German companies, the SE could be a relatively quick and efficient means to transform their board structure to meet international standards, whereas for other firms it constitutes a burdensome and costly alternative.

companies to switch to an EU-level business form. Both companies attempt to involve all European employees in the appointment procedure of the members of the supervisory board.[24]

Other companies in strict regulation jurisdictions, such as Germany and Austria, go a step further and also take the opportunity to choose a one-tier board structure. A recent example is Mensch und Maschine Software SE, a high-tech company that focuses on Computer Aided Design and Manufacturing (CAD/CAM) solutions. This German-based firm converted into an SE adopting the one-tier system because it is the preferable corporate governance structure for listed high-tech companies in which management holds a significant number of the outstanding shares. A single tier board makes prompt and flexible decision-making possible. This is viewed as a substantive benefit for firms that operate in a fast-growing and ever-changing business environment and explains why 71 per cent of the 'normal' SEs opted into the one-tier system offered by the SE Statute.

It should come as no surprise, moreover, that almost 20 per cent of the SEs are established as ready-made shelf companies. A shelf company can be a convenient option when firms promptly require to set up an EU-level business form without going through the complex and costly formation requirements. As we will see with *Centros* and its progeny, here too 'registration agents' play an important role in promoting new developments. For instance, the German Foratis AG, which according to its website is a market leader in shelf companies,[25] offers SEs for a purchase price of €132,000. With such an SE, buyers acquire an EU-level entity with a share capital of €120,000. Because the majority of SEs that are offered off the shelf by this agent are structured as a one-tier board, it could be concluded that corporate governance rather than mobility considerations are responsible for the creation of a niche market for shelf SEs.[26] The fact that Foratis AG focuses on the German market reinforces the conclusion that the SE is generally viewed as an additional 'national' business form which, besides the international allure, offers mainly advantages in the area of corporate governance. Two and half years after the introduction of the SE we can draw the tentative conclusion that this EU-level initiative has not resulted in the hoped-for increase of reincorporation

---

[24] See *Financial Times* (G Wiesmann and I Simensen), 'German Blue Chips Ponder Switch to SE Format', 12 April 2007; *Financial Times* (R Milne), 'Porsche's designs on VW lead it to steer to a different company structure', 12 April 2007; *Financial Times* (I Simensen and G Wiesmann), 'Unions Weakened on Supervisory Board', 12 April 2007; *Financial Times* (R Hönighaus and I Simensen), 'Allianz plans to raise €3.5bn in German Property Sale', 4 May 2007; *The Economist*, 'Locusts in Lederhosen', 20 October 2007.

[25] See <www.foratis.com>.

[26] It follows from the available data that two companies purchased a shelf SE at Foratis AG: (1) *Atrium Erste Europäische* VV SE was renamed Convergence CT SE in January 2006; and (2) Donata Holding SE was before the acquisition called *Atrium Fünfte Europäische* VV SE. Both companies have a one-tier board structure. In the first months of 2006, Foratis registered four new SEs. *Atrium Achte Europäische* VV SE and *Atrium Neunte Europäische* VV SE were registered in April 2006. *Atrium Dritte Europäische* VV SE and *Atrium Vierte Europäische* VV SE were established in March and February 2006 respectively.

mobility. However, we can foresee a trend that companies that are located in the new member states of the EU will value the European label of the SE more than companies in other member states.[27]

It is obvious that legislative developments, harmonization directives, and genuine EU business forms are insufficient to break down the strong non-mobility equilibrium that prevails in the EU. The involvement of the European Commission in developing a harmonization programme has tended to restrict innovations in company law in general. The harmonization process applies mainly to public corporations, but both national and European lawmakers tend to extend the directives' reach to other limited liability vehicles when introducing policy reforms. Quite apart from the normative concerns of employing a harmonization process to develop a system of uniform rules, the imposition of mandatory rules will have the effect of increasing the incidence of standardization in the field of company law, and may well lead to a number of legal and institutional barriers to reform initiatives. Consequently, given the so-called 'petrification' effect, the prospects for changing the main elements of company law in Europe were for a long time rather slim. What is more, even if member states are willing to take initiatives for deregulation, the possibility of undermining the directives could severely hamper such an operation. It is argued, however, that the harmonization process of EU company law has reached its inevitable terminus point and a new direction has been introduced to achieve the aims of the European economic integration. Indeed, the ECJ's triad of cases could, along with the pressure from increased corporate mobility, induce the member states to embark on company law reform processes and engage in some kind of competition to encourage entrepreneurship and innovation.

## 3. ECJ Case Law as the Foundation for Corporate Law Reform

### 3.1 The 'Incorporation Mobility' Case Law

Corporate mobility is a complicated notion which can be broken down into two separate categories. Legal scholars generally distinguish between incorporation of start-up firms and the reincorporation of existing firms. As for the first type of corporate mobility, it is now generally accepted that the post-*Centros* decisions have made it possible that if an entrepreneur in member state A, even if this is a classical real seat jurisdiction, wishes to incorporate their start-up company in member state B, they can do so and later establish a branch in state A, which will contain all of the activities and assets of the business. Even if the establishment in state B serves the purpose of avoiding state A's rigid corporate law rules, such as

---

[27] See for similar conclusions AETS, *Étude de faisabilité d'un statut européen de la PME*, July 2005. An unnoted, but equally important, development is the leading role played by registration agents in the market for shelf-SEs.

minimum capital requirements, the organizers normally obtain full recognition in state A without application of any of its corporate law.

The *Centros* case is an example of this scenario. *Centros* involved Danish nationals who, seeking to evade Danish minimum capital requirements, organized a close corporation in the United Kingdom. Then, seeking to establish the actual business in Denmark, the organizers sought Denmark's permission to register a branch. This permission was refused, and the ECJ decided that so doing was contrary to the freedom of establishment under Articles 43 and 48 of the Treaty. Denmark, like the UK, follows the theory of incorporation. The firm's primary establishment—its legal status as a corporation—was accordingly beyond dispute in Danish courts. The case solely concerned the 'secondary establishment' of a branch by an English private company in Denmark. Secondary establishment alludes to the setting up of agencies, branches, or subsidiaries. The ECJ expanded the scope of the term 'branch', reducing the difference between primary and secondary establishment to a minimum and ruling that it was contrary to the Treaty for Denmark to refuse to register a branch of a firm organized as a private limited company in the United Kingdom solely to evade the application of Denmark's minimum capital requirements (Ebke 2000). To be sure, under the *Cassis de Dijon* decision,[28] the Court does allow Treaty freedoms to be restricted when justified by the public interest, applying a multistep 'rule of reason' test. But the ECJ rejected the Danish justification for minimum capital. Creditors of closely held firms, said the Court, could look to other protections than minimum capital requirements, and governments seeking to protect creditors could adopt measures less burdensome on fundamental freedoms.[29]

*Centros* did not involve a country of origin holding to the real seat doctrine, and thus did not explicitly rule the real seat doctrine contrary to community law. Nevertheless the judgment has important implications for corporate migration. The English private company in the case had been incorporated by Danes who at all times lacked any intention to conduct operations in the UK. Read broadly, the case shows that actors can situate their incorporations in countries offering internal processes and legal regimes that lower their costs regardless of where the firm's assets, employees, and investors are located.[30] But there may be limits

---

[28] Case 120/78 (*Rewe Zentrale AG v Bundesmonopolverwaltung für Branntwein*) [1979] ECR 649.

[29] At the time of the *Centros* decision, most member states viewed minimum capital requirements as essential to obtaining limited liability protection. However, these requirements do not pass the four-factor test. See *Centros* § 34:

'[I]t should be borne in mind that, according to the Court's case law, national measures liable to hinder or make less attractive the exercise of fundamental freedoms guaranteed by the Treaty must fulfill four conditions: they must be applied in a non-discriminatory manner; they must be justified by imperative requirements in the general interest; they must be suitable for securing the attainment of the objective which they pursue; and they must not go beyond what is necessary to attain it.'

[30] This trend is far from new. In *Segers* (Case 79/85 *Segers v Bedrijfsvereniging voor Bank en Verzekeringswezen, Groothandel en Vrije Beroepen* [1986] ECR 2375), the court already decided that under Art 43 (ex 52) a Dutch sole proprietor could incorporate in England, because setting

on the privilege extended. *Centros* leaves open the parameters of the principle of mutual recognition. In a future case where a member state imposes higher minimum standards as a condition for recognition, said the ECJ, such measures must be proportional and non-discriminatory.[31] It still remains to be seen which minimum standards will prove proportional and non-discriminatory, in particular minimum standards protecting stakeholders other than creditors.

The ECJ continued along the *Centros* path in *Überseering*, opening the door to transfer of the real seat. The case holds that where a firm incorporated in member state B, in which it has its initial registered office, is deemed to have moved its actual centre of administration to state A, Articles 43 and 48 preclude state A from applying its law so as to deny the capacity to bring legal proceedings before its national courts.[32] As in *Centros*, refusal to recognize a firm's corporate status was held to be a disproportionate sanction for the mere transfer of the real seat. It could be argued that, strictly speaking, *Überseering* does not cover the incorporation process by a newly established firm in a member state different from its actual place of business. However, since the existing corporation did not move its statutory seat—and thus kept its corporate nationality—this case is considered to be a further clarification of *Centros* and not a different type of corporate mobility.

Both *Centros* and *Überseering* left open questions respecting the scope of a member state's privilege to apply national law to pseudo-foreign companies. *Inspire Art* answered some of these questions, extending the rule beyond recognition and standing to cover application of a member state's broader system of corporate law. *Inspire Art* involved a Dutch enterprise organized in the UK solely for the purposes of avoiding stringent rules of Dutch company law. The organizers registered a branch in the *Handelregister* of the Chamber of Commerce in Amsterdam, but refused to register as a pseudo-foreign company. Two questions went to the ECJ: (1) whether Articles 43 and 48 preclude the Netherlands from setting additional demands such as those found in Articles 2–5 of the *Wet op de Formeel Buitenlandse Vennootschappen* (WFBV-Dutch law on pseudo-foreign companies); and (2) whether, if the provisions in the WFBV are found to be incompatible with European law, Article 46 must be interpreted so that Articles 43 and 48 do not preclude the Netherlands from applying rules such as those set forth in the WFBV, on grounds of creditor protection.

The ECJ held that Article 1 of the WFBV, which required Inspire Art to register as a pseudo-foreign company, was contrary to Article 2 of the Eleventh Council

---

up a Dutch close corporation took considerably longer—even if he intended to continue to operate wholly in the Netherlands.

[31] See *Centros* §§ 31–8.

[32] The ECJ rejected German case law principles under which a Dutch corporation was denied legal entity status and, consequently, the right to bring an action in a German court. The ECJ took the view that since member states defer negotiating the mutual recognition of firms under Article 293, the denial to the Dutch corporation of the procedural right to bring an action fails to comply with Articles 43 and 48 of the Treaty.

Directive, which does not allow member states to impose disclosure requirements in addition to those provided by the Directive. In terms of the second issue before the ECJ, the Court referred to its earlier judgments and ruled that it was immaterial for the applicability of the freedom of establishment that a company, established in a certain member state, carries out its operations in another member state. Moreover, the ECJ held that the minimum capital requirements for pseudo-foreign companies mandated by the WFBV were in violation of the freedom of establishment, as they were not justified by the exception of Article 46 or any other requirement in the general interest.

Summing up, *Centros* introduced constitutionally mandated mutual recognition and constitutional review of minimum standards. It implied, contrary to the real seat doctrine, that incorporation in one member state cannot be called into question in another simply because the firm's central administration is not located in its state of incorporation. *Überseering* carries the line of reasoning to a transfer of real seat context. *Inspire Art* extends the ruling from mandated access to judicial process to substantive corporate law more broadly.

## 3.2 The 'Reincorporation Mobility' Case Law

The recent triad of ECJ decisions does not cover a reincorporation scenario, which could be achieved as follows. Company X wishes to reincorporate in member state B. To this end, company X plans to organize a shell company X1 in state B and then merge company X into the shell. Company X will retain its administrative headquarters in State A and remain resident there for tax purposes. The company law of neither state A nor state B includes provisions that facilitate a merger of a company formed thereunder with a company formed under the laws of another state.

The lack of corporate law provisions to facilitate company X's planned transaction was the rule rather than exception in the EU. Mergers of this kind were only possible in a small number of member states, specifically, Greece, Italy, Portugal, and Luxembourg. The other member states lacked this enabling legislation. National policy-makers, content to follow old patterns, have added few incentives for business parties to undertake cross-border combinations. Absent statutory recognition of the merger, company X literally must transfer its assets and liabilities to a new entity in state B, liquidating itself in state A prior to the transfer.

A robust freedom of establishment arguably should cover this type of cross-border merger. But also here, the ECJ comes close in its decision in respect of the merger between the Security Vision Concept SA and Sevic Systems AG. The case concerns a sale of all assets by a Luxembourg firm to a German firm in exchange for the German corporation's common stock. The parties structured the transaction so that the Luxembourg transferor liquidated after the asset transfer. German corporate law recognized such mergers 'by dissolution without liquidation' only among domestic firms, and the German register of companies refused the registration of the merger. The ECJ held the refusal violates Articles 43 and 48 of the Treaty, citing cost savings and brushing aside concerns like fiscal supervision and protection of creditors and minority shareholders.

Note that the merger in the *Sevic* case did not traverse the law of the transferor state, Luxembourg. The scenario we described above accordingly is not covered in all particulars—company X needs the right to exit state A's corporate law regime in addition to recognition of the merger in state B while keeping its headquarters in state A. *Sevic*, however, covers a merger that results in both the transfer of the statutory seat and the real seat. Exit from state A becomes complete only if state A recognizes the state B incorporation of an entity with a local administrative seat. State A's real seat doctrine could thus remain as an independent barrier.

## 3.3 The Effect of the Incorporation Mobility on Company Law Reform

The ECJ decisions in the *Centros, Überseering,* and *Inspire Art* cases only recently set in train the basis for the cross-border movement of administrative headquarters and the migration of new firms to more favourable jurisdictions. Economic evidence shows that these decisions have improved incorporation mobility because a significant number of continental European privately held firms have been influenced by the absence of minimum capital requirements to establish as a private limited company in the UK. For example, Marco Becht, Colin Mayer, and Hannes Wagner investigated new company formations in the UK between 1997 and 2005, revealing that the number of 'foreign' private limited companies increased from 3,460 per year in the pre-*Centros* era to 22,970 post-*Centros* (Becht, Mayer, and Wagner 2006). Moreover, they show that during this period 26,700 of the more than 77,000 'foreign' private limited companies were located in Germany alone.[33] One should bear in mind, however, that just over half of the private limited companies register their trading activities in Germany.

The resulting improvement of incorporation mobility allows the development of some arbitrage with respect to minimum capital rules. The mandatory capital maintenance rules with respect to the repurchase of issued shares, the reduction of capital, the issuance of new shares, and the minimum capital requirements mandated firms to hold on their books accounts often in excess of €8,000. The effect of these mandatory rules is to limit the flow of potential wealth-constrained entrepreneurs from starting up a business. As a consequence, the demand for low-cost company law vehicles unhindered by capital maintenance requirements is relatively high across the EU. One would expect that the jurisdictions without

---

[33] The data from the Becht, Mayer, and Wagner (2006) study suggests that the limited accounts for about 14.8% in 2005 and 14–15% in 2006 of the market for closely held corporations in Germany (Niemeier 2007).

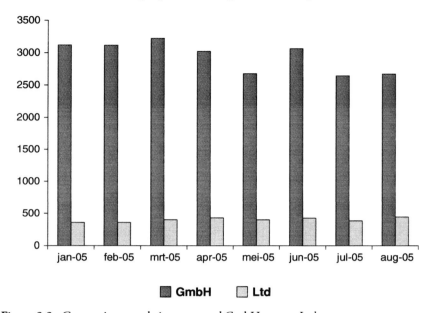

**Figure 3.3.** Comparison newly incorporated GmbHs versus Ltds

*Source:* Adapted from Deutscher Bundestag (BT)–Drucksache 16/283–16.12.2005–*Auswerkungen und Probleme der Private Limited Companies in Deutschland.*[34]

minimum capital requirements are likely to attract more registrations of start-up companies. This finding is corroborated by the German government's official data collection body (see Figure 3.3).

While Germany is absolute leader in post-*Centros* outflows, the Netherlands is a distant second in terms of new incorporations of private limited companies with their activities in the Netherlands. Despite fewer outflows and a relatively lower increase in the use of the UK private limited company by small local firms (see Table 3.2), the challenge posed by the limited has nevertheless triggered new legislative measures by the Dutch legislature which make it easier and less costly to establish a BV (Van Duuren et al 2006). These measures see to the abolition of the €18,000 minimum capital and the simplification of the formation procedures and the drafting of the articles of association. Naturally, given the relatively low number of private limited companies, this response by Dutch legislators may be adequate to reduce the outflows to pre-*Centros* levels.

Figure 3.4 shows the increasing popularity of the UK private limited company in the Netherlands. This analysis is based on the January 1997 to June 2007 Chamber of Commerce Registry, which surveys all of the private limited companies that were

[34] The data on limiteds in Germany, reflected in Figure 3.3 above, only include German limiteds that exclusively carry out business in Germany. The actual number of limiteds registered in Germany is therefore significantly higher (Niemeier 2006).

**Table 3.2.** The correlation between the increased use of the limited and formation requirements

| Country | Pre-Centros (1997–9) | Post-Centros (2003–6) | Relative increase | Minimum capital (required paid-in capital) | Costs (€) | Duration (days) |
|---|---|---|---|---|---|---|
| Germany | 2009 | 43,181 | 21.5 | 25,000 (12,500) | 1,000 | 24 |
| Denmark | 446 | 2291 | 5.1 | 16,800 (16,800) | 6,175 (–August 2003) | 23 (–August 2003) |
| Austria | 240 | 3141 | 13.1 | 35,000 (17,500) | 2,000 | 30 |
| Netherlands | 1590 | 6652 | 4.1 | 18,000 (18,000) | 2,000 | 10 |
| Belgium | 914 | 1841 | 2.0 | 18,550 (6,200) | 1,500 | 30 |

*Source*: Adapted from W Niemeier, 'GmbH und Limited im Markt der Unternehmensrechtsträger', *Zeitschrift, für Wirtschaftsrecht (ZIP)*, 73: (2007); M Becht, C Mayer, and HF Wagner, 'Where Do Firms Incorporate?' 1794–1801, ECGI Working Paper No. 70/2006, August 2007; <www.doingbusiness.org>.

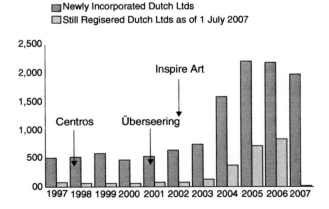

**Figure 3.4.** Registered private limited companies in the Netherlands established in 1997–2007 and still registered in July 2007

*Source*: Data from the Dutch Chamber of Commerce. The total number of private limited companies is extrapolated from the registration between 1 January 2007 and 30 June 2007.

established in the Netherlands in a particular year and are still registered in July 2007. The key question is how many of these private limited companies are economically active.[35] We focus on the data for 2006 and the first six months of 2007 which shows that more than 60 per cent of the 'Dutch' private limited companies are active in this respect. For economically active companies, the most popular sectors employing the UK private limited companies in the Netherlands are: wholesalers (20%), service providers (19%), retail companies (10%), construction and transport firms (10%), and IT and software (9%). To be sure, our analysis also indicates that the economically active private limited companies are actually very small firms, with more than 75 per cent employing at least one person. If we compare our findings with the 2003–2006 post-*Centros* data collected by Becht, Mayer and Wagner, we can observe that the rate of dissolution of these 'Dutch' limiteds is relatively high. From the more than 6,000 'Dutch' private limited companies registered in that period, approximately 2,000 were still registered at the chamber of commerce on 1 July 2007. These data also include branches from UK companies, but our data show that most of these companies have either Dutch names or a majority of directors that reside in the Netherlands making then 'Dutch' private limited companies.

We have to keep in mind, indeed, that those European firms incorporating in the UK are mostly 'round-trippers' (Becht, Mayer, and Wagner 2006). There are several reasons for this. First, evidence indicates that lower costs are a main factor inducing especially small companies to incorporate in the UK. Economic work shows that in the pre-*Centros* era, forming a private company is rather expensive, as a percentage of GNI per capita, and involves many long and complex formalities in most member states (Djankov et al 2002). Second, the reason the UK is attractive is that it often takes some days rather than several weeks to actually establish a company. Third, registration agents in continental Europe advertise and vigorously promote the UK as a major destination for small companies. It is common for agents to lure entrepreneurs by offering to create a company within twenty-four hours for insignificant sums. This trend provided incentives for lawmakers to reduce or eliminate outmoded minimum capital rules for private companies, which could be easily obtained by lowering the minimum capital requirements and providing simpler formation rules (Armour 2006). For instance, France already lowered its minimum capital requirement to €1 in 2003. Germany and the Netherlands will most likely continue to follow this trend.[36] In Germany, it is proposed to reduce the minimum capital from €25,000 to €10,000 and to provide smaller firms with the possibility of incorporating a variant of the GmbH without minimum capital, but with the legal requirement to save profits until a minimum

---

[35] The Netherlands considers a company as 'economically active' if it employs at least one person for at least fifteen hours per week.

[36] In making this projection, we must acknowledge that the jurisdictions that are most affected by the UK private limited company, such as France, Germany, and the Netherlands, take legislative actions.

level of minimum capital has been reached (the *Unternehmergesellschaft*). Dutch lawmakers seek to abolish the legal capital concept.

To the extent that small companies continue to select the UK private limited company to avoid costly and burdensome incorporation procedures, lawmakers will simply replicate the UK template to undermine the competitive advantage of the UK vehicle. Incorporation mobility is then only sustainable so long as there are sufficient other economic rents for small businesses and their agents. This suggests why it is so important for lawmakers to draft and modify their legislation to counter the forces stimulating the out-migration of smaller firms.

More importantly, the development of incorporation mobility reveals a number of significant disadvantages to adopting a foreign corporate law regime. When a German company employs a UK private limited company, it might face more costs than initially expected due to the different business environment.[37] These costs include loss of personal privacy, loss of competitive position, direct compliance costs, and administrative costs. Surprisingly, smaller firms in Germany rarely meet their disclosure obligations under the Fourth and Seventh EU Directives on the annual accounts and consolidated accounts of limited liability entities. From a small firm viewpoint, they would prefer to pay a fine rather than reveal information that could be used against them by competitors.[38] In contrast, what usually occurs in the UK is that small businesses tend to make their financial disclosures in a timely and accurate manner. Registration agents predict that German companies will adapt to UK business practices. The first wave of directors of 'German' private limited companies were not adequately informed of their personal responsibility for filing of annual returns and accounts under UK criminal law or did not take seriously the criminal charges which could be brought against them. However, research conducted by Companies House shows that the compliance rates have improved significantly.[39] In 2007, the main prosecution warning letter was translated into German and forwarded to home addresses of directors of 'German' private limited companies. It turns out that this initiative has resulted in higher compliance rates. Importantly, Companies House has avoided during the post-*Centros* period taking steps to prosecute non-UK-resident directors.

---

[37] The costs for creating a British limited for a foreign company are not excessive. For example, the German registration company Go Ahead offers a UK limited for €260. However, there are some additional costs that users of the UK private limited company tend to discount or overlook. For instance, VAT registrations, opening a bank account, domain and website charges are not included. Also, there are major legal costs associated with the translation and legalization of the incorporation documents. See Robert Drury, 'The EPC Versus the Private Limited Company', presented at the Fifth European Company Law and Corporate Governance Conference, Berlin, 28 June 2007.

[38] See also *Financial Times* ( Hugh Williamson), 'Germany's love of the "Limited"', 3 October 2006.

[39] Correspondence of 13 July 2007 with Thomas Smith, Director of Communications of Companies House (on file with the authors).

The above discussion highlights an important point about incorporation mobility in the EU. For the most part, it is only the smallest start-up firms—namely those which are unusually responsive to lower costs rather than to the actual corporation law provisions that deal with internal governance structures—that are considering the adoption of a British limited. Given this, it should not be surprising that the survival rate of 'German' private limited companies, similar to the Netherlands, is extraordinarily low. For example, the German evidence shows that about 50 per cent of these firms fail already after one year, and more than 90 per cent are dissolved after two years of trading (Niemeier 2007).

The evidence also suggests a second observation about incorporation mobility in the EU. Figure 3.5 shows that there is an explicit upward trend at the outset of the post-*Centros* period, which takes into account the pent-up demand for a low-cost vehicle. Not surprisingly, the level of German and Dutch directors has levelled off since the first months of 2006. The figure shows the number of directors

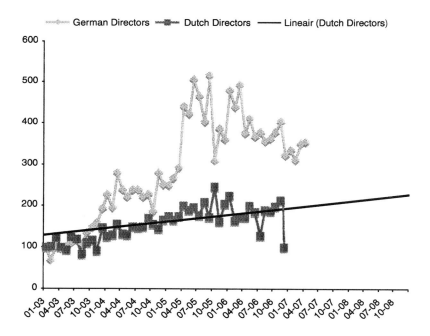

**Figure 3.5.** Trends in the number of appointments of German and Dutch directors in UK private limited companies (January 2003=100)

*Source*: The Dutch trend is adapted from information available at Companies House (UK). The German trend is adapted from W Niemeier, 'Die "Mini-GmbH" (UG) trotz Marktwende bei der Limited', *Zeitschrift für Wirtschaftsrecht (ZIP)*, 38: 2237–50 (2007).

appointed in private limited companies who are nationals of Germany and the Netherlands, but also includes the number of directors in a UK branch or companies that have a majority of British nationals as directors. From this data, we assume that the number of real UK private limited companies is relatively constant. Hence, the noticeable differences that we observe in Figure 3.5 are due to the changes in total number of 'German' and 'Dutch' private limited companies respectively.

One further piece of evidence shows that specific reforms made by some member states during the post-*Centros* period served to stem the outbreak of foreign private limited companies in these countries. Consider the case of Denmark where lawmakers modified their private company law to fast track (from two to three weeks to two to three hours by using a web-based registration system) their formation procedures without altering in effect the minimum capital requirements. As a result, there was a 20 per cent drop in the use of the limited in Denmark, i.e., from the 2,291 post-*Centros* 'Danish' private limited companies only 446 were established in 2004 and 2005 (see Table 3.2).

The analysis in this section confirms that the incorporation mobility resulting from the ECJ case law is rather trivial. Since the cost of incorporation cannot be seen as the most important factor in 'choice-of-business-form' decisions, arguably it does not provide sufficient incentive for national legislatures to engage in regulatory competition.[40] Indeed, member states are only likely to reduce incorporation costs without undertaking fundamental changes to the core elements of their corporation law regime, or introducing innovations that would enable firms to better adopt the most effective governance structures. As a matter of fact, economic and political pressures have not built up sufficiently to force through German legislative action that would involve substantial costs to incumbent groups. For example, it has been proposed that changes involving the reduction of minimum capital requirement (involving a reduction from €25,000 to €1), the transplant of the British wrongful trading rule,[41] and the option allowing firms to choose a single layer member-managed GmbH, would lead to a more flexible and lower-cost structure and thereby overcoming the path dependence forces which have successfully blocked the introduction of a more market friendly structure so far.[42] The German legislature had a two-phased reform in mind, First, a compromise proposal should have lowered the capital requirement from €25,000 to €10,000. Subsequently, a

---

[40] Scholars have made a similar point for the USA (Ayres 1992; Bratton and McCahery 1997; 2006).

[41] The wrongful trading regulation requires directors to monitor the firm's health and, if necessary, to take some remedial or preventive measures that stop their firms from sliding into insolvency.

[42] To be sure, the German legislature introduced a professional limited liability partnership (*Partnerschaftgesellschaft*) in 1995 and updated the legislation in 1998. However, the procedures involving the formation and operation of this partnership form appear too costly and cumbersome to economic actors. For instance, the *Partnerschaftgesellschaft* statute is linked awkwardly to both the civil and commercial partnership rules.

more fundamental reform should have further adjusted the GmbH legislation to the social and economic changes. However, due to the change in government after the federal election in September 2005, the proposed reform path has not seen the light of day. The point here is that not only have reform groups failed to overcome the system's barriers, but they have also failed to effectively alter society's perceptions about the need for legislative change in this field. Major reforms that involve deviations from the current rules on the preservation of the share capital and the notarial deed requirement for the transfer of the shares are unlikely to find support in the near future. Indeed, in order to limit the increasing popularity of the limited, a new proposal to introduce a modernized GmbH was published on 29 May 2006. The proposed Act—*Gesetzes zur Modernisierung des GmbH-Rechts und zur Bekämpfung von Missbräuchen* (MoMiG) is built on three main functions of the GmbH law (Seibert 2006): (1) The incorporation of a GmbH should be fast, cheap, and simple; (2) the new GmbH should offer a transparent shareholder structure; and (3) creditors should be better protected against illicit exploitation and rent-seeking strategies of the owners of a GmbH.

The reform measures serve to simplify the registration system, making a fast and electronic registration with the Chamber of Commerce possible for GmbHs. The availability of a public shareholders' list at the Chamber of Commerce emphasizes the importance of the electronic registration as such an up-to-date list should help prevent the acquisition of the company from non-shareholders. It is the intention of the new Act to consider only registered persons as shareholders. In order to make the GmbH an attractive export product, the new Act proposes to abolish the requirement that the registered office of a firm is located in the same country as its corporate seat. Surprisingly, however, the upgraded GmbH would still require a minimum capital of €10,000 (see Table 3.3). Moreover, as a trade-off for the reduction of the minimum capital requirement, the government proposes to increase the managing director's liability in the event of the firm's insolvency.

Given this proposal, it seems that Germany's law-making elite endeavours to secure the popularity of the GmbH by enacting a compromise legislation that mainly focuses on the relations of shareholders and managers to persons dealing with the GmbH. However, on 23 May 2007, the German government submitted a revised version of the MoMiG Act to the Parliament. Besides the *Unternehmergesellschaft* without the immediate need for paid-up share capital, it is possible for the founders of small firms with a maximum of three shareholders to simply sign the model articles of association—which will be attached to the corporate statute—and have the signatures legalized. This procedure will streamline and expedite the incorporation process as it will dispose of the need for a notarial deed in the event of a small business setting up a company.[43] Down

---

[43] The increased incorporation mobility arguably puts some pressure on the formal use of lawyers as notaries in the incorporation process. That is not to say that their function is outdated in the modern business world. Much will depend on the value-added content of the services they provide.

**Table 3.3.** Legal characteristics 'new' GmbH (Germany)

| Characteristic | GmbH (revised) |
|---|---|
| Legal Personality | Yes |
| Management | At least one managing director |
| Formation | Articles of Incorporation + notarial deed + registration at the Registry of Commerce + audit by the Local Court + publishing in a legal gazette |
| | Small firms with a maximum of three shareholders can use the model articles of association (*Mustergesellschaftsvertrag*) without the need for a notarial deed. |
| Autonomy of Articles of Incorporation | Some provisions are only valid if they are included in the Articles. Agreements and resolutions with effect for the future or that lack the agreement of all shareholders are null and void or voidable |
| Notarization of Articles of Incorporation | The Articles must be recorded in a notarial deed, otherwise the Articles are null and void |
| | The notarial deed is not needed when the model articles of association are used |
| Fiduciary Duties | Statutory shareholder's right to information/case law duty of good faith and loyalty |
| Financial Rights | Shareholders have a right to share profits in proportion of their investment |
| Transferable Interests | No public offerings allowed; a transfer of shares requires a notarial deed in order for the transfer to be valid |
| Continuity of Life | Yes |
| Limited Liability | Yes, minimum capital requirement of EUR 10,000 |
| | It is possible in the new proposal to establish an *Unternehmergesellschaft* without the minimum capital, but with the requirement to save profits until a minimum level of minimum capital has been reached |
| Financial Statements | Mandatory disclosure |
| Taxation | Corporate taxation |
| Linkage | Management structure of public corporation (*Aktiengesellschaft*, AG) |

the road, these measures will certainly have similar effects on the use of the private limited company as the fast track registration system in Denmark, which will again show the triviality of the corporation mobility.

Conversely, the *Sevic* case indicates that medium-sized and large firms, which are most cost sensitive, will undertake to relocate their seat based on the legal rules they prefer in the operation phase of the company. As we have seen, this is the main reason why larger companies make use of the SE: it offers firms a legal form that allows them to pursue their corporate objectives. However, it will be impossible to conclude with any certainty whether the *Sevic* case will lead to an increase in the reincorporation mobility in the EU. In the next section, we will analyse barriers to corporate mobility. We will then be able to assess the possible alternatives to open up the mobility choices for European companies that are currently considered by policy-makers, lawmakers, academics, and alike.

## 4. Barriers to Reincorporation Mobility in the EU

In the United States, corporations are able to do business outside their state of incorporation with the certainty that the corporation law of the formation state will apply. This arguably leads to more efficiency as it could decrease transaction costs and stimulate transfers of the statutory and/or administrative seat, mergers among firms of different member states, the use of branches, and cross-border cooperation in general. However, US law does not offer constitutional protection for 'foreign' corporations. It is therefore no wonder that US scholars find it remarkable that corporate mobility is still so underdeveloped in the EU. The absence of a common history, culture, and language may, of course, prevent the emergence of US-style corporate mobility in the EU (Kirchner, Painter, and Kaal 2005). But the ECJ's case law and Commission's legislative measures, such as the harmonization Directives and the introduction of genuine European business forms, make the European Union arguably more conducive to corporate mobility than the United States (Ribstein 2002).

Two barriers could explain the inertia of European firms to jump on the corporate mobility bandwagon. First, lawmakers and powerful interest groups are very successful in defending the strong non-mobility equilibrium. Ronald Gilson, for example, explains that 'some European lawyers have read *Centros* narrowly, "merely referring to a case of abuse, without general significance. From the perspective of an American, and therefore of an amateur at parsing the opinions of the European Court of Justice, so narrow an interpretation seems like wishful thinking." For better or worse, the Court explicitly ruled that denying branch registration to a company whose foreign incorporation has the sole purpose of "evading application of the rules governing the formation of companies" in the nation in which the company's principal place of business will be located, "is contrary to Articles 43 and 48" (Gilson 2001).' Second, even if corporate mobility enjoys a constitutional mandate in the EU, member states can cheaply put up effective exit tax barriers that limit freedom of establishment. Hence, so long as member states retain any discretion they will not easily be confronted with out-of-equilibrium threats that force them to reassess their cooperative strategy to limit corporate mobility.

## 4.1 The Status Quo Barrier

We now take a look at the other factors that constrain corporate mobility. It follows from the above discussion that corporate mobility in the EU is constrained by factors other than language and cultural differences. Even though the ECJ opened the door to increased corporate mobility by requiring the removal of national measures that impede cross-border market access and free choice of legal regime, defenders of the *status quo* are very inventive in finding ways to circumvent any disturbance of the non-mobility equilibrium (Halbhuber 2001). It seems that this strategy could largely be explained by strong path dependence factors, such as the influence of legal elites and traditions, and the effect of increasing returns on the law-making process. Naturally there are varying degrees of path dependence which are reflected in the diversity of recent company law developments. However, in terms of generalization, strong path dependence is a common phenomenon in legal systems that are dominated by legal elites and traditions bereft of the 'law-as-a-product' dimension. Ironically, if legal products—like regular products—gain popularity and expand utilization, increasing returns can magnify the benefits of defending the status quo, resulting in a similar evolution pattern. This partly explains why European jurisdictions are still loath to overhaul their corporate laws even though the ECJ, as noted above, has opened the door towards a market for company law products.

Let us assume that legislators, judges, practitioners, regulatory agencies, professional groups, and legal scholars constitute an elite law-making group that is responsible for interpreting, preserving, and developing the law (Watson 1985). These legal professionals produce different kinds of texts, such as statutes, judicial decisions, and scholarly writings, which one school of comparative law academics calls 'legal formants' (Sacco 1991; Monateri and Sacco 1998). The law does not consist solely of these texts, but should instead be viewed as a series of formulations that complement each other (Schlesinger et al 1998). Still the law and its evolution appear more like a battleground on which law-making elites compete for hegemony than a system of checks and balances (Bourdieu 1987).

What are the factors that tend to block corporate mobility, thereby reinforcing legal rules and institutions that are in place? Generally, there are two factors which operate to make law conservative. Firstly, the law-making elite treats the law as existing in its own right. In this view, the law is largely autonomous and operates in its own sphere (Kelsen 1967). As one commentator puts it: 'the means of creating law, the sources of law, come to be regarded as a given, almost as something sacrosanct, and change in these even when they are obviously deeply flawed is extremely difficult to achieve' (Watson 1985). Secondly, the law is justified in its own terms. Lawmakers, i.e., persons trained in law and nothing else, search for the legitimacy of legal change, which makes the law typically backward-looking. To a large extent, this insulates legal evolution from social and economic change and it therefore displays a serious degree of path dependence.

To what extent does the evolution of the legal rules and institutions reflect social and economic change? Lawmakers, who genuinely disagree as to which rules and institutions are 'best' (Bebchuk and Roe 1999), could be viewed as legal elites that produce competing legal formants. It is possible to distinguish between conservative and reform-minded legal elites. Because the law is viewed as autonomous, lawmakers historically employ two strategies when entering the competitive arena of legal reform. On the one hand, conservative lawmakers deploy the existing legal doctrines, principles, and culture to protect the status quo and thwart reform. On the other hand, reform-minded lawmakers tradition-ally make reference to foreign rules and institutions to propose legal change and to induce the controlling elite of the receiving system to believe that the offered model meets their expectations (Watson 1974).

If we take this a step further, it could be argued that the development of the law takes place mainly by transplantation of legal rules. Yet in order to be effective, a borrowed legal rule or institution must be understood and appreciated by the dominant, and usually conservative, law-making elite. Indeed, it is submitted that a legal transplant increases its own receptivity when adaptations to the domestic formal and informal legal order are made or the borrower is already familiar with basic legal principles of the donor jurisdiction (Berkowitz et al 2002).

It is in the legal actors' nature to attach considerable importance to authority in the transplanting process. It is often very difficult for a law reformer to 'sell' his ideas without the support of some kind of authority whose expertise is widely rec-ognized by the legal community (Sacco 1991). That authority could be inherent in a foreign legal system or institution due to its prestige, common legal tradition, or high accessibility. Reform-minded lawmakers attempt to convince the con-trolling elite that borrowing should occur by juxtaposing black-letter law reports, and consulting intuition and any available facts to show the foreign legal system's supremacy (Ogus 1998; Fanto 2002). Yet, the results of comparative legal studies often lack a clear theoretical or empirical explanation of why a particular foreign system or institution is the most suitable model, given the needs of the social and economic environment. When legal parochialism is strong and jurisdictions are largely resistant to transplants (which is often the case where jurisdictions are convinced of the effectiveness of their own legal system), reform-minded elites adopt a different strategy. They deny the fact that a model is borrowed, and use local authority to bolster their opinion (Mattei 1994). In this view, legal change could be explained largely by 'hidden' transplants, which are a mixture of foreign and indigenous doctrines and principles (Horowitz 1994).

However, it might be argued that if a jurisdiction becomes part of a common market such as the United States or the European Union, convergence of important principles of company law is likely to become greater, as the number of firms that not only do business in more than one state, but have among their members residents of different states, increases. In this context, national-level company law reforms in the EU have been encouraged by changes in European Court of Justice case law, which have encouraged firm mobility for start-ups, giving reform-minded lawmakers an incentive to intensify their efforts to modernize their domestic company laws. But, as noted earlier, the dominant reform strategy of most national-level policy-makers is still influenced by a 'patching up' approach designed to ensure prevalence of the status quo.

For instance, the elimination of the capital maintenance rules for private companies appears relatively easy. These rules, where the content is less important than their uniformity (Charny 1991), had already been applied to public corporations and subsequently were harmonized by the European Commission to reduce costs for third parties transacting with the firm. Having served simply as an authoritive focal point rule for legislators engaged in company law reform, the decision to eliminate the rule for private companies—in light of the increased mobility—is hardly surprising as it could be accomplished without causing too much disturbance of existing expectations of the controlling and conservative law-making elite. In this view, the array of mandatory legal capital rules only seems to benefit several interest groups (Carney 1997). In fact, incumbent management may have influenced the EU legislature to supply provisions that limit dividend payments and share repurchases so as to obtain more leeway to reinvest firm's profits. Accountants, who play a pivotal role in the required valuation, also have a substantial interest in exerting influence on the legislative outcome.

But also members of the law-making elite, such as lawyers and other legal practitioners, seem to benefit from guiding their clients through the complicated harmonized rules (Enriques and Macey 2001). Thus, since legal elites that benefit from the existing legal rules arguably have incentives to block innovative measures, reform-minded groups are confronted with the daunting task of replacing the existing legal rules with new measures and techniques.[44] Still, it is not surprising that bringing about change can be more troublesome than merely having to protect the incumbent interests. This partly explains the inherent shortcomings of this legal reform strategy.

But there is another factor of path dependence that is responsible for creating barriers that hinder reform-minded lawmakers from persuading the legislature

---

[44] As discussed, the blocking power of the conservative law-making elite differs from country to country. For instance, the French legislature reacted immediately to the possibility of losing new incorporations to England by reducing the minimun capital requirement to €1. On the other hand, the German legislature, which experienced a much higher number of businesses opting for the English limited, seems only to be able to agree on a compromise which lowers the capital requirement from €25,000 to €10,000.

to overhaul company law. This factor of path dependence, which is generally labelled as increasing returns, can explain the survival of particular institutions and traditions that were once effective in solving serious problems in the business environment, but no longer provide strong support of lawmakers given changing economic and social circumstances.

It is now commonplace that if firms use a particular business form more frequently, its value increases, thereby decreasing incentives to introduce legal reform. Increasing returns engender the standardization of rules and institutions over time (Kahan and Klausner 1996). Standardization, in turn, accounts for the lock-in to a suboptimal framework.[45] The increasing returns approach corroborates the hypothesis that lawmakers are prone to inertia and inflexibility. The models pertaining to the appearance of increasing returns are often used to explain why the widespread adoption of products and technologies that become more valuable as their use (or the use of compatible products) increases could lead to a suboptimal outcome (Arthur 1994, 1996). When increasing returns are associated with competing products, inferior products may prevail over products that are inherently better. More importantly, they may stand in the way of innovations.

The literature points to the success of the QWERTY keyboard, VHS video recorder, and DOS/Windows operating system over allegedly superior alternatives (Arthur 1994; Katz and Shapiro 1986).[46] Three related but conceptually different mechanisms are responsible for the possible dominance of increasing returns over inherent benefits: (1) sunk costs; (2) learning effects; and (3) network effects. The end result is that if new adopters of a product or technology are only interested in their own benefits without any consideration of the effect of their decision on other 'network users', the development of new products and technologies will be impeded, thereby fostering lock-in to the inferior standard.

Unsurprisingly, law and economics scholars have asserted that similar increasing return mechanisms help to explain inertia and momentum in the evolution of legal rules and institutions (Klausner 1995; Kahan and Klausner 1996).[47] Comparable increasing return effects appear to play a pivotal role, especially in the field of business forms, which, as we have seen, should be viewed as legal products traded in a market (Posner 1982). Consider, for example, statutory provisions and cases under company laws. In most western jurisdictions, the majority of firms are organized under the provisions of a corporate statute (see Chapter 2). Such statutes

---

[45] Bebchuk and Roe (1999: 155) state that

'rules might be path-dependent because the identity of the locally efficient legal rule—the rule efficient for a given country—might depend on the rules and structures that the country had at earlier times.'

[46] These allegedly superior products are the Dvorak Simplified Keyboard (DSK), Sony's Beta format and Philips V2000 format for VCRs, and Apple's Macintosh system respectively. But Liebowitz and Margolis (1995; 1998) demonstrate that the evidence for the superiority of a particular product is weak and, hence, the extent of network effects may be much more limited than is commonly assumed.

[47] But see Gillette (1998); Lemley and McGowan (1998); Ribstein and Kobayashi (2001).

not only confer substantial network effects to users of those statutes, but firms also expect to obtain further benefits as new enterprises incorporate. The use of the corporate statute could be valuable to a particular firm, regardless whether other firms have incorporated under the same statute. All the same, widespread use of the corporate form could have network effects analogous to those of the QWERTY keyboard. As more firms adopt the corporate form, networks of legal actors specializing in this particular business form (eg, lawyers and legal scholars) will develop, thereby offering legal services of a higher quality and lower cost. Furthermore, firms may choose the corporate form to attract and accommodate investors who expect firms to use it.[48]

Learning effects further reinforce the application of increasing returns processes to business forms, including legal doctrines, statutory provisions, and case law (Bratton and McCahery 1995).[49] These effects, which come from the use of the corporate law statute, for instance, also explain why most of the parties that originally opted into the corporate form have an incentive to continue to use the regime. Factors that arguably add to the value of the traditional corporate form include avoidance of formulation errors, ease in drafting relational agreements, availability of case law on the interpretation of the statute, and the familiarity to legal actors (Clark 1989). If these benefits are taken into account, newly formed businesses are likely to migrate to the business corporation statutes that confer these benefits to the user. This will mean that demand will be higher than it otherwise might be, which in turn will lead to the supply of standardized statutory terms, rather than customized ones that benefit a particular firm in a particular situation. Because standardized terms offer certainty (Goetz and Scott 1985), when advising their clients about incorporation decisions, business lawyers will recommend a standardized term—even if it is suboptimal—rather than draft a customized term that could lead to a higher expected value for a client.

The result of network and learning effects is that continuous use of the dominant business form, even if it is not ideally suited to some firms, will reduce the incentives for lawmakers to engage in reform processes. As in other areas of law reform, the reluctance to diverge from the existing framework means that even if essentially new business forms were created, parties might be unwilling to substitute the standard form for non-standard terms. In short, the benefits that accrue

---

[48] Klausner (1995) argues that where information asymmetries exist and signalling is costly, marketing network externalities may exist. Network effects provide a purely academic explanation for the fact that US high-tech start-ups are structured predominantly as public corporations, despite tax disadvantages. Venture capitalists would rather avail themselves of the predictable corporate form, for which many contractual mechanisms have been developed and standardized, than rely on new customized governance and organizational structures.

[49] If, for instance, case law creates a legal rule that goes beyond the statute, such as enhanced fiduciary duties for close corporations, increasing returns derive directly from precedent and the doctrine of *stare decisis* (Rasmussen 1994; Stone Sweet and McCown 2001).

to a standardized regime may be sufficient to outweigh the benefits that firms could gain by shifting to a new or modernized statute.

These 'switching costs', ie, the costs of switching from a standardized form to a new company law regime, constitute yet another reason for conservative law-makers defending the status quo or only engaging in patching-up reforms.[50] The uncertainty about the future benefits of the introduction of new legal business forms leads to the persistence of traditional rules and governance structures, and delays genuine legal innovation (Parisi, Fon, and Ghei 2001). Like R&D invest-ments into high-tech products and technologies, initial law-making costs are partially sunk costs. In this respect, legal intervention is costly, not only due to the research, legislative, and publication costs of new law, but also because vari-ous legal actors must invest substantial amounts in human capital and modes of operation that 'fit' the new rules and institutions. If the new legal regime proves to be undesirable over time, these costs cannot easily be recovered.

As we have seen, the EU harmonization programme itself retards the scope of diversity among the member states and thus lessens the salience of free choice. EU Directives have given the substantive corporate law of the member states a mandatory and petrified quality, insulating them from evolutionary pressures at home, much less from competition from abroad. Indeed, the harmonization programme has created legal and institutional barriers to corporate mobility. This 'petrification externality' is evidenced by statements made by the German and Dutch governments in the *Sevic* case in which they argue that corpor-ate mobility, in particular in the context of cross-border mergers, requires spe-cific rules designed to protect stakeholders' interests. They were of the opinion that these protective rules could only be promulgated through a harmonization Directive. This would severely minimize the prospects for changing the status quo in the EU. Moreover, even if a harmonization Directive is adopted, the implementation could be hampered by a member state's desire to undermine the Directives. The ECJ's response that harmonization rules are not necessary to accept cross-border movement initiatives by European firms is therefore a leap in the right direction.

Even if the problems posed by the implementation of the cross-border merger directive have been effectively redressed by the ECJ in *Sevic*, this does not entail an increased number of cross-border mergers. There are a number of obstacles which remain that could serve to frustrate or unduly delay transactions. Firstly, shareholders, especially, if well organized, can impact the effectiveness of the cross-border merger process. For example, minorities under German law may

---

[50] Research in behavioural psychology has indicated that people in general show a natural bias toward the status quo, in that they have a tendency to prefer to leave things as they are. Moreover, evidence from laboratory experiments shows that people exhibit a so-called endowment effect: people often demand significantly more to give up an object than they would be willing to pay to acquire it, even when the transaction costs associated with reacquiring a similar object are very low (Arlen 1998).

object to a merger resolution by making claims for additional compensation where the ratio applicable to the exchange is too low or if becoming a shareholder in the new company is not an option. Such challenges can impose great costs and impede the approval of the merger, particularly in cases involving jurisdictions that do not have procedures that are equivalent to Germany. In such transactions, minorities can file an avoidance of the merger resolution that may frustrate the transaction because the filing itself bars registration of the merger in the commercial registry.[51]

## 4.2 The Exit Tax Barrier

Reincorporation costs make European firms highly immobile. Reorganizing under a foreign corporate law statute often triggers taxes on hidden reserves, effectively restricting the demand for firms to opt into different national governance systems. If the tax burden exceeds the expected cost savings held out by the alternative legal regime, migration has no point even if there is a complete and consistent set of harmonization Directives in place. Indeed, the still current ECJ's decision in *Daily Mail* on hidden reserves will do little to stimulate demand for reincorporation.[52]

*Daily Mail* concerned a UK company that wished to transfer its administrative seat to the Netherlands. Its purpose was tax avoidance. The company planned to dispose of a large capital asset. The transfer of its central office to the Netherlands implied a transfer of its tax residence. Dutch tax residence in turn meant a stepped-up tax basis on assets, averting a substantial UK capital gains tax on the planned asset sale. Meanwhile, no transfer of the firm's UK domicile of incorporation was contemplated. Since both the Netherlands and the United Kingdom followed the incorporation doctrine, transferring the administrative seat raised no questions concerning the governing corporation law. On the other hand, UK tax law[53] required the Treasury to consent to the transfer of the company's seat and tax residence abroad. *Daily Mail* argued that the UK consent provision was contrary to Articles 43 and 48 of the Treaty.

The ECJ treated the claim as a corporate law matter, holding that Article 43 of the Treaty does not grant a company the right to transfer the administrative seat while retaining corporate status under the law of the jurisdiction of origin unless that jurisdiction's law allows for the transfer.[54] The ECJ underscored, however, that 'the rights guaranteed by [the Treaty] would be rendered meaningless if the member state of origin could prohibit undertakings from leaving in order

---

[51] See S Maul, 'Corporate Mobility', presented at the Fifth European Company Law and Corporate Governance Conference, Berlin, 28 June 2007.

[52] See Case 81/87 *The Queen v Treasury and Commissioners of Inland Revenue, ex parte Daily Mail and General Trust* [1988] ECR 5483.

[53] Section 482 (1) (a) of the Income and Corporation Taxes Act 1970.

[54] The more particular ground was that no agreement on the mutual recognition of companies or firms within the meaning of Article 293 (ex 220) had been reached. See *Daily Mail* (§ 21–5).

to establish themselves in another Member State.'[55] The key point on the facts of the case, stressed the ECJ, was that the UK exit regulation applied in cases where the company wished to transfer its seat while maintaining UK corporate status. In such cases, it held, the national legislation may freely impose conditions, such as obtaining consent of the Treasury.

Significantly, the ECJ has revised the issue of the permissibility of exit taxes in the context of the transfer of residence by an individual, self-employed person. In *Lasteyrie du Saillant*,[56] the ECJ prohibited discriminatory taxation of an exiting taxpayer. Mr. de Lasteyrie left France in 1998 to settle in Belgium, transferring both his professional practice and tax residence. At that time, he held securities that exceeded 25 per cent of the profits of a company subject to corporation tax in France, securities whose market value exceeded their acquisition price. The Code *Général des Impôts* includes a provision that prescribes a levy of income taxes on such differences in value of securities when a French resident leaves the country. The plaintiff challenged this provision and the case was referred to the ECJ, which held that the legislation in question impeded the exercise of free establishment. The Court reasoned that the rule was discriminatory because taxpayers who transfer their residence abroad are taxed on latent increases in value, while taxpayers remaining in France are taxed only on increase in value after they have actually realized such gains. Thus, *Lasteyrie du Saillant* provides that exit taxes cannot hinder the exercise of the free establishment exercised by a natural person and that exit tax regimes must comply with the criteria established in *Centros*.[57]

Clearly the case is important because it challenges the discretion of member states to use of exit taxes on the basis of freedom of establishment, if only in relation to individual taxpayers. But the ECJ in *Lasteyrie du Saillant* distinguished between natural persons and corporate residents and therefore left untouched its judgment in *Daily Mail*. It is difficult to assess whether the ECJ will extend its freedom of establishment jurisprudence to legislation hindering corporate emigration, such as seat transfers and mergers. Because the ECJ has accepted exit taxes as a central defence in restricting firm mobility and free choice, few expect that the ECJ will issue a judgment that disrupts the regulatory structure of company law in the EU.

Indeed, in cases where taxes have inhibited or traversed Treaty freedoms, the ECJ has recognized three justifications under the rule of reason: (1) the protection of fiscal cohesion of the national tax system; (2) the need for effective fiscal supervision; and (3) the prevention of abuse of law. It has been suggested that exit taxation should be permitted, despite its deterrent effect on migration, on fiscal cohesion grounds. But the fiscal cohesion defence, while it has proved

---

[55] See *Daily Mail* para 16.
[56] See Case C-9/02 *Hughes de Lasteyrie du Saillant v Ministerie de l'Économie, des Finances et de l'Industrie* [2004] ECR I-2409.
[57] See the four-factor test described in n 29 above.

successful in a few ECJ tax cases, has most often been applied very restrictively (Gammie 2003).

To be sure, the Council Directive on the Common System of Taxation applicable to Mergers, Divisions, Transfer of Assets and Exchanges of Shares concerning Companies of Different Member States, adopted in 1990,[58] covers a range of cross-border transactions that do not trigger any tax issues. These include (1) legal mergers, which can involve either (a) two or more existing companies merging into one with the original companies ceasing to exist; (b) a merger of one company into a second company that carries on the business; or (c) the merger of a wholly owned subsidiary into a parent company; (2) the direct acquisition by an acquiring company of voting control of a transferor company through acquisition of shares from the shareholders of the transferor in exchange for shares of the acquirer;[59] and (3) transfers of the assets of one or more branches of a firm in exchange for firm stock followed by dissolution of the transferor company.[60] Two important conditions apply respecting the assets in the transferor state. First, the acquiring company must continue to use the same tax base and depreciation method, and, second, the assets must be 'effectively connected with a permanent establishment of the receiving company' within the state of the transferor.[61] In other words, the assets of the transferor firm must be left in place by the merger. The conditions follow from the fact that the resident state of the transferor company needs to be able to collect the previously deferred capital gains tax in the future when the receiving company disposes of the assets. Note, however, that the second condition implies a limitation on mobility—the capital gains deferral is available only if the state of the transferor retains its tax jurisdiction over the assets in the form of a permanent establishment. The Directive does thus not deal with all possible exit tax questions. Also, because the Directive does not provide

---

[58] Council Directive 90/434/EEC.

[59] A share merger occurs when a company acquires a holding in the capital of another company obtaining a majority of voting rights and in exchange it issues securities to the shareholders of the company in which it acquired majority holding. The Directive does not, however, indicate which share acquisitions qualify for tax benefits. There are at least two competing views: (1) where there are several connected share acquisitions in a company for the purpose of reaching majority as a result of the separate purchases, the Directive should apply to even the first package of shares purchased; or (2) the Directive could be applied restrictively only to the acquisition of one share that provides actual majority (50% plus one share). Naturally, the Directive covers public takeover bids, as well as any further acquisitions above 50% (Terra and Wattel 2005). Unsurprisingly, the Directive does not include corporation tax provisions for share mergers. It only regulates the taxation of shareholders, including both corporations and individuals.

[60] It is unclear whether the Directive under 'branches of activity' covers all types of activities or whether the case law of the ECJ on the interpretation of the Directive on the taxation of capital raising, Council Directive 69/335/EEC concerning indirect taxes on the raising of capital, in the *Muwi* case, Case C-164/90 *Muwi Bouwgroep BV v Staatssecretaris van Financiën* [1991] ECR I-06049, applies here as well, and the term 'branch of activities' should be interpreted similarly to that of the Capital Raising Directive.

[61] The acquiring firm need not become resident in the transferor state, but the state maintains its right to tax any profits created by the remaining establishment as a tax at the source of income. It also maintains the right to tax the assets upon exiting the state in the future.

explicitly for free emigration of companies, it is likely, given the preference to defend the status quo, that member states impose exit taxes for transactions the Directive does not cover.

## 4.3 Possible Solutions to the Reincorporation Mobility Barriers

### 4.3.1 EU-level Legislative Measures

At the outset, we would like to emphasize that, while the formal and de facto seat transfer lies at the heart of the corporate mobility discussion in the EU, the need for a Fourteenth Company Law Directive on the transfer of seat from one member state to another seems more acute than ever (Wymeersch 2007). The European Commission's Action Plan on 'Modernising Company Law and Enhancing Corporate Governance in the EU' acknowledges the importance of both a Directive on cross-border mergers and a Directive on the transfer of seat.[62] The introduction of the SE offered acceptable solutions for the issues relating to board structures and employee participation. While, as we have seen, the SE gave the necessary impetus to the approval of the Directive on cross-border mergers, the seat transfer Directive is still in the drafting phase. Under the existing equilibrium, however, the deadlock situation is not likely to be solved easily (Ventoruzzo 2007).

An earlier draft version of the Fourteenth Directive dealing with the transfer of a firm's seat intended to reconcile the real seat and incorporation doctrines by providing that member states shall take all measures necessary to allow firms to transfer their registered office or de facto head office, together or separately, to another member state. According to Article 3 of this draft proposal, such a transfer will involve a change in the law applicable to the firm. Even so, this draft proposal refrains from eliminating the real seat doctrine: employee rights will be governed, where they are more firmly enshrined, in the home state.

However, the earlier draft is not in line with the post-*Centros* view that firms should be allowed to incorporate as foreign business forms (Vermeulen 2003). In this context, a recent corporate mobility proposal drafted by the German Council for International Private Law could serve as an alternative basis.[63] The

---

[62] See Commission of the European Communities, *Modernising Company Law and Enhancing Corporate Governance in the European Union: A Plan to Move Forward*, COM (2003) 284 final, Brussels, 21 May 2003. In this respect, we should also mention the need for the introduction of a European Private Company. However, proponents claim that it is needed for the creation of companies and conversion purposes rather than enhancing corporate mobility. See Eurochambres and BusinessEurope, Document prepared for the symposium organized by EUROCHAMBRES and BUSINESSEUROPE under the auspices of the European Economic and Social Committee, 'The European Private Company—EPC: A European Structure Intended for SMEs', Brussels, 15 May 2007.

[63] See HJ Sonnenberger and F Bauer 'Proposal of the *Deutscher Rat für Internationales Privatrecht* for European and National Legislation in the Field of International Company Law'.

incorporation doctrine is the starting point of this proposal. Under this principle, a corporation as well as a partnership will be governed by the formation state's law. This includes rules regarding the legal nature, the internal governance structure, legal representation, and limited liability. A host state can only apply its corporate law rules if a legal system is chosen abusively. According to the proposal, it is necessary to follow the respective legal rules for all companies involved in a cross-border reorganization, such as mergers and legal splits, which is more or less a codification of the *Sevic* case. The proposal offers a simple principle for voluntary migration to a foreign legal regime. First, it should comply with the corporate law rules of the new regime. In addition, it is obvious that the transferring company should regard the laws of the departing state with respect to the rights of shareholders, creditors, employees, and other stakeholders.

This proposal could be compared to the US Restatement of Conflicts Law. Recall however that model measures are not widely accepted in the EU despite their apparent positive benefits. At first blush, the German initiative could offer focal point solutions to the coordination problems among states. It purports to codify and summarize the ECJ case law, but also attempts to fill the gaps with respect to the scope of corporate mobility and the type of business forms eligible for cross-border incorporations and reincorporations. If accepted, it could be cited by lawmakers and judges as if it were authoritative, representing each member state's expectations of what states should do when dealing with corporate mobility issues. When more states have adopted the solution, it becomes increasingly difficult for a dissenting member state to lag behind. As we will see in other contexts in Chapter 7, voluntary and codified standards are considered an effective means for implementing better practices by European businesses.

### 4.3.2 ECJ Case Law

Although legislative measures would directly facilitate corporate mobility, these reforms are not presently the leading techniques in challenging the EU non-mobility equilibrium.[64] Therefore we expect that, as long as most member states gain few significant advantages from increasing mobility, fiscal barriers and national vested interest are likely to remain significant impediments. Under existing arrangements, challenges to the dominant equilibrium are

---

[64] It should be noted, however, that the EU Commission's SLIM (Simpler Legislation in the Internal Market) Initiative is also aimed at improving cross-border mobility in the EU. This Initiative, which was launched in May 1996, resulted in the adoption of Directive 2003/58/EC of the European Parliament and of the Council of 15 July 2003 amending Council Directive 68/151/EEC, as regards disclosure requirement in respect of certain types of companies. This amendment gives companies the option to voluntarily file their documents and particulars in other EU languages so as to improve cross-border access.

still defeated by policy preferences that allow few alternatives, leading either to deadlocks or compromise legislation that yields few political gains. This chapter has explained why the alternative measures are a prerequisite for introducing US-type mobility.

In the context of these circumstances, it is important to recognize two issues. Firstly, the ECJ has clearly resolved in the *Centros* triad of cases difficult questions regarding incorporation mobility. Secondly, the ECJ's interpretation in the *Sevic* case is an important first step towards bringing forward the arrangements needed to support a reincorporation regime. Therefore, this suggests that the ECJ's role is likely to be crucial in altering the dominant preferences of member states through new decisions that provide the key mechanisms for creating free mobility in the EU (Schön 2007). To be sure, the ECJ is constrained in pursuing its own agenda within carefully reasoned legal analysis in order to avoid member state criticism.[65]

With regard to the reincorporation mobility, it is worth noting that there is a referral case pending.[66] The Court of Appeal Szeged (Hungary) seeks, among other things, answers to the following three questions. First, what is the applicable law, if a company, organized under the corporate law of member state and entered in its commercial register, wishes to transfer its seat to another member state? Second, can such a company transfer its registered office under Articles 43 and 48 of the Treaty? Third, is it possible to subject such a transfer to conditions and approvals by either the state of incorporation or by the host member state?

In this case, Cartesio, a Hungarian legal entity, requested the Court of Registration to register the transfer of its registered office to Italy. Cartesio wished to remain registered in Hungary. The Court rejected this request holding that Cartesio should follow the Hungarian corporate law procedures. If the ECJ confirms this view, Cartesio must first be dissolved and liquidated and then again be incorporated in Italy. The new Italian company must register as a branch in Hungary. The questions in this case could give the ECJ an opportunity to clarify its position on both the statutory seat transfers (which entail the application of a different legal regime) and de facto seat transfers (which do not affect the applicable corporation law) before the adoption of the Fourteenth Directive. Following the development of the ECJ's new jurisprudence, the court may well extend the decision in *Lasteyrie du Saillant* to legal entities (Hopt 2007). Sensibly the European Commission announced that it has abandoned plans to introduce a Fourteenth Directive, against this background.[67]

---

[65] See Pollack, (2003)(explaining the slow pace of institutional change by the ECJ).

[66] See Case C-210/06 OJ C 165 of 15 July 2006—*Cartesio*.

[67] C. McGreevy, Speech by Commissioner McGreevy at the European Parliament's Legal Affairs Committee, Brussels, 5 October 2007 (Speech/07/592).

## 5. The Effect of Reincorporation Mobility on Company Law Reform

The EU remains committed to the goal of increasing mobility in Europe. However, as we have argued in this chapter, mobility is still largely constrained by member state discretion. Even though the ECJ has reduced the scope of the real seat doctrine and its barriers to the freedom of establishment, the Court has not effectively eliminated it. As we have seen, the ECJ case law does not explicitly resolve matters involving a domestic company wishing to exit its state of incorporation. This chapter has documented the serious obstacles preventing an outbreak of mobility, including the absence of a reincorporation procedure and exit taxes that continue to block freedom of establishment and restrict cross-border mobility. To unblock the remaining obstacles to cross-border mobility, we argued that the ECJ will inevitably have to follow through on its new line of reasoning. Finally, we predicted that a new threat of ECJ interventionism, perhaps complemented by legislative measures, would only make domestic lawmakers more responsive, reacting by adjusting their regulatory and fiscal strategies more deeply and frequently in order to avoid losing domestic firms.

To illustrate this point, let us consider the introduction of the Limited Liability Partnership (LLP) in the United Kingdom. While the decision to introduce an LLP was motivated by diverse factors, including election politics, which contributed to its speedy passage, the Department of Trade and Industry (DTI) was directly involved in the establishment of the LLP. The DTI, which was motivated by the threat of regulatory competition from offshore LLP statutes, particularly that of Jersey,[68] promulgated the Limited Liability Partnership Act in 2001.[69] The legislation introduced a new limited liability vehicle that has legal personality, a partnership governance structure, and partnership tax treatment.[70] In drafting this legislation, the DTI responded to the pent-up demand from multinational professional service firms wishing to transfer to LLP status.[71] Importantly, the reform-minded law-making elite, side-stepping traditional elites, exploited the lobby

[68] Limited Liability (Jersey) Law, 1996. Motivated by liability and tax considerations, British accountants (in particular Ernst & Young and Price Waterhouse) provided a wholly crafted statute to the Jersey legislature, a largely passive and accessible body that decided to enact the statute. In speedily adopting the LLP, Jersey signalled its commitment to a comprehensive set of business forms for foreign organizations. However, high switching costs and doubts about the prospective benefits of incorporating as a Jersey LLP may explain Jersey's failure to capture a share of the UK partnership market.
[69] The Limited Liability Partnerships Act 2000, the Limited Liability Partnerships Regulations 2001, and Limited Liability Partnerships (Fees) (No 2) Regulations 2001 came into force on 6 April 2001.
[70] The Limited Liability Partnership Act 2000 and the Finance Act 2001 provide that LLPs are classified as partnerships for tax purposes.
[71] In its draft Regulatory Impact Assessment, the DTI made a 'tentative estimate' that around 60,000 regulated firms might eventually become LLPs.

**Table 3.4.** Legal characteristics UK LLP

| Characteristic | UK LLP |
|---|---|
| Legal Personality | Yes |
| Management | Decentralized; in absence of agreement every partner may take part in management, however designated members have particular responsibility for certain statutory requirements |
| Formation | Registration at Companies House on a prescribed form LLP2 together with a statutory fee – two or more partners |
| Autonomy of Articles of Incorporation | N/A |
| Notarization of Articles of Incorporation | No |
| Fiduciary Duties | No general duty of good faith; specific duties in the regulations to account for competing activities and use of partnership property |
| Financial Rights | In absence of agreement equal sharing rights |
| Transferable Interests | No public offerings allowed |
| Continuity of Life | Change in membership of partners does not lead to dissolution |
| Limited Liability | Yes |
| Financial Statements | An annual return and annual statutory accounts must be filed |
| Taxation | Pass-through taxation |
| Linkage | Linked to corporate law provisions |

groups' pressures to extend the scope of the UK LLP to other non-professional firms. In this view, the linkage of the UK LLP to the corporate law provisions, such as the requirement to comply with many of the provisions of the Companies Act and Insolvency Act, constituted a trade-off for gaining access to limited liability. Equally, conservative lawmakers made it mandatory that accounts must be audited to show a 'true and fair' view under UK GAAP.[72] The Consultative Committee of Accountancy Bodies published its Statement of Recommended Practice (SORP) on accounting by LLPs.[73] SORP confirms that UK LLPs must disclose their financial statements in line with those of limited companies.[74] Table 3.4 gives an overview of the most important legal features of the UK LLP.

It follows that innovative change differs across systems depending on mobility factor and the organization of reform-minded interest groups. In fact, these features help explain the capacity of the UK legal systems to establish hybrid legal vehicles for different forms of business relationships and professional firms. The next chapter will explain in more detail how competitive pressures could instigate reforms despite the presence of considerable path dependence effects. It seems that the influence of high-powered, reform-minded interest groups is pivotal to the direction of change in company law reform. Furthermore, the chapter will show that legal evolution is also not immune to exogenous shocks, such as social and economic changes, international competition, and foreign pressures, which have been sufficient to trigger new company law statutes in Japan and Singapore.

[72] There are exemptions from audit for LLPs with turnover up to a certain threshold. On 26 May 2000, this threshold was set at an amount of £1 million.

[73] See SORP Accounting by limited liability partnerships at: <www.ccab.org.uk>.

[74] Initially there was significant resistance to the UK government mandating financial disclosure for LLPs. Many commentators assumed that the high cost of disclosure and privacy issues would limit the interest in the LLP. The Limited Liability Partnerships Regulations and accounting standards require that the financial statements should include, unless exempted by the requirements of the Companies Act 1985 as modified by the Regulations, the following items: (1) profit and loss statement, consolidated in the case of a group preparing accounts; (2) a statement of total recognized gains and losses pursuant to FRS 3, consolidated in the case of a group preparing accounts; (3) cash flow statement pursuant to FRS 1, consolidated in the case of a group preparing accounts; (4) a balance sheet, and a consolidated balance sheet in the case of a group preparing accounts; and (5) notes to the financial statements disclosed.

# 4

# Company Law Developments in the United States and Asia

## 1. Introduction

Ideally, company law vehicles should be the result of legislative processes that are initiated for the most part to create mechanisms designed to reduce agency costs and satisfy the contracting interests of business parties, such as investors, firm founders, and joint venture partners (Kraakman et al 2004).[1] The voluminous literature on law and society explains that lawmakers are public regarding actors who will identify which rules are efficient across different firms and time, and replace inefficient rules accordingly. Thus conceived, the ideal and actual function of law-making is to attempt to increase social welfare by correcting market failures. Lawmakers supposedly regulate company forms in the public interest.[2]

Criticism of this public interest theory of law-making has largely focused on two shortcomings. First, legislation is not primarily the result of efficiency considerations. Second, despite similar external market pressures, differences in company law forms continue to persist. Even though there have been recent instances of formal legal convergence, current law-making procedures and pre-existing conditions tend to lock the evolution of company law structures into a particular path, thereby maintaining diversity between individual jurisdictions.[3]

To be sure, domestic legislators and judges have offered several judicial and statutory solutions to meet the special needs of the variety of closely held firms. Even though the framework of corporate law is not optimal for these types of firms, courts have attempted to resolve intra-firm conflicts by reference to

---

[1] See also Chapter 1.
[2] This view corresponds to the 'public interest theory'. The public interest paradigm of law-making emphasizes the government's role in correcting market imperfections such as monopoly pricing and pollution (Laffont and Tirole 1993).
[3] Gilson (2001) distinguishes between functional convergence (when existing institutions are flexible enough to respond to the demands of changed circumstances without altering institutions' formal characteristics) and formal convergence resulting in legislative action necessary to alter the existing institutions.

partnership law principles. However, an acknowledged problem with this approach to the legal control of closely held firms is the risk of ignoring the needs of other types of firms that operate as close corporations. It is well known that legal rules for firms with capital symmetry should differ from the rules for those without. For instance, equal rights in management, automatic buyout rights, and broad fiduciary duties that govern 'partnership corporations' are not automatically suitable for start-up corporations financed by venture capital. The deregulatory approach tends to increase the cost of statutory ambiguity, including legal research, litigation, and judicial system costs (Ramsay 1992). A more efficient regulatory response, which involves determining the appropriate level of regulation, ultimately requires cost-benefit decisions to ascertain the necessary policy changes. In pursuing this goal, lawmakers should, as we have seen, view legal business forms as products and focus on designing legislation that contains clear and simple fall-back provisions tailored to the requirements of firms characterized by multi-ownership. Because participants in these firms sometimes start their business ventures with a handshake rather than an articulate agreement,[4] a business form statute should ideally supply a set of default terms that the majority of parties would have bargained for in a costless world (Easterbrook and Fischel 1991). By doing so, lawmakers not only help to minimize transaction costs for firms that wish to enter into customized agreements, but also reduce the costs of statutory ambiguity.

This suggests that there may be significant benefits for businesses and investors in jurisdictions that make available more productive business forms. Why do we not see a proliferation of new (hybrid) business forms in continental Europe? After all, the European Court of Justice decisions in *Centros*, *Überseering*, and *Inspire Art* only recently set in train the basis for the cross-border movement of administrative headquarters and the migration of new firms to more favourable jurisdictions. The ECJ case law has improved corporate mobility dramatically as a large number of continental European privately held firms have been influenced, by the absence of minimum capital requirements, to incorporate in the UK as limited companies.[5] We have to keep in mind, however, that those European firms incorporating in the UK are mostly 'round-trippers', which means that a large percentage of businesses in continental Europe could benefit directly from the development of more efficient hybrid entities in their own jurisdiction. But they need a coalition of groups to crack open the policy-making agenda and induce national legislatures to introduce new limited liability vehicles. These reasons may be enough to explain that the impact of the ECJ's decisions has so far only led to patching-up initiatives in most member states, influencing some legislatures to eliminate or reduce minimum capital for private companies. As

---

[4] Even billion-dollar joint ventures often operate under a short and simple agreement (Lewis 1999).
[5] See Chapter 3.

a consequence, the demand for upgraded company law unhindered by capital maintenance requirements is relatively high across the European Union, while the introduction of new hybrid business forms is mainly viewed as unnecessary since they contribute to increased costs attributed mainly to transition issues and enhanced choice (Freedman 1999).

However, in recent years, hybrid, unincorporated, business forms that combine the best of partnership and corporate law, have attracted a great deal of attention from policy-makers and entrepreneurs. Indeed, the increase in interest is both wide and deep. During the last two decades, the expansion of activity in this area in the United States has been substantial. In the USA, the rapid increase in limited liability partnership (LLP) and limited liability company (LLC) business forms has grown much faster than anticipated. Several factors contribute to the growth of new and more efficient partnership law structures. First, states have responded to the needs of a wide variety of firms for a more flexible set of forms, which has reduced reliance on or eliminated inefficient older forms. Second, the liberalization of partnership law has been accompanied by the virtual elimination of the distinctions between partnerships and corporations accompanied by a move toward the recognition of partnerships as entities. Third, the increase in the choice among business forms has resulted in the erosion of traditional restrictions of the internal structure of legal business forms.

As the influence of 'legal transplants' from the USA is felt more and more in company law reform projects in both Europe and Asia, it might be expected that non-US jurisdictions will eventually display similar patterns of legal evolution as we currently see in the USA. For instance, the last decade has witnessed the rise of new legal entities and US transplants in countries that represent both common law and civil law traditions. In the United Kingdom, the promulgation of the LLP was prompted by competition from offshore LLP statutes, particularly that of Jersey, where Price Waterhouse and Ernst & Young promoted the new legislation based on a similar law enacted in State of Delaware. The Department of Trade and Industry (DTI), which was directly involved in the introduction of the LLP in the United Kingdom, did not, however, just adopt the US LLP—which simply added the limited liability feature to its general partnership law provisions. Ultimately, the DTI created a stand-alone, hybrid company form that is situated between a partnership and a corporation.

Similarly, a Limited Liability Partnerships Act 2005, inspired by the Delaware LLP, came into effect on 11 April 2005 in Singapore. The Company Legislation and Regulatory Framework Committee (CLRFC) spurred the introduction of an LLP in Singapore in order to expand the governance options to be considered by small and medium-sized businesses, professionals, and investment funds. Importantly, Japan, which has a tradition to follow Germany's company law model, has recently been inspired by the success of legal innovation in the United States and the United Kingdom, resulting in the introduced two new legal forms: the J-LLP (*Yugensekinin-jigyo-kumiai*) and J-LLC (*Godo-kaisha*). These hybrid entities, which are intended to supply Japanese firms with more contractual flexibility, are arguably more suitable for firms involved in multinational joint ventures in the human capital-intensive and financial services sectors.

As politicians and business groups across Asia reflect on the changes in Japanese company law, which are seen as offering organizational advantages to firms in knowledge-intensive industries, lawmakers in other Asian competitive countries, such as India, Malaysia, and China, are already sequencing reforms that will lead to the introduction of the LLP. To the extent that India, for example, is a latecomer in adopting LLP legislation, the delay seems to have provided opportunities for lawmakers to learn from the tried and tested experiences in other jurisdictions. Effort to improve on the LLP structure, based on learning outcomes in other countries, may well benefit Indian professional firms, who are increasingly involved in international transactions, by giving them a business form that is adaptive to their competitive and litigious environment. The reform is seen as desirable, moreover, as it can help induce the introduction of more business start-ups. Similar arguments are used to the same effect by the Chinese Standing Committee of the National People's Congress, which already adopted major revisions to China's company law on 27 October 2005, including the introduction of one-person companies, lower capital requirements,[6] improved information and minority protection rights, and other corporate governance techniques. This laid the basis for China's top legislature to open the discussion, in April 2006, on introducing LLPs in order to stimulate venture capital investment and create a level playing field to facilitate a competitive advantage for Chinese professional firms that increasingly operate in the global market. Importantly, the type of reforms proposed in Asia point to significant inherent benefits in terms of increased flexibility for the firms that adopt new hybrid legal forms. As they are cheaply available and combine the best of the partnership and corporate world, these flexible legal forms contain features that make them better suited to professional firms, start-ups, small family firms, and financial funds.

In Chapter 2 we examined the contractual theory of the firm. The contractual theory gives important insights into the legal structure of business organizations. Not only does this approach have the capacity to point to common problems that arise in this environment, but it also emphasizes the key function of law in defining the governance structure of the firm, supplying important contractual provisions *ex ante*, and supporting the enforcement of implicit contracts and internalized norms *ex post*. From this perspective, statutory and judicial company law should offer standardized, contractual products that help to economize on transaction costs, such as drafting, information, and enforcement costs, and to limit opportunism and fill gaps in the business context. In other words, efficient

---

[6] For limited liability companies, the minimum capital has been decreased from RMB 100,000 to RMB 30,000 (approx. US$3,750). A one-person company could be set up with a minimum capital of approx. US$12,500.

company law offers models that cover the relationships between the business participants inside the firm and the representation of the firm in its dealings with outside participants, such as creditors. Company law statutes act thus as a set of 'off-the-rack' terms upon which business participants can fall back when establishing the distribution and allocation of powers and responsibilities for varying levels of control and commitment. Finally, the theoretical and empirical contributions to the literature on incomplete contracts emphasizes that providing a set of default rules that deal with every possible contingency is a complex and uncertain process. Building on this literature, economic theories of the firm suggest that, besides the statutory and judicial default rules, the incentive and ownership structure of company law forms and the interaction between explicit and implicit contracts help the parties and institutions involved in filling the inherent gaps in the relationship, thereby preventing possible conflicts.

Although the function of company law as a means for incentive design and transaction planning appears to be underrated by lawmakers and academics (Freedman 2004), the introduction of new hybrid business forms indicates that contractual rule-making sometimes prevails over so-called elite and traditional rule-making (Clark 1989). In that case, it is submitted that the path dependence story does not necessarily imply that legal innovations are inherently inefficient. This chapter argues that devising new and separate company law forms is more efficient as they offer distinct sets of rules and norms for businesses. Indeed, a separate set of legal arrangements has substantial contracting benefits for the firm's participants by allowing them to define their expectations *ex ante*—less hindered by existing doctrines and traditions—and, hence, assist judiciaries in solving governance problems and other conflicts *ex post*. As a matter of fact, practising lawyers and business advisers appear to be willing to embrace new company law convinced that from both a tax and business perspective hybrid business forms obtain the most efficient result. This chapter provides empirical evidence for the popularity and effectiveness of new legal products not only in the United States, Asia, but also Europe. It seems that the selection of legal entities requires balancing limited liability protection against, on the one hand, tax benefits and, on the other hand, contractual freedom to organize and structure the firm. Empirical research from the United States confirms the importance of forms that combine limited liability with partnership-type taxation and flexibility. The recent developments in Asia suggest that lawmakers and academics cannot afford to remain in denial that hybrid business forms will eventually prevail over the existing partnership and corporate forms.

## 2. Developments in the United States

We ended Chapter 3 with the statement that the evolution of company law may well generate a new transformation if national lawmakers find a compelling reason to abandon the defence of well-entrenched legal forms and increasing returns that reinforce their position and block the diffusion of new innovative legal rules and institutions. Studies on the political determinants of legislative change have examined the connection between public welfare and legislative outcomes, calling into question the motivation of lawmakers to undertake reforms on this basis. Given this, the introduction of new company law forms in response to social and economic concerns would seem unlikely. Nevertheless, the recent emergence of new business forms strongly suggests the presence of some kind of incentive to innovate.

A general implication for a broad theory of legal evolution is that lawmakers do not always dominate the law-making process. This is especially true of company law, which is influenced not only by lawmakers, but also by politicians and— more importantly—interest groups (Becker 1983; Grossman and Helpman 2001). To fully explore this phenomenon, this section discusses the incentives for the introduction of new legal forms. This analysis builds on the economic theory of legislation, which assumes that legal rules are demanded and supplied in much the same way as other products. Legislation ensues from the jointly maximizing relationship between interest groups and political actors. Promising political or personal support,[7] interest groups persuade political members of the legislature, and specifically those who run the supply and demand process of legal products, to pass or veto legislation (Tollison 1988).

A key question concerns the identification of which groups of firms are able to lobby successfully for business organization law reform and the prospect of success. Within the economic theory of legislation, legislatures have no incentive to adopt efficient provisions for firms that lack sufficient resources to lobby for laws (McCubbins and Schwartz 1984). Generally, the legislature, consisting of risk-averse politicians and conservative lawmakers, tries to avoid innovations. Yet if powerful interest groups demanded that provisions of business forms be changed, political pressures within the legislature would attempt to satisfy the demand with beneficial legislation.

In terms of assessing the likelihood of the enactment of modernized or new business forms into national law, there are several classes of firms that might be directly attracted by the cost-saving benefits. The first class is made up of prospective firms that will only come into existence if modern, flexible, and responsive business vehicles are available. For instance, it is expected that simplicity and low formation costs will not only appeal to firms, but will also encourage the formation of joint ventures and other combinations. The second class consists of

---

[7] Interest groups have several means of influencing the so-called brokers of legislation. For instance, they can offer hoped-for future employment. Another pervasive means is political support, i.e., monetary contributions to political campaigns and votes. In addition, personal relationships make members of the legislature particularly responsive to interest groups (Laffont and Tirole 1993; McCormick and Tollison 1981). Because politicians care about their re-election, they seek information on how their position on a particular issue will affect the outcome of the next election. As a result, it is submitted that 'lobbying and information provision by interest groups to politicians is the most important factor in explaining governmental policy outcomes' (De Figueiredo 2002).

future start-ups which would use either the traditional partnership or close corporation form. For the most part, these start-ups are small, closely held firms that would not consider the law *ex ante*, but may unwittingly fall foul of unexpected and disruptive rules *ex post*. The third class is made up of potential portfolio firms that will convert into the newer business form in order to have a chance of attracting outside capital. A fourth and related class consists of existing firms for which cost savings will accrue in the event of reorganization to a new business form, with the savings exceeding the cost of reorganization. This class includes professional service firms which, but for a limited liability partnership form, would continue to use a traditional partnership form.

A wide array of business firms may deviate from the status quo to demand a new company law form. Economic evidence shows that only certain firms will have sufficient influence to achieve positive legislative results, either because they are more powerful than others or because they perform collective lobbying through a common body which gives them an advantage over other firms in the procurement of favourable legislation (Macey 1998). Small and medium-sized enterprises (SMEs), for instance, are not likely to play a featured role in the development of business organization legislation. While this type of firm could derive much benefit from legal changes that dispose of the cumbersome formation and operation requirements, information and organization costs arguably inhibit its efficacy in attaining its preferred legislative goals (McCormick and Tollison 1981). In the event of SMEs making the lobbying effort independently, they must first incur information costs in discovering the effects of the choice of business forms on their own welfare.[8] Consequently, since SMEs may be severely budget-constrained in their ability to influence the legislature (De Figueiredo and Tiller 2001), they have incentives to join up with firms with whom they share common interests so as to lobby for legislation. The organization costs (ie, the costs of identifying other similarly situated firms) must not exceed the overall benefits from lobbying. This is especially true if firms encounter collective action problems. Rational firms have incentives to free-ride on the costly lobbying efforts of others. Attempts to engage in collective lobbying will therefore fail if a few firms bear the entire cost, but receive only a portion of the benefits (Olsen 1965). Additionally, even if small and medium-sized firms can overcome these problems and have adequate resources to lobby legislatures, they are likely to expend their efforts on more pressing operational and special considerations relating to a particular industry.

It can therefore be predicted that company laws will not adequately reflect the needs of SMEs. But even if this class of firms has high-powered incentives to lobby for innovative business forms (Bernardo and Welch 2001),[9] their efforts

---

[8] As small firms are unlikely to consider business organization laws, except in major relational crises, it is costly to ascertain the effects of different rules and provisions in advance.

[9] Bernardo and Welch (2001) argue that overconfident entrepreneurs are relatively less likely to imitate their peers and more likely to explore the environment leading them to adopting new innovations.

might not be successful. In terms of assessing the prospect of success, two factors may play a crucial role. First, legislative procedures and political processes reduce the stakes interest groups have in regulation. Legislatures have developed administrative structures and mechanisms (ie, the political and regulatory institutions, voting rules, rules of order) to control the opportunistic conduct of politicians and legislators who are sensitive to lobbying (McCubbins, Noll, and Weingast 1989; Schwartz and Scott 1995). As a result, the supply side plays a decisive role with respect to company law reform (Laffont and Tirole 1993). Second, although amendments to the menu of business forms would arguably make smaller firms more efficient, it may not be in the interests of other more powerful lobby groups to modify the law to allow new legal forms to emerge. Consequently, legislatures are likely to respond by failing to adopt value-increasing legislation.

Consider, for instance, the notaries (lawyers who specialize in incorporations and are qualified to issue a notarial deed) who could organize themselves as a significant interest group, blocking innovative measures and frustrating attempts to effectively implement the easy availability of limited liability for small businesses.[10] In Germany and the Netherlands, a notarial deed is required for all incorporations. Given the importance that firms attach to the regulation and cost of market entry (Djankov et al 2002), the extension of limited liability protection to partnership forms would preferably not require the issuance of such a deed. Yet, if a limited liability partnership were to gain adherence amongst investors and popularity with entrepreneurs,[11] the notaries' fee revenues might drop substantially. If their losses are more acute than the possible gains of business lawyers who would be involved in the formation process of a new limited liability vehicle, the notaries will have a particularly high-powered incentive to block such a new form.

That is not to say that legal professionals will not lobby for modernized company law legislation. Indeed the US experience points in the opposite direction. As experts in law with a well-entrenched position and proximity to the law-making process, they have a strong ability to influence the legislature (Ribstein 2002). As noted, the increase in recent years of the number of hybrid entities offering limited liability can be attributed to the legislatures' responsiveness to the interest group activities of professional services actors. Well-organized

---

[10] It might be argued that the persistence of the system of notaries is an example of the path dependence role of interest groups as a serious source of path dependence. In the twelfth and thirteenth centuries, the function of notaries was to register long-term contracts, including relational contracts—such as partnerships. Apparently, the merchants used notaries when

'reputation via word of mouth alone was insufficient to support honest behaviour and that a third party without any binding authority to enforce obligations was nonetheless quite valuable for promoting honest exchange'

(Milgrom, North, and Weingast 1990). In continental European jurisdictions, the formal use of lawyers as notaries evolved into a requirement to obtain legal personality.

[11] It is submitted that the developments with respect to the 'quasi-partnership' close corporation demonstrate the demand for business forms that combine the combination of partnership and corporate features (Ribstein 1995).

professional firms may lack enough choice to shield their liability, giving them adequate incentives to exercise political influence over legislatures to enact an LLP-type form.[12] In addition, innovative legal professionals who seek to design and implement new arrangements for their clients may have a financial incentive to persuade the legislature to enact a new business form.[13] If the existing menu of business forms does not satisfy a pent-up demand for firms to employ new and improved frameworks,[14] 'innovative form entrepreneurs' will endeavour to capture the market, thereby increasing their fee revenues (Banoff 2001). In the event of these professionals strongly favouring reform, given both types of incentives, the legislature is likely to respond by referring back to, and evolving from, existing doctrines and rules. For instance, they will bear in mind the key role of the notaries in the formation and operation of business forms. In fact, the current role of the notaries in business formations makes it likely that they will be able to defend the status quo, or expand their power in the future.

The upshot is that the political economy of hybrid business form legislation tends to reflect the compromise between the legislature and powerful organizations of professional lawyers. It is by no means certain that a new framework that meets the perceived interests of professionals is efficient and equally beneficial to other business firms, SMEs in particular. Nevertheless, legislatures are likely to allow these other firms to use such a framework without the value of corresponding advantages for these firms.

This effect is most obvious in the United States where the relatively simple landscape of company law has changed dramatically over the last two decades. For instance, the LLP emerged in Texas in 1991 to provide 'peace of mind' insurance for innocent partners. Thereafter, the LLP spread rapidly from two states in 1992 to all fifty states and the District of Columbia by 2001. In the original Texan conception of the LLP, general partners in professional firms were allowed to avoid joint and several malpractice liabilities. As the LLP evolved, most states expanded the scope of this business form by allowing non-professional firms to use the statute. In addition, most states expanded the original shield of limited liability protection beyond malpractice or other torts of their fellow partners to include all liabilities of the firm, whether based on tort, contract, or other basis.

---

[12] The professional lobbies could be very powerful if they are in fact the by-products of organizations that obtain their strength and support because they perform some functions in addition to lobbying for collective goods. Because membership is in fact mandatory, the organization can overcome information, organization, and collective action problems (Olsen 1965).

[13] The role of business lawyers as interest groups is of course closely related to their role as lawmakers in the arena of legal formants (Sacco 1991).

[14] Since there is a prevailing view that tax issues play a crucial role in choice-of-business-form decisions, innovative lawyers are inclined to design statutes or combinations of statutes with a view to helping firms obtain favourable tax treatment. Section 4 of this Chapter shows that there are other choices of business form drivers, such as contractual flexibility and the autonomy of firm participants in structuring, free from court interference, the internal affairs of the firm.

The LLC is yet another, and more successful, legal production that combines partnership features with corporate characteristics. The introduction of the LLC bundled together limited liability, a flexible governance structure, and preferential tax treatment and also required less ongoing paperwork than corporations. Also, it provides an almost total shield against personal liability without cumbersome formation and capital maintenance rules. In 1977, the first modern LLC statute was promulgated in Wyoming at the behest of lawyers and accountants acting as a lobby group for an oil company wishing to combine limited liability and pass-through tax treatment.[15] Before the Internal Revenue Services (IRS) generally secured the favourable partnership taxation for this new business form, Florida was the only other state that enacted LLC legislation, which it did in 1982 so as to attract foreign investors, particularly from South and Central America. However, the uncertainties with respect to the tax treatment of the new business form severely hampered the rush to conduct business under this new statute, and consequently did not lead to the expected upsurge of economic activity in Florida. As late as 1988, the IRS clarified the tax treatment of the LLC by issuing a ruling stating that the eligibility for partnership tax treatment is conditional upon the business form's corporate features.[16] If the LLC lacked two of the four corporate characteristics considered by the IRS to be crucial (continuity of life, centralization of management, limited liability, and free transferability of interests), then the Treasury regulations would treat the LLC as a partnership for tax purposes.[17] After this ruling, other states jumped on the LLC bandwagon, slowly and hesitantly at first, but after 1990, LLC legislation swept rapidly through the United States, largely because of competitive pressures and domestic interest groups, especially legal practitioners who viewed the LLC as better suited to the needs and expectations of their clients. LLC provisions had been adopted in all fifty-one US jurisdictions by the close of 1996 (see Table 4.1).

The emergence of and experimentation with the LLC forced the tax authorities to explain in more detail the distinction between partnership and corporate tax treatment, which eventually led to a new federal 'check-the-box' tax rule. Under the IRS 'check-the-box' regulations, which became effective on 1 January 1997, 'unincorporated' associations are taxed as partnerships unless they affirmatively elect to be taxed as corporations (see Figure 4.1). The partnership taxation—pass-through tax treatment—is based on the assumption that a partnership is a mere aggregate

---

[15] In 1975, lawyers and accountants advising Hamilton Brothers Oil Company devised the 'limited liability company', resembling the Panamanian *limitadas*. After a failed legislative effort in Alaska, they lobbied successfully for enactment of the LLC statute in Wyoming. In 1980, the IRS issued a favourable private letter ruling to Hamilton Brothers Oil Company regarding its Wyoming LLC structure (Hamilton 2001).

[16] Revenue ruling 88-76, 1988.

[17] The test for determining entity classification was set out in section 301.7701-2 of the Treasury regulations, known as the '*Kintner* regulations'. These regulations had a profound influence on the development of the early LLC statutes. A so-called 'bulletproof' statute was designed so that the entity would be treated as a partnership for federal income tax purposes.

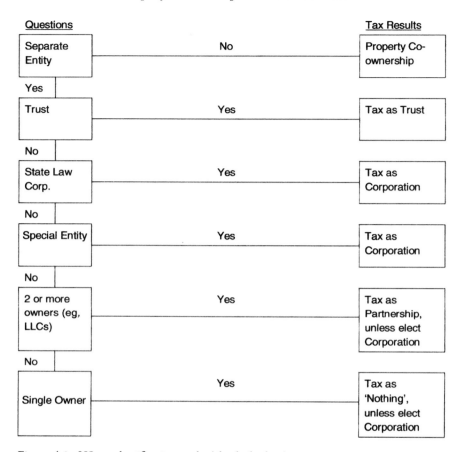

**Figure 4.1.** US tax classification under 'check-the-box'
*Source*: Callison (2001).

of individual partners who redistribute profits among themselves. Consequently, members of an LLC report their income and losses as if they were personally realized by the members, and income is taxed to the members as individuals.[18]

The 'check-the-box' regulations triggered yet a third wave of amendments of the LLC statutes, thereby encouraging the development of corporate-type LLCs and the adoption of a wide variety of LLC statutes. Table 4.1, for example, shows the variety in enactment dates and the type of fiduciary duties regime. In terms

---

[18] IRC § 701 provides that an LLC classified as partnership pays no tax on its income, but each member pays tax on the distributive share of the LLC's tax items, see IRC §§ 701 and 702. In contrast, corporate income is taxed first to the corporation and later, if it is distributed as dividend, to the shareholders individually.

Table 4.1. The development of LLC legislation, in particular fiduciary duties, in the United States

| State | Enacted | Adopted ULLCA | ULLCA § 409 | UPA § 21 | 8 Del. Code § 144 | MBCA § 8.30 | RULPA § 107 3rd Party Analogy |
|---|---|---|---|---|---|---|---|
| Alabama | 1993 | Yes | Yes | | | | X |
| Alaska | 1994 | | | | X | X | |
| Arizona | 1993 | | | | | | X |
| Arkansas | 1993 | | | X | | | |
| California | 1994 | | | X | | X | |
| Colorado | 1990 | | | | | X | |
| Connecticut | 1993 | | | X | | | X |
| Delaware | 1992 | | | | X | | |
| Florida | 1982 | | | | | X | |
| Georgia | 1994 | | | | | X | |
| Hawaii | 1997 | Yes | Yes | | | | |
| Idaho | 1993 | | | X | | | |
| Illinois | 1994 | Most | Yes, but not exclusive | | | | |
| Indiana | 1993 | | | X | | | |
| Iowa | 1992 | | | | X | X | |
| Kansas | 1990 | | | | | | X |
| Kentucky | 1994 | | | X | | X | |
| Louisiana | 1992 | | | X | X | X | |
| Maine | 1994 | | | X | | X | |
| Maryland | 1992 | | | | | | X |
| Massachusetts | 1995 | | | | | | |
| Michigan | 1993 | | | X | | X | |
| Minnesota | 1993 | | | | X | X | |
| Mississippi | 1994 | | | | | X | X |
| Missouri | 1993 | | | X | | X | |

**Table 4.1.** *(Cont.)*

| State | Enacted | Adopted ULLCA | ULLCA §409 | UPA §21 | 8 Del. Code §144 | MBCA §8.30 | RULPA §107 3rd Party Analogy |
|---|---|---|---|---|---|---|---|
| Montana | 1993 | Yes | | | | | |
| Nebraska | 1993 | | | | | | |
| Nevada | 1993 | | | | | | |
| New Hampshire | 1993 | | | X | | | |
| New Jersey | 1993 | | | | | | X |
| New Mexico | 1993 | | | X | X | | |
| New York | 1994 | | | | X | X | |
| North Carolina | 1993 | | | X | | X | |
| North Dakota | 1993 | | | | X | X | |
| Ohio | 1994 | | | | X | X | |
| Oklahoma | 1992 | | | X | | X | |
| Oregon | 1994 | | X | | | | |
| Pennsylvania | 1995 | | | X | | | |
| Rhode Island | 1992 | | | X | | X | |
| South Carolina | 1994 | Yes | Yes | | | | |
| South Dakota | 1993 | Yes | Yes | | | | |
| Tennessee | 1994 | | | X | X | X | |
| Texas | 1991 | | | | X | | |
| Utah | 1991 | | | | | | |
| Vermont | 1996 | Yes | Yes | | | | |
| Virginia | 1991 | | | | | X | X |
| Washington | 1994 | | | X | | | |
| West Virginia | 1992 | Yes | Yes | | | | |
| Wisconsin | 1999 | | | | X | | |
| Wyoming | 1977 | | | | | | |
| Washington DC | 1994 | | | | | | X |

*Source:* Adapted from <www.LLCweb.com> and Murdoch 2001.

of fiduciary duties, the table distinguishes between: ULLCA § 409 (Uniform Limited Liability Company Act), which mandates the duty of loyalty and care in a member-managed company; UPA § 21 (Uniform Partnership Act), which requires the members to act as a trustee for any profits derived without the consent of other partners; 8 Delaware Code § 144, which deals only with one aspect of the duty of loyalty, namely, the obligation to disclose self-dealing transactions in which there is a conflict of interest; MBCA § 8.30 (Model Business Corporation Act), which provides the standards of duty of faith and duty of care for directors; and RULPA § 107 (Revised Uniform Limited Partnership Act), which does not bind parties to fiduciary duties.

The development of corporate-type LLCs is also reflected in the recent revision of the Uniform Limited Liability Company Act of 1996. The Revised Uniform Limited Liability Act of 2006 (RULLCA) provides a modern, updated legislation governing the formation and operation of LLCs. The noteworthy new provisions clarify the ability of members to define and limit the duties of loyalty and care that members owe each other and the LLC. Moreover, the revised Act codifies buyout remedies similar to those found in close corporation statutes. To be sure, section 701(5)(B) of the Revised Act permits a member (but not a transferee) to seek a court order 'dissolving the company on the grounds that the managers or those members in control of the company...have acted or are acting in a manner that is oppressive and was, is, or will be directly harmful to the [member]'. However, as in the close corporation context, section 701(5)(B)(b) allows courts to craft a lesser stringent buyout remedy (unless the LLC's operating agreement states otherwise). Lastly, although the Act preserves the distinction between manager-managed and member-managed LLCs, it gives members a more corporate-type authority to bind the company. Section 301 explicitly states that a member of an LLC is not an agent solely by reason of being a member. The Act thus recognizes that the partnership doctrine of 'statutory apparent authority', by which a member can bind the LLC for apparently acting in the ordinary business of the LLC, does not belong in an LLC statute. The development towards a more corporate-type LLC would undoubtedly convince more states to adopt the model provisions that are stated in the uniform act. However, the Revised Act seems to ignore the fact that the absence of statutory guidance may have a detrimental effect on the members of the LLC and the third parties dealing with this entity. For instance, commentators point out that the new Act does not provide a clear default rule with respect to a member or manager's ability to bind the LLC (Ribstein 2007; Ribstein and Kobayashi 2007). Even though, as the prefatory note to the Act rightly explains, this omission will not significantly alter the commercial reality that exists between LLCs and third parties, legal certainty would be better served if the Act dealt explicitly with power-to-bind questions.[19]

---

[19] Another example of an omission is the failure to adopt 'series LLCs'. The Delaware Code (Del Code Ann Tit 6 § 18-215) states that 'A limited liability company agreement may establish or

## 2.1 The LLC: The Entity of Choice for US Non-listed Firms

The LLC is a separate legal entity that attempts to take proper account of the concerns of economic actors in an increasingly competitive and litigious business environment. The most important feature is that it offers limited liability protection. By doing so, the LLC allows easy access to the limited liability feature and hence puts a legal shield between individuals and creditors, thereby encouraging entrepreneurship and start-ups. The LLC keeps the price of limited liability down by providing for flexible tax rules and the tax planner with the chance to opt for the most optimal taxation. Due to the over-regulatory nature of the marketplace, clear and flexible business forms that shun formation and operation formalities, like the LLC, were heralded in the United States.

### 2.1.1 Entity Status

Entity status is bestowed on the LLC by statutory law.[20] An LLC in its own name acquires rights and obligations, acquires property and other legal rights in immovables, and can sue and be sued. From a law and economics perspective, legal entity status is a necessary shorthand device to define the property rights over which participants within a firm can contract. In the absence of entity status, it would be practically impossible to shield the assets of the LLC from creditors of the firm's owners. First, the transaction costs of drafting and inserting provisions in all contracts between the participants inside the firm and the firm creditors on the one hand and their personal creditors on the other will be prohibitively high. Second, the firm participants, including the business creditors, would face a moral hazard problem, viz. it is virtually impossible to assure the business creditors of the existence of the necessary agreements with the personal creditors.

### 2.1.2 Capital Structure and Contributions

The capital structure of the LLC is based on principles similar to the public corporation. It determines the members' voting rights, profit and loss sharing, and received distributions.[21] As with the corporation, the statute enunciates that rights of members are allocated in respect of their financial interests. To be sure,

---

provide for the establishment of 1 or more designated series of members, managers, limited liability company interests or assets. Any such series may have separate rights, powers or duties with respect to specified property or obligations of the limited liability company or profits and losses associated with specified property or obligations, and any such series may have a separate business purpose or investment objective.' Although the drafters of the Revised Uniform Limited Liability Act acknowledge in the Prefatory Note that these series are used in practice, they decided not to include any reference to this practice in the Act. They thought 'it made no sense for the Act to endorse the complexities and risks of a series approach', thereby failing to understand the function of the Act to clarify the law and offer practice a standard set of default provisions.

[20] RULLCA §104(a).

[21] An operating agreement may establish the manner in which LLC members allocate amongst themselves the profit and losses of the LLC. In the absence of an express agreement, most LLC

members could adopt per capita sharing in some LLCs, where they supply a personal guarantee, make unsecured loans, or undertake a management role in the firm. As a consequence, members can expect to receive additional votes or other rights in exchange for such additional contributions.

As for the consideration for the payment of shares, most LLC statutes provide that contributions may be made to the firm in many different forms, such as 'tangible or intangible property or other benefits to the firm, including money, promissory notes, services performed,[22] or other agreements to contribute cash or property, or contracts for services to be performed'.[23] The relationship—matters such as contribution, distributions, admission and withdrawal, management, and so forth—between the members of an LLC is under US law governed by the informal 'operating agreement', which may even be oral. To be sure, states differ in their requirements regarding whether both an oral and written agreement are necessary in respect of the contribution obligations. The LLC does not require minimum contributions in exchange for a membership interest.[24] As a default rule, the Revised Uniform Limited Liability Act provides that a member's inability is not an excuse for not making payments or delivering property or services.[25]

Most states mandate that the members maintain a central record of each contribution to ensure the rights of members are respected. Therefore, a member could make a claim regarding a past contribution that has not been registered and seek to update the central record. Thus, if an LLC has more than one class of units, it may be necessary to create two sets of books, one that records the economic relationships among the members ('inside basis') and another for tax purposes ('outside basis').

## 2.1.3 Distributions

In general, LLC statutes do not demand that members receive any distribution before they exit the firm. In some cases, the distributions from an LLC will be tax free.[26] Consistent with what we have seen in the previous section, the LLC statutes

---

statutes provide a default rule which states that the profits and losses of the LLC are shared in proportion to the value of the members' contributions.

[22] The treatment of a member's contribution of services to an LLC in exchange for an interest may vary depending on whether a member receives an interest in capital and profits of the LLC or an interest in the future profits of the LLC, see *Mark IV Pictures, Inc v Comm* 969 F2d 669, 673 (CA8 1992).

[23] RULLCA § 402. It is worth pointing out that the initial basis of a member's interest in an LLC will depend on the method by which the interest was obtained. The initial basis of a member's interest is employed to reflect the gains and losses that are passed on to the member from the LLC and to calculate the amount of gain or loss that a member must recognize on the sale of the interest, see IRC § 1001 (a).

[24] Whilst contributions of cash or property to an LLC are considered tax neutral, investors must also recognize that if the LLC is an 'investment company', a member may thereby recognize gains but not losses on a transfer of property to the LLC, IRC §§ 721(a)–(b).

[25] RULLCA § 403.

[26] Generally, most *pro rata* distributions of the LLC's net profits will be tax free. Clearly, IRC § 731(a) provides that an LLC member recognizes gain on a distribution of an LLC only where the extent of the money distributed exceeds the adjusted basis of the member's interest in the LLC.

that include a distribution clause rely on the members' contributions rather than per capita as for the sharing of profits, losses, or retained earnings. If a member receives distributions, it is likely to be in the form of cash. In circumstances where a member would demand a non-cash distribution, some states simply deny this right.[27]

Should a member receive excessive distributions, a creditor may have a remedy—in some states—in case the firm would not recognize his claim. There is some variation across the states regarding what constitutes an excessive or wrongful distribution. The statutes attempt to proxy excessive or wrongful distribution by reference to those transactions that tend to induce an LLC's insolvency. Managers and members are liable to creditors in circumstances where they return contributions while making the LLC insolvent and leaving creditors unpaid. Naturally, a valuation is required to determine if the distribution entails a return of contributions in a firm that is unable to discharge its debt and other obligations.

Arguably liability for wrongful distributions is similar to fraudulent conveyance law. Law reform experts argue that partnership and corporate law are not the optimal mechanisms for regulating creditors' claims against members in the case of excessive distributions and posit the general tort remedy is better tailored to achieving the policy objectives in this area. In fact, a number of scholars have recommended on efficiency grounds abandoning veil piercing in favour of a fraudulent conveyance remedy (Bainbridge 2005).[28] On this view, increasing the liability of members will discourage the transfer of members' interest to their most valued use.

### 2.1.4 Members' Interests

Members' interests consist of (1) financial rights to share in the profit and losses and receive distributions; and (2) governance rights to participate in management and control.[29] Generally these rights are defined by the statute and relevant case law. It is commonly agreed that, in the absence of contrary agreement, members may only transfer their financial rights.[30] The governance rights may only transfer by consent of the non-transferring members. To be sure, there is some conflict over the precise interpretation of financial rights. For instance, some question whether financial rights include indemnifications, repayment of loans, and salaries. Of course, this defect can be addressed by the promulgation of precise legal measures that clearly specify the transferable financial rights.

With respect to assignments, some jurisdictions mandate that assignors can be released from liability when all members have given their consent to the transfer. In some states, the assignee will not automatically obtain governance rights in

---

[27] RULLCA § 405(c).
[28] RULLCA 304 emphasizes that failure to meet legal formalities is not a basis for veil piercing.
[29] As discussed earlier, these rights are characteristic of closely held firms.
[30] The general rule is that with the sale or exchange of a member's interest in an LLC, the member's interest is treated as a capital asset and the gain or loss on the sale or transfer is a capital gain or loss, see IRC § 1221.

the LLC even when the financial rights have been transferred. The restrictions on the transferability of a member's interest obviously preclude the development of a liquid market in members' interests. To be sure, a number of states have introduced publicly traded units—which are nothing more than depository receipts for the owners' property interests. However, the efficiency of selling units is called into question because underwriters are unwilling to offer units on a wide scale. Further, the introduction of units could trigger obligations for securities law purposes that will in turn entail additional costs for members.

Legislators have determined that the interests of members that pass to heirs are strictly limited to financial, but not to other rights. In effect, they are entitled to the same rights as an assignee. To be sure an exception is allowed for a divorced spouse who not only is entitled to receive distributions, but is also entitled to receive an interest in the firm's property, including good will. Naturally, these beneficiaries are not entitled to become members of the firm.

## 2.1.5 Internal Organization

The LLC statutes are largely linked to general and limited partnerships, and corporations. To the extent that LLC statutes do not contain explicit linking provisions, the 'pick and mix' of provisions of other business forms could entail implicit linking problems. If the statutes are silent on a particular issue, the import of general partnership provisions could imply that gaps should be filled with other partnership law rules. In the absence of statutory authority, courts could decide to extend general partnership principles to the LLC and to treat different business forms alike. For instance, since the Uniform Limited Liability Company Act of 1996 (ULLCA 1996) uses identical language to the Revised Uniform Partnership Act (RUPA) for its fiduciary duties,[31] it is obvious that there would be some undesired spill-overs from one business form to the other. Second, even though most LLC statutes provide for decentralized management by default, it is also possible to opt for centralized management.[32] This raises the issue of whether other default rules should also differ according to the parties' choice. In this respect, ULLCA 1996 provides for different fiduciary duty provisions, but similar dissociation and dissolution provisions. Courts could view this as a legislative omission and decide to apply corporate law rules to centralized management LLCs when the underlying relational contract remains silent.

This explains why the National Conference of Commissioners on Uniform State Laws decided in 2006 to promulgate a 'second generation' uniform act. The Revised Act is arguably more consistent with the preferences of the majority of the users of the LLC statute. For instance, by expanding the members' freedom

---

[31] ULLCA (1996) § 409.

[32] See eg ULLCA (1995) § 203 (stating that the articles of association must set forth whether the company is to be 'manager managed'). RULLCA §407 alters this regime by stating that a limited liability company is a member-managed limited liability company unless the operating agreement expressly provides that the company is manager managed.

through their operating agreement to state the rules that will govern their relationship as well as the conduct of the business, the Revised Act codifies the case law's position on the function of the operating agreement and the scope of fiduciary duties.[33]

### 2.1.6  Minority Protection

It is submitted that extra-legal mechanisms, such as trust and loss of reputation, can lessen but not eliminate the inefficient subtraction of firm-specific investments. When gains of opportunism can be very large, legal standards are needed to prevent parties from engaging in opportunistic behaviour. As prerequisites for these standards of performance, minority and majority opportunism must be discouraged, and the self-enforcing character of the relationship must be preserved. In this respect, US legal scholars usually point to the function of fiduciary duties (Bratton and McCahery 1995).

Fiduciary duties have evolved differently across a range of contexts involving different types of parties and consensual relationships. For instance, traditional partnership law has developed broad and strict fiduciary duties. It is submitted that in the context of partnerships, enhanced fiduciary duties are justified because the consensual relationship is built upon mutual trust and the utmost good faith. Broad fiduciary duties are a core principle of traditional partnership law in all jurisdictions. Partners expect honesty, fair dealing, and mutuality of effort from each other. As in a marriage, they owe each other the duty of the highest loyalty and trust. In his famous and often quoted opinion in *Meinhard v Salmon*,[34] the American Judge Cardozo emphasizes that fiduciary relations are about trust by stating that 'many forms of conduct permissible in a workaday world for those acting at arm's length are forbidden to those bound by fiduciary ties. A trustee is held to something stricter than the morals of the marketplace. Not honesty alone, but the punctilio of an honour the most sensitive, is then the standard of behavior.'

In this view, even though partnerships can be described as contractual in the broad sense that the partners have entered the relationship voluntarily, fiduciary duties are moral concepts of the highest order, and are not contractually modifiable. The keystone of the partnership relationship lies in the partners' commitment to abnegate short-term self-interest and to promote the welfare of the aggregate of partners rather than their own. Partnership law therefore traditionally provides for broad fiduciary duties that lessen the risk of opportunistic conduct. These duties are necessarily open-ended standards of performance that can be separated into (1) a duty of care and loyalty; (2) a duty to disclose information;

---

[33] For instance, an Ohio appeals court found that where an operating agreement expressly allows competition between other businesses, the operating agreement overrides any claim based on the breach of fiduciary duties. See *McConnell v Hunt Sports Enterprises*, 132 Ohio App 3rd 657, 725 NE2d 1193 (1999).
[34] *Meinhard v Salmon*, 249 NY 458, 164 NE 545 (1928).

(3) a duty to preclude from self-dealing transactions, personal use of partnership assets, usurpation of partnership opportunities, and competition with the partnership; and (4) a duty of good faith and fair dealing. Because fiduciary duties are open-ended and vague, it might be argued that a breach of fiduciary duty is often hard for an outside party such as a court to verify, and consequently will only assist in preventing opportunism to a limited extent. For instance, even though fiduciary duties reflect concern about the potential abuse of automatic exit rules in endgame settings, the moral mandate approach rejects the notion that fiduciary duties have only a limited remedy function, which is only brought into play when the trust-based relationship breaks down and *ex post* renegotiation is cumbersome. Yet proponents of strict and broad fiduciary duties suggest that these high standards of performance have a distinct function that supplements the remedial actions provided by statute. Fiduciary duties help to foster the development and internalization of trust and norms in a particular business relationship. These rules not only perform an important role in diverting expropriation, but also assure business stability by encouraging the partners to surrender autonomy and abnegate self-interested behaviour. In this way, the open-ended, overly broad judicial language levels the playing field in relational contracts and induces trust behaviour in firms, in that fiduciary duties provide a legal incentive for the parties to cooperate and forego opportunistic behaviour. In this respect, fiduciary duties have a prophylactic function.

Traditionally, the broad scope of the fiduciary duties distinguishes partnerships from corporations. While managers stand in a fiduciary relationship to the corporation and its shareholders, managers of corporations appear to have a more relaxed set of fiduciary duties. In corporations, the legal concept of fiduciary duty has two quite different functions. First, managers are generally expected to perform their duties with the care of a prudent person who manages his own affairs of equal gravity. Second, the managers owe the corporation a duty of loyalty that limits the possibility of self-dealing transactions, prohibits managers from usurping corporate opportunities, and forbids unfair competition with the corporation. In short, fiduciary duties offer protection against the managers' pursuit of personal interest and excessively negligent behaviour. They cannot be used to discipline directors in the performance of their official duties, thereby second-guessing managers' business judgements.

Because the corporate law fiduciary standards applicable to publicly held corporations generally apply equally to close corporations, it is not quite clear whether shareholders in the latter owe each other a fiduciary duty. As noted in Chapter 2, in some jurisdictions courts increasingly extend the application of strict partnership-type fiduciary duties to shareholders of close corporations. Because there are no capital market forces that help to constrain opportunistic behaviour, and complete contingent relational contracts are unfeasible, there really is something to the partnership metaphor. It might be argued that in close corporations, where management functions are (at least to some extent) transferred from directors to shareholders, strict fiduciary duties are justified to prevent the greater threat of opportunistic behaviour. However, the convergence of fiduciary duties in partnerships and close corporations also seems to have its limitations. Some law and economics scholars argue that strict and broad fiduciary duties at all levels of closely held firms could be counter-productive (Ribstein 2001). In this view, broad fiduciary duties could encourage parties to engage in over-monitoring at the expense of productivity.

Moreover, a strict interpretation of fiduciary duty raises the vexed question of the possibility of opting out of fiduciary duties. In order to answer this question, one should distinguish between the fiduciarian and the contractarian views (Vestal 1993). While the former defends restrictions on fiduciary waivers in closely held business forms, the latter considers fiduciary duties as default rules that the parties should be permitted to opt out of upon mutual agreement. Even though the critics of the fiduciary approach seem to acknowledge that opting out is possible by selecting another business form, they argue that bargaining around fiduciary duties could contribute to norm erosion in the short term, and may induce a norm change in the long term. In the contractarian approach, the parties to a particular transaction are in the best position to reflect their relational wishes in a contract.

The drafters of the ULLCA 1996—by using similar language to RUPA— have struggled to take the viewpoints of both groups into account. As a result, ULLCA 1996 reflects both the fiduciarian and the contractarian approach, thereby causing confusion and ambiguity. ULLCA 1996 has defined the scope of fiduciary duties within a partnership. ULLCA (1996) § 409 provides that the only fiduciary duties a partner owes to the partnership and the other partners are those of loyalty and care, and defines these duties in exclusive terms. The duty with respect to the disclosure of information is contained in § 408 and so is not a fiduciary duty. The obligation of good faith and fair dealing, imposed on the partners in § 409(d), is also viewed as a contractual concept rather than a fiduciary duty. In this respect, ULLCA 1996 conceives the partnership relationship merely as a contractual relationship, thereby restraining the judicial discretion to impose other fiduciary duties than those defined in the statute. It may be argued that the courts will be left some leeway to expand the partners' duties and obligations, which are included within the non-fiduciary obligation of good faith and fair dealing. However, ULLCA (1996) § 409(d) appears to preclude claims based on bad faith and unfair dealing by stating that the partners have (only) an obligation of good faith and fair dealing in the discharge of their duties. RULLCA, however, reverses the earlier move to define and codify members' fiduciary duties and opens the door for partnership-type broad fiduciary duties.[35] This is especially imminent in the context of a member seeking a remedy for oppressive conduct.[36]

---

[35]  RULLCA § 409.          [36]  RULLCA § 701.

This brings us to the question of whether the notion of fiduciary duties should be mandatory or a default rule that the parties could tailor or waive contractually. ULLCA (1996) § 103 greatly limits the parties' freedom to contract around fiduciary duties and good faith obligations. The fiduciary duties of loyalty or care and the obligation of good faith and fair dealing can be modified by agreement, subject to a reasonableness test. Moreover, the members are not allowed to entirely eliminate these duties and obligations. Because members may want to state their preferences in an operating agreement *ex ante*, they should be allowed to tailor the scope of the fiduciary obligations contractually or to opt out of the statutory regime entirely. To be sure, it is argued that a mandatory rule is desirable in partnership law, since it (1) emphasizes the importance of trustworthy behaviour; (2) levels the playing field between the partners by protecting parties against oppressive contracts and unforeseeable harm; and (3) prevents deleterious social consequences in that the ability to opt out fosters exploitation and abuse. However, mandatory fiduciary duties in LLCs may do more harm than good when parties do not seek to completely surrender their autonomy upon entry into the LLC. It should, therefore, come as no surprise that the Revised Act protects the operating agreement from judicial second-guessing by (1) clarifying that the members are able to define and reshape fiduciary duties in the agreement; and (2) providing guidance to courts to decide in cases where a member seeks to escape the agreement because the provisions are 'manifestly unreasonable'.[37] Table 4.2 compares the LLP—as regulated in the RUPA—and the LLC—as it appears in the Revised Uniform Limited Liability Company Act and the Delaware Limited Liability Act. The comparison shows that the Delaware LLC evolved most in the direction of a corporate-type LLC with narrow fiduciary duties and restrictive exit clauses.

If we agree that company law legislation is incomplete and view lawmakers as just another producer in the overall economy, the introduction of the hybrid business forms appears to be nothing more than product innovation based on the compelling logic of firms seeking easy access to a range of governance structures designed to have limited liability protection, reduce complexity, and limit transaction costs. However, it follows from the above discussion that new business forms do not immediately provide business parties with an optimal and comprehensive governance structure. Opponents to new legal forms attempt to frustrate and ridicule the need of hybrid business forms. One common view is that a firm can tinker with the existing legal framework by simply adjusting the statutory provisions or combining existing legal forms to a structure that is responsive to its needs. The balance of evidence suggests, however, that substantially modifying the company law statutes involves significant costs (eg increased information costs and uncertainty, distortions in the signalling function of business forms, decreased coherence of terms, erroneous gap filling by courts, and other negative

---

[37] RULLCA § 110.

Table 4.2. Comparison US LLP and US LLC

| Characteristic | LLP (RUPA) | LLC (RULLCA) | LLC (Delaware LLC) |
|---|---|---|---|
| Legal Personality | Yes | Yes | Yes |
| Management | Decentralized | Decentralized (default) Centralized (opt-in) §407 RULLCA<br><br>RULLCA refers power-to-bind questions to other laws, such as the law of agency. | Decentralized (unless otherwise provided in the LLC agreement, the management is vested in LLC members in proportion to the then current percentage or other interest of members in the profits)<br><br>Unless otherwise provided, each member and manager has the authority to bind the LLC |
| Formation | Informal by two or more partners | Public filing of the articles of organization with the secretary of state (one or more members) | In order to form an LLC, one or more authorized persons must execute a certificate of formation, which must be filed in the office of the Secretary of State |
| Autonomy of Articles of Organization | Partnership: relationship governed by written and oral agreements | If operating agreement is inconsistent with the Certificate of Organization: (1) the operating agreement controls the internal affairs, (2) the Certificate controls as to third parties who reasonably rely on this document (the Certificate must set forth only limited and specific information, such as the name of the company and the address of the initial designated office) | It is the policy to give maximum effect to the principle of freedom of contract and to the enforceability of limited liability company agreements |
| Notarization of Articles of Incorporation | No | No | No |

| | | | |
|---|---|---|---|
| Fiduciary Duties | Duties of loyalty and care. Obligation of good faith and fair dealing | Duties of loyalty and care. Obligation of good faith and fair dealing, RULLCA increases and clarifies the power of the operating agreement to define, reshape or eliminate fiduciary duties. Moreover, it provides some guidance to courts when a person seeks to circumvent the operating agreement by stating that its provisions are manifestly unreasonable. §110 RULLCA | The elimination or restriction of fiduciary duties is allowed. The contractual duty of good faith and fair dealing is left intact. |
| Financial Rights | Equal sharing (default rules) | If no agreement, sharing in proportion to the members' contribution to capital | If no agreement, profits and losses will be allocated on the basis of the agreed value of the contributions |
| Transferable Interests | Generally, no | Yes, restrictions are imposed by the Act, securities laws, and operating agreement | Yes, restrictions are imposed by the Act, securities laws, and operating agreement |
| Continuity of Life | Withdrawal does not automatically dissolve the LLP | Withdrawal does not automatically dissolve the LLC | Possibility to resign from an LLC is limited; resignation does not automatically dissolve the LLC |
| Limited Liability | Yes | Yes | Yes |
| Financial Statements | No need to disclose records publicly; partners have access to records | Members have access to records. No mandatory disclosure | Members have access to records. No mandatory disclosure |
| Taxation | Pass-through ('check-the-box') | Pass-through ('check-the-box') | Pass-through ('check-the-box') |
| Linkage | Linked to general partnership form | RULLCA has a more delinked character than its predecessor ULLCA which contains some provisions that are similar to RUPA | Delinked |

spill-over effects) that outweigh possible benefits. In the next section, we show why lawmakers in Japan and Singapore considered new separate business statutes to be more efficient in providing firms, at different levels, with a legal structure that does not impose burdens or create distortions and, hence, would have significant cost advantages.

## 3. The Introduction of Hybrid Business Forms in Asia

In this section, we discuss how existing institutional arrangements may be called into question by economic shocks, increasing global competition, or war (Roe 2006; Rajan and Zingales 2003). The large-scale effects of these events can lead to reversals of expectations and consequently supply incentives and opportunities for reform-minded groups to create new legal rules and institutions. Even though there are few genuine exogenous shocks in history, it is generally recognized that the Asian economies experienced a major financial crisis in 1997 which, combined with earlier underlying weaknesses, prompted policy-makers to consider altering the taken-for-granted institutional arrangements. A most conspicuous example of external-shock-induced organizational changes is the corporate governance and securities law reforms in Japan, which were introduced by governmental regulators in response to the so-called lost decade of the 1990s.

Japan has a long history of responding to external threats. Consider the period before the Meiji reforms when Japan was essentially a closed country and carried out only limited commercial and cultural exchanges with the Hollanders.[38] At the end of the Edo period (1603–1867), the Japanese government responded to the external shock of confronting new social and economic pressures of the Russians, and later Europeans and Americans, which attempted to establish trade contracts with Japan. Yet, it was only in 1854 that Japan ratified the Japan–US treaty of peace and amity forced by Commodore Perry of the US Navy. But, it took some time for the trade, which remained very limited until the beginning of the Meiji period (1868–1912), to develop. Foreign nations demanded the ratification of treaties, which provided for immunity for foreigners from Japan's existing penal system. At the same time, these treaties granted foreign traders economical and legal advantages over domestic business people. In order to regain independence and dignity in their own country, Japan reacted, among other things, by adopting legal reforms, including a legislative regime to govern the internal affairs of companies, inspired by German law. The transplantation of a civilized, Western-style legal system was viewed as the only rapid and effective solution to force the foreign powers to abrogate the treaties.

---

[38] The Meiji period (1868–1912) is known for bringing about the modernization of Japanese economic, political, and social institutions.

Thus, company law in Japan could be viewed as a German transplant (Milhaupt 2005). Despite the 1950 amendments introduced during the American occupation, the general corporate form (*Kabushiki Kaisha*) remained relatively formal and later reforms continue to show a tendency to transplant German legal rules.[39] For instance, the enactment of the *Yugen Kaisha*, a closely held business form based on the German GmbH in 1938, reflects the German legacy.

Subsequently, radical attempts to change Japan's company law system emerged in the late 1990s. In general this period is considered to be a 'lost decade' as Japan experienced a long-lasting severe recession that followed the burst of the preceding bubble economy. The Japanese economy was hit hard as large corporations defaulted and banks suffered under an increasing weight of non-performing loans. The 'shock' not only hit the financial economy but also destroyed Japan's self-esteem as a 'technopower'. The weakening of domestic confidence, manifested in the involvement of the Japanese bullet train, Shinkansen—once a symbol of the reliability of Japan's technological superiority—in multiple accidents in 2000, has become increasingly important for Japan. Moreover, large firm confidence was further weakened by the successful commercial strategies of European and American high-tech companies, collaborating through US hybrid entities, that have eroded the position of many Japanese technology-oriented firms.

All of this raised concerns about the rigidities and shortcomings of Japanese law. The growing emphasis on institutional reform and change, in response to globalization and the corresponding competitive pressures, has been stimulated by a new constellation of interest groups which have significant political clout to bring about a variety of reforms, including the facilitating of stock options, to spur the knowledge-based sector and encourage investment.

Besides traditional governance measures, policy-makers have focused on creating hybrid business forms, similar to those developed earlier in the USA and UK, that offer more flexibility in the decision-making structure and governance framework as well as resource management mechanisms needed to support the efforts of firms working in the human capital-intensive sector. Moreover, there are numerous indications that policy-makers have devoted considerable attention to the concerns of the largest and most established companies seeking to develop new technology, spin-off new opportunities and intellectual property, which can form the basis of joint ventures and alliances.[40] Thus, by 2003, the Ministry of Justice had established

---

[39] Such as strengthening the statutory auditors' powers.

[40] In 2002, realizing this adverse change in the competitive situation, Japan used its prior and existing 'Research Association for Mining and Manufacturing Technology Law' (Koukougyo Gijutsu Kenkyuu Kumiai Hou), and established EUVA (EUV association, 2002–8) aimed at catching up to the EUV-LLC, but so far, this effort has not borne fruit. To worsen the situation, the US-European group has just initiated their stage by starting the INVENT partnership (2005–12) to which IBM, AMD, Infineon, and Micron Technology have contributed roughly JPY 70 billion (about US$700 million) which is also a closely held firm aimed at carrying out similar R&D activities (similar to EUV-LLC) on technologies to form a super-fine semiconductor integrated circuit by using extreme ultra-violet (EUV) light.

a number of priorities involving the amendment of the Commercial Code. The end result was a package of legislative reform measures, collected in the New Company Law, which were submitted to the Diet in March 2005.

Generally, the New Company Law (Kaisha Ho) abolishes the *Yugen Kaisha* (YK), the close corporation, and leaves a modernized *Kabushiki Kaisha* (KK) in place (grandfathering the existing YKs). The KK regulation is liberalized through the relaxation of the minimum capital requirements (reducing the threshold from net assets of JPY 10 million to JPY 3 million). Further, closely held KKs, which restrict in their articles of association the free transferability of shares, will only require one director to be appointed instead of three. The appointment of a statutory auditor for the KK is not mandated if an officer is appointed who has the qualifications of tax accountant or accountant. While a suitably modernized KK will surely attract a number of closely held firms, the legislature acknowledged that the amendments introduced will not be sufficiently attractive to those individuals or established companies that are interested in selecting a more flexible business form.

It is therefore not surprising that the New Company Law provides for the introduction of a new company law form, the Limited Liability Company or *Godo Kaisha*. The LLC is a partnership-type form that bundles together limited liability, decentralized management by default, unanimous consent to transferability of members' interests, fiduciary duties, and no requirement to audit and disclose financial records. The Japanese vehicle bears a strong resemblance to the US LLC (eg voting and distribution rights are proportionate to the members' contributions), but diverges in a number of important respects, including: (1) contributions to the LLC will be limited to cash or property, but no services, know-how, or other agreements are permitted; and (2) the LLC will receive corporate, but not pass-through, tax treatment.

It may be that the adoption of a US-style LLC can be seen as the effect of a strong triggering event, which is the determinative force of domestic institutional change. It is difficult at this juncture, however, to be certain that these changes are only the result of such an exogenous trigger. Moreover, it is hard to distinguish between endogenous and exogenous pressures as the determinative force of institutional change. In any event, it could be argued that the sequence of institutional changes marked by the new hybrid entities is ultimately the result of both pressures. On the one hand, the effects of decreasing returns on key actors within the commercial system, notably through the growth and internationalization of the financial system and the integration of product markets as a whole, actually influences the course of legal and institutional development, undermining complementary institutions and policies. Further, pronounced disruptions to the existing path not only altered intrinsically the interests of key pressure groups, but also modified their incentives to invest in the development of new types of legal institutions and rules. That said, the scope for both exogenous and endogenous pressures to bring about major structural reforms in Japan is evidently great.

On the other hand, controlling legal elites and incumbent interest groups were initially strongly resistant, regardless of the pressures, to adopting a business form that combines important attributes of the corporate form and the partnership form, such as limited liability, flexibility, and pass-through taxation. In order to overcome resistance to change, the Ministry of Economy, Trade, and Industry (METI) stepped in and submitted, subsequent to the introduction of the *Godo Kaisha*, the Limited Liability Partnership Bill to the Diet in February 2005. As a consequence, the LLP or *Yugen Sekinin Jigyou Kumiai* came into effect on 1 August 2005 to encourage the creation of new business ventures, joint ventures, and other strategic partnerships between high-tech companies and research institutions. The LLP Law provides for the introduction of a vehicle that is characterized by limited liability, a flexible organization structure, pass-through taxation, and restrictions on the free transferability of partners' interests. Despite these attractive features, the legislation mandates a number of highly restrictive and costly features including: (1) registration of the LLP agreement; (2) disclosure of financial information including the profit and loss statements and the balance sheet upon the request of creditors; (3) the mandatory obligation of partners to participate in LLP management and its operation; and (4) the right of partners to exit at will. Notwithstanding these arguable shortcomings, which reflect political compromises, the LLP may, as will be discussed in the next section, provide significant cost advantages to firms.

Viewed from the perspective of an entrepreneurial government faced with exogenous pressures, such as global competition (Bratton and McCahery 1997), rapid changes in technologies and evolving market conditions, it is more likely to promote the competitiveness of indigenous industries through adoption of a cost-effective, reliable, and flexible legal regime. If the future brings a substantial increase in business activity, a shift in interest group pressures for efficiency-based law-making could well be expected. Such a jurisdiction may consider entering the competitive law-making environment for the supply of law as product. In the company law context, a jurisdiction could reap the benefits by coming forward with a set of contractual-based rules ideally suited to closely held firms. If this jurisdiction were to engage in a law reform process along such lines, it could very well create a focal point leading to a significant number of domestic and even foreign firms selecting this legal innovation.

Singapore is an example of an entrepreneurial jurisdiction. As a result of increased competition in Asia and the rapid development of China and the increase of Chinese firms being engaged in cross-border activities, the Singapore legislature enacted, among other things, an LLP (which came into effect on 11 April 2005). This evolution reflects 'the acute awareness of the need to recognize and accommodate current international business and commercial practices'.[41] The Singapore LLP (S-LLP) is a new type of business vehicle in Singapore based on

---

[41] See <www.singaporelaw.sg>.

the Delaware LLP and to a lesser extent the UK LLP. An S-LLP is a legal entity that can sue and be sued and acquire and hold property. Like the Japanese counterpart, it offers a flexible management structure and pass-through taxation. The LLP is a stand-alone business form explicitly delinked from the existing partnership law.[42] The partners are not personally liable for the firm's debts and obligations.[43] This protection shall not affect the personal liability of a partner in tort for his own wrongful act or omission. The internal relationship between the partners is governed by the limited liability partnership agreement. In the absence of an agreement or when the agreement is silent, the First Schedule, which acts as a model agreement, will apply. Although the S-LLP is required to keep accounts and other records, it is not necessary to prepare profit and loss accounts or balance sheets or to have them audited and disclosed. Table 4.3 provides a comparative overview of the revised and introduced business forms in Japan and Singapore.

The transformation described above provides a framework for evaluating the economic role of new hybrid business forms. On this basis, the next section will review the new legal entities that emerged in the USA, UK, and Asia and are attracting more and more businesses to their relatively new network. It is suggested that these hybrid business forms, compared to the traditional menu, can provide effective choices for controlling opportunism while limiting transaction costs. Three fundamental questions will be asked: (1) whether closely held firms would prefer to select a new, redesigned hybrid legal entity, which sets forth the joint ownership structure and provides important contractual provisions in advance; (2) whether new business forms ideally suited to particular businesses are better positioned to offset the inefficiencies resulting from the lock-in effects and path dependence factors; and (3) how many products a menu of legal business forms should contain.

## 4. The Impact of Hybrid Business Forms on the Economy

We have so far distinguished between the three reform strategies which roughly lead to the emergence of three distinct statutory products. First, a legal upgrade, which has been the main reaction of the European member states to the European Court of Justice's post-*Centros* decisions, arguably provides an easy-to-use vehicle that supplies lawyers and firms with familiar provisions that are 'tried and tested' and consequently offer learning and network benefits to users of the form. Second, a linked, but new, legal business form similarly holds out continued network and learning benefits along with the prospect of superior cost advantages due to better suited statutory provisions. Third, in contrast, a non-networked product holds

---

[42]  See Section 6 of the Limited Liability Partnerships Act 2005.
[43]  The LLP may recover distributions from partners that know or ought to have known that the LLP was insolvent or the distributions caused insolvency of the LLP.

**Table 4.3.** Comparison: new company law in Japan and Singapore

| Characteristic | KK (new) | J-LLC | J-LLP | S-Private Company | S-LLP |
|---|---|---|---|---|---|
| Legal Personality | Yes | Yes | No | Yes | Yes |
| Management | Corporate structure (shareholders-board of directors) | Flexible—no restriction | Flexible—mandatory participation of all partners | Corporate structure (shareholders-board of directors) | Flexible—default: partnership like management structure |
| Formation | Registration of the articles of incorporation with the Legal Affairs Bureau (*hōmukyoku*)—registration fee = JPY 150,000 | Formed by articles of incorporation signed between members—registration of operating agreement and corporate seal with the Legal Affairs Bureau (*hōmukyoku*)—registration fee = JPY 60,000 | Registration and disclosure of the LLP agreement with the Legal Affairs Bureau (*hōmukyoku*)—registration fee = JPY 60,000 | Registration of the Memorandum (subscribed by at least 1 person) and the articles of association | Online Registration at <www.bizfile.gov.sg /> Registration Fee is S$ 165 / Registration takes 15 minutes |
| Autonomy of Articles of Incorporation | Yes | Operating agreement | LLP agreement | Yes | LLP agreement |
| Notarization of Articles of Incorporation | Yes—notarization fee = JPY 50,000 | No | No | No | No |
| Fiduciary Duties | Directors must act in good faith | Managers have similar duties to legal duties of KK directors | Defined by LLP agreement (Incomplete law) | Duties of directors: (1) to act honestly; (2) duty to disclose shareholdings; (3) duty to convene general meetings | Defined in LLP agreement or, if the agreement is silent, the provisions in the First Schedule (full disclosure of relevant information and non-compete clause) |

**Table 4.3.** *(Cont.)*

| Characteristic | KK (new) | J-LLC | J-LLP | S-Private Company | S-LLP |
|---|---|---|---|---|---|
| Financial Rights | Distribution of profits and losses allocated according to equity participation ratio (however, distributions of profits require net assets of at least JPY 3 million) | Profits and losses may be allocated at a different rate from equity participation rate if specified in operating agreement | Profits and losses may be freely allocated with the unanimous approval of partners | Dividends shall be apportioned and paid proportionately to the amounts paid or credited as paid on the shares during any portion or portions of the period in respect of which the dividend is paid; | Defined in LLP agreement or, if the agreement is silent, the provisions in the First Schedule (equal sharing rule) |
| Transferable Interests | Shares are freely transferable. Restrictions (by making transfer subject to board approval) in the articles possible | Members' unanimous approval required | Partners' unanimous approval required (mandatory rule) | A private company restricts the right to transfer its shares | LLP agreement—default: assignment of financial rights |
| Continuity of Life | Yes | Yes—even with one member | Yes, but minimum of two partners | Yes | Yes—the Court may order the winding up if the LLP carries on business with less than two partners for more than two years |
| Limited Liability | Yes, no minimum capital requirement, but in practice some paid-in capital is necessary | Yes | Yes | Yes | Yes (claw-back provision for distributions made three years before insolvency) |

| | | | | | |
|---|---|---|---|---|---|
| Financial Statements | Disclosure of annual balance sheet | No disclosure of annual balance sheet—financial statements must be made available to members and creditors | LLP must disclose its balance sheet and profit and loss statement to creditors (upon request) | Submission of an audited profit and loss account and balance sheet at a general meeting | Accounts and other records should be kept and retained for seven years. No mandatory audit and disclosure requirements |
| Taxation | Corporate | Corporate | Pass-through | Corporate | Pass-through |
| Linkage | Company Law | Company Law | Law Concerning Limited Liability Partnership Agreements | Companies Act | Non-applicability of partnership law clause |

*Source:* Adapted from <www.singaporelaw.sg> and <www.jetro.go.jp>

out greater costs for adopting firms as switching costs affect prospective users negatively, and the absence of an established set of precedents—which are needed to fill the gaps in the inherently incomplete law—provide few incentives for parties to adopt an entirely new type of legal product.

It would not be surprising, given the relative cost advantages of upgrading, that the first approach is the obvious alternative. A modified statute could be attractive as there are no new learning costs involved. Because there are usually few alterations needed, it is easier for practitioners and business parties to adjust to the new round of changes. Given that the changes are unlikely to touch the core components of the legal tradition and its legitimating features, parties will have an incentive to learn the new rules. Nevertheless, the upgrade model has been criticized for not only making innocuous, albeit necessary, changes but for being out of step with innovative social and economic change. Although the upgrade approach seems attractive, particularly if the existing statutory framework is functionally obsolete, it is unlikely to benefit users unless accompanied by genuine cost-saving changes.

Despite the apparent ease with which jurisdictions can engage in producing statutory upgrades, this phenomenon has proved more costly and time-consuming than anticipated. This is evidenced by: (1) the difficulty in the design of acceptable upgrades; and (2) the reluctance of lawmakers to agree and quickly implement the proposed changes. Apparently, lawmakers when committed to incremental reform are less concerned with the pace and practical consequence of legislative change.

Even though most jurisdictions still employ the upgrade strategy to reform, an increasing number of countries embrace a new product approach by following either the second or third reform strategies as described in the previous section. This can be seen in the cases of the UK, Japan, and Singapore, which moved quickly into unchartered territory when embarking on a new legal reform strategy that complemented their existing upgrade legislative reform approach. Surprisingly, this development seems better able to ensure speedy and effective legislative action. The length of time to develop and reform new company statutes is reflected in Figure 4.2.

It follows from this figure that it is probably easier for lawmakers to understand and appreciate the alleged benefits of the new forms across political systems. The complex tax and doctrinal issues that can hamper and delay law reform projects are more effectively avoided when a new vehicle is proposed which leaves untouched the existing company law framework. Reforms along these lines, moreover, are supported by interest groups due to the measurable benefits they yield, including a new business form's (1) greater flexibility; (2) response to specific market problems and pressures; (3) ability to resolve conflicts between agents; and (4) value-added features in the structuring of transactions and business planning. Thus seen, the introduction of new legal products results in inherent benefits for businesses leading to major changes in the bargaining environment in which firms operate.

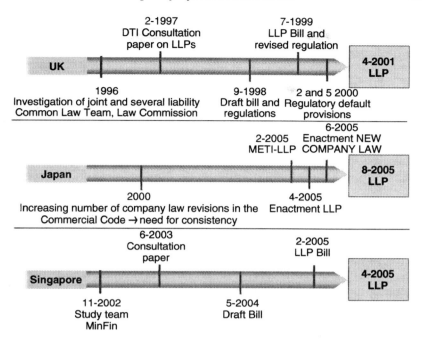

**Figure 4.2.** The time needed to introduce the LLP

## 4.1 The Inherent Benefits of Hybrid Business Forms

### 4.1.1 Limited Liability and Pass-through Taxation

New statutory products often involve an optimal mix of legal and fiscal attributes (Thompson 1995). Empirical research supports the view that a new legal product eventually outweighs the benefits that arise due to learning and network effects (Ribstein and Kobayashi 2001). While there is great appeal to the utilization of existing frameworks, firms are now more inclined to structure their business in a framework that is largely free from legal oversight and allows experimentation. Figure 4.3 shows the number of LLP formations in the United Kingdom for the period 2001–6. On 1 July 2007, 26,520 LLPs were registered in the United Kingdom.

Figure 4.4 and Figure 4.5 show respectively the categories of businesses that have adopted the S-LLP and J-LLP.

Rather than the professional firms that the LLP form was initially designed for, there are numerous other categories of businesses which, due to a variety of drivers, have selected this new form. There are a number of common factors that induce firms to choose hybrid forms (e.g., limited liability and tax advantages). Limited liability is the most important attractor of businesses to

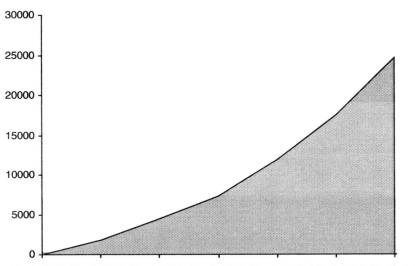

**Figure 4.3.** Total number of LLPs in the United Kingdom
*Source*: Companies House.

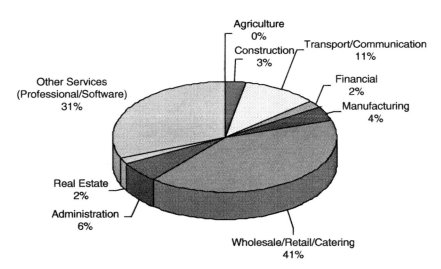

**Figure 4.4.** LLPs in Singapore (11 April 2005–11 April 2006)
*Note*: Total number 1,697.
*Source*: Based on data from BizFile Singapore.

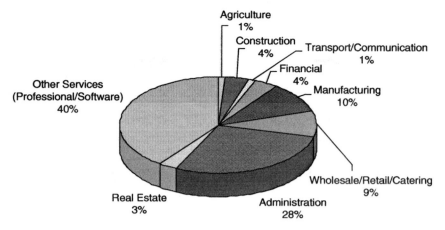

**Figure 4.5.** LLPs in Japan (August–December 2005)

*Note:* Total number 327.

the hybrid entities. Surprisingly, empirical research shows that, despite tax benefits, the emergence of the LLC did not affect the total number of new incorporations. It appears that the first LLC statutes were not able to attract firms that typically incorporated (Ribstein and Kobayashi 2001). As we have seen in Chapter 1, observers questioned, for example, why high-tech start-up firms chose to forgo tax savings by selecting the public corporation. However, the popularity of the LLC in the fastest growing business segment of the market in the United States is increasing. Approximately 30 per cent of the 100 fastest growing firms in the United States are structured as LLCs. These companies are less than five years old, but their annual sales exceed US$1 million.[44] This trend is to some extent driven by the recent tendency of venture capital and private equity funds, faced with an ever-growing fierce and global competition, to embrace complex structures that help optimize the financial results for each group of investors. Figure 4.6 shows, for instance, how the pass-through feature of the LLC, in combination with a corporate blocker, could increase the options for fund managers to better tailor the tax structure to the needs of their investors.[45]

---

[44] See <http://www.entrepreneur.com/hot100>. These 100 firms had a total sales of US$1.7 billion in 2005 and employed a total number of 6,920 people.

[45] From a US tax perspective it may be more efficient if the 'Target' is organized as a pass-through LLC. However, if, for instance, a foreigner invested in a chain of pass-through vehicles, he or she would be liable for US 'effectively connected income' taxes. Since foreign investors prefer to avoid the US tax system, a so-called blocker corporation is used to file US tax returns (Fleischer 2003). A detailed coverage of the US tax aspects is outside the scope of this chapter.

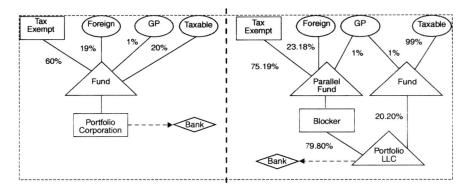

**Figure 4.6.** Tax-driven business planning
*Source*: Blashek and McLean (2006).

Certainly, there is some evidence that similar flow-through vehicles, such as the Canadian Business Income Trust, Energy Trusts, and Real Estate Investment Trust, are associated with tangible tax benefits that attract a significant number of firms (see Table 4.4).[46]

While the Canadian vehicles, for example, can be employed more widely than in other jurisdictions, their enhanced popularity, compared to similar vehicles in the USA, seems mainly related to the fact that an IPO does not affect their tax treatment.[47] In contrast, US listed entities are by definition taxed as a corporation. A similar pattern would likely emerge if US tax authorities were to adopt the same fiscal measures. Such a development would naturally tip the balance in favour of the LLC since the possible benefits of incorporation, like network effects, would not weigh up against the advantages of hybrid forms.

There is already a trend which shows a high number of firms selecting the LLC over the corporate form in the USA. The decrease in new incorporations is not only attributed to tax advantages, but also to the flexibility surrounding the formation and operation of an LLC as well as the higher costs associated with satisfying corporate governance mandates arising from the Sarbanes–Oxley Act (Ribstein 2004). Figure 4.7 shows that the number of new corporations in the USA has declined while the LLC continues to gain in popularity.

[46] Consultation Paper by the Department of Finance Canada—Tax and Other Issues Related to Publicly Listed Flow-Through Entities (Income Trusts and Limited Partnerships).
[47] The popularity of the Canadian Trust is evidenced by 255 trusts listed on the Toronto Stock Exchange in 2006. However, the income tax structure raised concerns for lawmakers faced with the imminent prospect of declining tax revenue. It is not surprising therefore that the Canadian Finance Minister responded by subjecting existing trusts to the same rate of taxation as corporations. The trusts will have a four-year transition period to adjust to the new regulations. See *Financial Times* (B Simon), 'Corporate Canada Takes a Deep Breath', 5 November 2006.

**Table 4.4.** Comparison of the taxes paid under different structures $

|  | Corporate Structure | Income Trust | Limited Partnership |
|---|---|---|---|
| Entity level | 35.00 | NIL | N/A |
| Investor level |  |  |  |
| Taxable Canadian | 5.70 | 14.82 | 14.82 |
| Non-resident | 2.15 | 3.30 | 8.36 |
| Tax-exempt | N/A | N/A | N/A |
| Total Tax | 42.85 | 18.12 | 23.28 |

*Source*: Department of Finance Canada (2005).

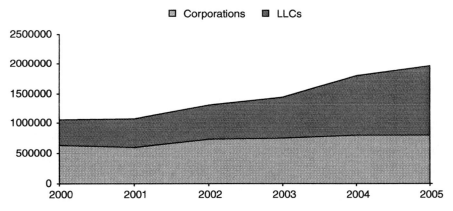

**Figure 4.7.** New filings of corporations and LLCs in the United States
*Source*: 2006 IACA Annual Report of Jurisdictions.

LLCs are now widely employed for real estate and energy ventures, the exploitation of patents, corporate joint ventures, acquisition vehicles, and venture capital and private equity funds as well as high-tech start-ups. As a matter of fact, the 2006 increase of revenues collected by the Delaware Division of Corporations—from US$626.1 million to US$665.3 million—is mainly due to the increase in LLC tax collections and filing fees (see Figure 4.8). It should be noted, moreover, that the Delaware LLC increasingly attracts foreign investors that establish subsidiaries and joint ventures in the United States.

### 4.1.2 Limited Liability and Private Ordering

It is a common refrain in the evolution of the corporate form that firms, in exchange for certain privileges, go through a number of formalities to incorporate their businesses, varying from, at first, the governmental approval of a

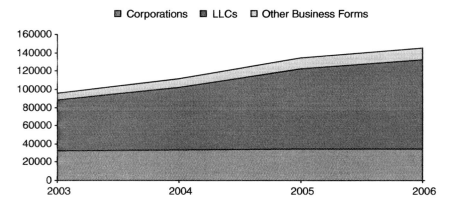

**Figure 4.8.** New business formation in Delaware (2003–2005)

Source: 2006 Annual Report, Delaware Department of State, Division of Corporations.

corporate charter to the obligation to abide by the terms and provisions of the corporate statute, particularly the rules surrounding the separation of ownership and control. Before the Industrial Revolution the privileges consisted mostly of a monopoly over trade or the exclusive right to act on behalf of the government in developing a country's infrastructure. With the growth of commercial and industrial activity, the pressures from politically influential industrialists to abandon the specific governmental approval of a corporate charter grew steadily and resulted eventually in the adoption of relatively simple incorporation procedures in the United States and continental Europe.

In its developed form with fully-fledged limited liability protection, the corporation was the choice-of-business form for large-scale firms which were compelled to amass substantial sums of equity capital in order to give effect to capital-intensive industrial and technological innovations. The principle of limited liability was widely acclaimed as an industrial breakthrough and it took only until the late nineteenth century for the corporate limited liability feature to become available to smaller, closely held firms. In this respect, we have already discussed in Chapter 2 two legal developments. First, a separate close corporation form, the *Gesellschaft mit beschränkter Haftung* (GmbH), was enacted in Germany in 1892. Another, second, development demonstrates the importance of case law in furnishing smaller firms with the much-coveted limited liability feature. A decision of the House of Lords in *Solomon v Solomon & Co Ltd* overturned the assumption that only passive investors were granted limited liability under the Companies Act of 1862. These developments gained a widespread popularity across jurisdictions. To date, most countries recognize a form of close corporation which, although it has become increasingly flexible in terms of permissible

**Table 4.5.** Comparison: French business forms

| | Société Anonyme (SA) | Société à Responsabilité Limitée (SARL) | Soiété par Actions Simplifiée (SAS) | *Most advantageous* |
|---|---|---|---|---|
| Minimum capital | €37,000 | No | €37,000 | SARL |
| Minimum number of shareholders | 7 | 1 | 1 | SARL - SAS |
| Management structure | 3-18 board members (mandatory)—the president must be an individual person | One or more managing directors who must not be corporate entities | Flexible—at least one president | SAS |
| Tax | Corporate | Corporate | Corporate | SA – SARL - SAS |
| Transfer of shares | Free transferability | Restricted | Free, but Articles may restrict | SAS |
| Limited Liability | Yes | Yes | Yes | SA – SARL - SAS |
| Accountant | Mandatory | Exempted below a certain threshold | Mandatory | SARL |

*Source*: Data from *L'Entreprise* 222 (April 2004).

deviations from the statutory provisions, is still modelled on the public corporation and its capital-oriented management structure.

This raises the question as to whether corporate-type business forms, without the pass-through tax treatment (as discussed in the previous section), but with the partnership-type feature to devise the most efficient management and governance structure, would gain a foothold in the modern business environment. The answer to this question can be found in France. Recent data concerning the use of the French *société par actions simplifiée* (SAS), a limited liability vehicle that is considered to be the most flexible company form in France, which allows parties to freely contract into an optimal decision-making arrangement, indicates that not only tax, but also contractual flexibility is a main driver for business form selection.

Table 4.5 shows the eschewal of tax as the driver for hybrid forms. Clearly, this runs against commentators' expectations that tax considerations predominately explain entity selection (Ribstein 1995).[48] Obviously, the driving force

---

[48] That is not to say that tax issues do not play a pivotal role in choice of entity decisions. See, for example, Petska et al (2005).

behind SAS is the freedom of contract which enables firms, in an incomplete contracting world, to adapt to changing market circumstances and increased global competition.

That said, the key driver behind the success of the new hybrid business forms, such as the LLPs and LLCs, is the concept of maximum flexibility and autonomy of firm participants to structure the firm's internal affairs free from legal principles and doctrine. It seems that, even though economic and path dependence factors prevent the emergence of complete law, the extended private ordering principles enhance the ability of business parties to experiment with these new forms. Businesses in need of debt and equity capital cannot therefore be expected to be tied up with corporate or partnership forms that only offer costly and burdensome statutory measures, such as mandatory management and decision-making structures (in the case of the corporation) or broad fiduciary duties (in the case of partnerships). This is especially true if these business forms—explicitly—fail to allow for the possibility to waive or contract around statutory rules and standards. For instance, the fact that parties may be subject to broad fiduciary duties, which may require a party to forgo personal interests, appears to act as a deterrent to venture capitalists and joint venturers. If parties are allowed to bring an action based on a breach of fiduciary duty when their high-risk gamble does not pay off, thereby circumventing the contractual mechanisms put in place to overcome information problems, the transaction costs arising from legal uncertainty and statutory ambiguity will increase significantly (Stevenson 2001).

To be sure, a new hybrid business form has the potential drawback of being a relatively untested entity that has not yet generated a large body of case law and academic research. The fact that company law is inherently incomplete and the parties are boundedly rational inevitably necessitates the involvement of the judiciary in the resolution of intra-firm disputes. Indeed, it might be argued that new legal products only survive because the judiciary plays an important role in *ex post* dispute resolution and the development of legal precedent. Empirical research indicates that new business forms create a new network of cases dealing with, among other things, the nature of new business forms, formation requirements, fiduciary duties, limited liability and veil piercing, transfer of interests, and dissolution. However, given the spur for new company law products that offer the maximum contractual flexibility, courts should 'permit persons or entities to join together in an environment of private ordering'.[49] In order to enhance legal certainty, courts should first respect the contractual arrangements. Only if both the statute and agreement are silent should courts endeavour to fill the contractual gap by looking at the parties' intentions *ex ante*.

That is not to say that greater contractual flexibility will automatically lead to efficiency. It follows from the discussion in Chapter 2 that an efficiency-minded legislature has the task to develop improved statutory default rules when

---

[49] See *Elf Atochem North America, Inc v Jaffari*, 727 A 2d 286 (Del 1999).

**Table 4.6.** Amendments to the Delaware LLC-Act

|  | 2004 | 2005 | 2006 |
|---|---|---|---|
| Number of sections in the amendment | 15 | 18 | 38 |
| **Amendment** | | | |
| Freedom of Contract | 7 | - | - |
| Clarification of Default Rules | 3 | 10 | 6 |
| Domestication/Conversion | 4 | 6 | 26 |
| Effective Date of the Amendment | 1 | 1 | 1 |
| Other amendments | - | 1 | 5 |

*Source*: General Assembly of the State of Delaware.

enhanced certainty and guidance are needed. In order to increase the success of new business forms, legislators are advised not only to keep the statute up to date, but must also ensure it meets the coveted social and economic requirements over time. For instance, if the mandatory participation provision in the Japanese LLP entails problems for the internal stability of firms, the legislature may eventually offer new rules that are clearer and give better guidance on dealing with agency problems in a business environment. In this context it is worth noting that Delaware legislature strives to maintain legislative pre-eminence by periodically amending, among other things, the Delaware Limited Liability Company Act. Table 4.6 highlights the amendments to the Act in 2003, 2005, and 2006.

Table 4.6 shows that Delaware frequently updates the LLC-Act to give maximum effect to the principle of freedom of contract and to the clarification of default rules.[50] We should point out that interest group pressures mandate the introduction of amendments facilitating domestication of and conversion to Delaware law. If we take this point a step further, it is not difficult to explain the importance of the clarification of the default rules. Since the selection of business forms is a choice made *ex ante*, interest groups, e.g., business lawyers, have an interest in informing the legislature of shortcomings in existing provisions and providing technical support in devising amendments.

As we have seen, the freedom of contract is a priority of Delaware lawmakers and in this respect it could be argued that amending the LLC statute into an all-purpose 'contractual entity' is necessary to confront the technological advances and the internationalization of the economy. There is something to the introduction of a 'contractual entity' that can be tailored to the business needs and expectations of each type of firm. Parties in joint ventures, for instance, are likely to reduce agency problems and contract into the preferred structure of their particular relationship even if business form statutes do not contain any

---

[50] Del Code Ann Tit 6 § 18-1101(b).

default rules. Still, the function of statutory company law—as a standard form contract—must not be underestimated. In the context of non-listed firms, company law should first offer a relatively small group of unsophisticated—and often unmotivated—business parties a ready-made business contract. Second, company law should give statutory guidance to mostly larger firms that do not fare well when ownership and control are integrated.

Table 4.6 reflects the Delaware's concern about emphasizing the importance of offering a coherent and consistent set of provisions. The larger point, then, is that Delaware, by continuously updating its legislation, signals to investors and creditors what they can expect in terms of the internal decision-making process and external representation model of a company. The foregoing discussion suggests that, given the importance of statutory guidance and the two types of governance structure—integrated and differentiated—a menu of business forms should contain at least two closely held limited liability entities, a manager-managed entity and a member-managed business form.

## 5. Conclusion

In Chapters 3 and 4 we distinguished three different positions along the reform strategy spectrum of company law. The first position is located on the left side of the spectrum and closest to stasis—where virtually no effective legal changes can occur and where only the idea of reform clashes with legal tradition and standardization pressures. Along or near the mid-point of the spectrum, company law changes are less impeded by tradition and standardization factors, but more influenced by interest group pressures. We see the United Kingdom occupying this position. Japan can be seen as a more adaptable jurisdiction located toward the right end of the spectrum and therefore better able to create and introduce more functional legal rules and institutions that turn the traditional view of company law around. It is submitted that Singapore is located on the right side of the spectrum as its legislature is aware of the need to adapt the legal system to international business practices in order to develop a distinct jurisprudence, acclaimed for its efficiency and integrity, which is set apart from the English legal system.

As we have seen in the case of the introduction of new hybrid business forms, interest group pressures and exogenous pressures can open up opportunities for reform-minded lawmakers previously blocked in their efforts to undertake legislative reforms. This does not imply that reform-minded legislators will create first best measures that satisfy the demands of users. Yet, despite certain inefficiencies identified in this chapter, there are some inherent benefits for firms in employing the new hybrid business forms. Besides pass-through taxation, the hybrid vehicles offer parties the freedom to contractually establish the rights and obligations within the organizational structure. They combine the corporate feature of fully-fledged limited liability with the partnership law principles of flexibility and informality. In this respect, the hybrid business forms usher in a new era in which the statement 'when in doubt, don't incorporate' is increasingly applicable to innovative businesses. The introduction and popularity of the hybrid business forms as depicted in this chapter are but a small step in that direction.

Indeed, these hybrid business forms often offer better standard form contracts that help to economize on transaction costs such as drafting, information, and enforcement costs. They offer models that cover the relationships between the participants inside the firm and the representation of the firm in their dealings with outside participants, such as creditors. The business statutes act as a set of 'off-the-rack' terms which business parties can fall back on when establishing the distribution and allocation of powers and responsibilities for varying levels of control and commitment. That is not to say that the statutes provide the parties with a set of all-encompassing standard form agreements. Given the large variety of business arrangements, it is simply impossible for lawmakers to provide a set of default terms that deal with every possible contingency. The parties in non-listed companies should therefore also rely on carefully drafted and other customized agreements. To see this, the next chapter analyses the contractual relationships in family-owned businesses, joint ventures, and venture capital-backed firms.

# 5

# The Second Pillar:
# Contractual Arrangements

## 1. Introduction

As noted in the first part of this book, the full applicability of the publicly held corporate governance framework to non-listed companies is questionable. Specific problems that are related to publicly held firms are not necessarily present in non-listed companies. In particular, participants in non-listed companies have fewer (stock) market mechanisms, such as the monitoring activities by stock exchange institutions and rating agencies, to restrict opportunistic behaviour and detect fraud. Non-listed companies, therefore, have to rely on different corporate governance techniques that deal with the establishment of the ownership structure and the prevention and resolution of conflicts. This chapter will show that the corporate governance framework of non-listed companies is highly contractual in nature. For instance, empirical research shows that the shareholders of non-listed companies usually enter into a shareholders' agreement.[1] In these agreements, the business parties bargain for different corporate governance principles and norms, thereby relying more or less on 'softer' mechanisms, such as trust and reputation. Mandatory and default rules of the applicable legal business form fill gaps in the agreement. In order to show the interaction between statutory and contractual norms and practices, this chapter will focus on four types of non-listed firms that increasingly attract both practitioners' and academics' attention: (1) joint ventures; (2) family-owned businesses; (3) venture capital-backed firms; and (4) private equity funds and hedge funds.

Because the contractual decisions are made before the actual outcome of the venture is clear, the business parties must engage in an *ex ante* search for the contractual terms that improve their governance structure and maximize the value of their investment. They tend to bargain over four fundamental elements—risk of losses, return, control, and duration—subject to three major constraints: conflict of interest, government regulation, and limits on specifying in complete detail all the terms of the

---

[1] Empirical research conducted by ABN AMRO shows that in 60% of the surveyed Dutch non-listed companies with a turnover of more than 25 million euros, shareholders had entered into a shareholders' agreement. See ABN AMRO, *Vrijwillige Verplichtingen? Een visie op corporate governance bij niet-beursgenoteerde ondernemingen*, 2006.

relationship *ex ante* (Klein and Coffee 2007). Two questions, which follow the bargaining elements and constraints, are crucial to efficient contracting. First, what is the relationship between the business parties inside the firm? The choice here is a function of the governance structure, break-up provisions, and incentive mechanisms. Second, what is the relationship between the firm and outsiders? This question focuses mainly on liability regimes. From an efficiency perspective, business parties will bargain into contractual arrangements that offer an optimal combination of solutions to these problems. In this chapter, we will discuss how the internal governance structure can be designed to encourage cooperation between the venturers, despite having differing private interests and incentives. These different, ambiguous, and conflicting expectations are never so obvious as in joint ventures among independent partners, which we will discuss in the next section.

## 2. Joint Ventures

When multinational enterprises are looking for new ways to cooperate with similar style firms in a cross-border setting, the establishment of a joint venture is an attractive option for these companies to further develop economies of scale and scope and to explore new markets. Even though the benefits of joint ventures are relatively straightforward, they are, for structural reasons, highly sensitive to conflict-of-interest situations. First, the independent joint venture partners are often simultaneously competitors outside the scope of the venture. Second, since joint ventures usually involve the development of a particular product, the average lifespan is usually not very long (see Figure 5.1). Third, joint venture partners mainly rely on renegotiation and reputational incentives to limit the worst effects of moral hazard. In their effort to align interests, joint venturers employ contractual defaults and remedies. By contracting their way into a governance structure, they endeavour to make credible commitments that serve as a means of creating a relationship of mutual reliance (Williamson 1985).

Joint ventures are normally creatures of contract, but the business parties often need a shelter to reduce their business risks and liabilities, as well as to organize the tax structure of the venture optimally. As we have seen in Chapter 4, limited liability and taxation are not the only factors that influence business form decisions. Ideally, the shelter should provide a perfect fit between the joint venture agreement (and any other complementary agreements, see Table 5.1) and the articles of association or operating agreement of the business form.

Indeed, besides the contractual documents, such as a joint venture agreement and shareholder agreement, statutory law and the articles of association usually govern the relationship between the joint venturers and management.[2]

---

[2] A number of thorny agency problems arise in many joint ventures. First, the most obvious concerns the fundamental agency problem between a controlling and a minority joint venture partner. Second, diverging market and strategic interests of the parent companies may result in

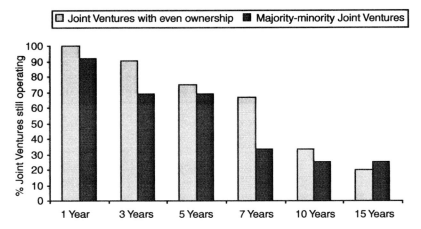

**Figure 5.1.** Lifespan of joint ventures
*Source*: 'McKinsey & Co' (published in Ernst, 2003).

For companies that are unable to achieve a contractual solution, for example, the business form statute is considered to be a gap-filling mechanism. Yet, these statutes often require that firms disclose essential information in their filed articles of association, such as the capital structure, a company's objectives, and the deviations from the default rules supplied by the statute, among other things e.g., the system of voting, supervision, and rules concerning the convening of and attendance at the general meeting of shareholders. In practice, business lawyers often struggle to translate the shareholders' preferences into a comprehensive set of articles of association. They find it difficult to transpose the coveted equity and control arrangements of the joint venture into the formal share capital and ownership structure of the corporation (Miller et al 1997).[3] In addition, some provisions of a joint venture agreement are not easily inserted in the articles due to, on the one hand, the restrictive quality of 'old' corporate law statutes and, on the other hand, the filing and disclosure obligation of the corporation's articles.

conflict with the management of the joint venture company. Third, members of management of the joint venture company are usually employed by one of the partners which may exacerbate latent tensions within the joint project.

[3] Business lawyers routinely encounter difficulty in translating the joint venture parties' preferences into the corporate form which, as is well known, is tailored to meet the needs of passive investors. Evidence indicates that nearly 85% of the joint ventures required at least six months to negotiate successfully the terms of the agreements, while 20% took more than eighteen months. The most difficult problem in such negotiations is the equity structure. It is usually not intended that majority shareholders acquire control of all aspects of a joint venture's operations. To be sure, dual class share arrangements could resolve some of the problems that arise, but such legal solutions are not easily conveyed to the joint venture parties. Naturally, they would prefer a straightforward structure, which, as we have seen in Chapter 4, could be explicitly written into an LLC operating agreement.

**Table 5.1.** Frequently used joint venture documents

| Documents | Topics |
| --- | --- |
| Feasibility (or joint study) agreement | (1) the viability of a joint venture<br>(2) the structure of the joint venture |
| The letter of intent | Informal document, mostly not binding, which contains an open agenda of the main points of how the parties will collaborate |
| Formation agreement | A formal document, more detailed than a Letter of Intent, which contains all the basic elements that will be incorporated into the joint venture |
| A confidentiality agreement | A separate document or a binding clause in the Letter of Intent, which (1) prevents confidential information being used by the party acquiring the knowledge; and (2) impedes further disclosure |
| A joint venture agreement | This document states the terms of the joint venture and defines the conditions on which the joint venture is formed |
| The agreed due diligence procedures | This document is intended to permit the investigation of legal and financial aspects of the parties' contributions |
| A shareholders' agreement | This document sets forth the special rights of the partners, such as, for instance, the right of a minority partner to appoint a certain number of directors or the need for a unanimous decision to make capital contributions |
| A board of directors' agreement | This document establishes how voting will be done on a variety of issues at the board of directors' level |
| A management agreement | This document could be used when the parties disperse among themselves certain management responsibilities |
| An adherence agreement | This document intends to bind new adherents to the joint venture |
| Agreed budget and operating plan for a specific period | An indication of what parties planned, the financial limitations of the joint venture, its expansion possibilities, and how money would be spent and on what. |

*Source*: Adapted from Wolf (2000).

For example, provisions on annual budget, capital expenditure limitations, business-plan-related issues, and additional internal control procedures are not easily incorporated in the articles of association. This might be problematic in the case of a conflict between the joint venture partners, since provisions of the articles could very well trump the terms set forth in the joint venture agreement (or any of the complementary agreements). To be sure, breach of the agreements could trigger a legal battle in court. However, such a remedy would not only be time consuming and costly, but also of very limited practical value if corporate acts are already consummated under the legal statute. The upshot is that conflicts may dilute the value of the agreements between the joint venture partners. In order to resolve these drafting problems and, at the same, encourage joint ventures, some jurisdictions, like Japan and Singapore, have embarked on company law reforms based on recent developments in the United States and the United Kingdom, where hybrid business forms have entered the scene.

These hybrid business forms offer parties often the complete freedom to contractually establish rights and obligations, such as mutual reliance and dispute resolution provisions, within their organizational structure, which usually make the drafting of complicated complementary agreements unnecessary. In fact, this flexibility has made the LLP a very popular vehicle for property development joint ventures in the United Kingdom. The almost complete freedom for its members to organize the governance structure in whatever manner they see fit makes this business form highly attractive to the players in risky businesses. The fact that almost any of the imaginable protective provisions, such as first charges over profits, casting votes, and buyout provisions, can be included in the LLP agreement entails that the internal structure is less complex than in the case where the parties opt for the close corporation form, the private limited company. Recall that the corporate default rules are designed for larger firms with often passive investors.[4] As we shall see in the next section, contractual provisions usually prevail over company law measures.

## 2.1. Mutual Reliance Provisions

Company law usually provides for some kind of fiduciary duties that either require the venture partners or venture managers to act in the venture's interest and prohibit them from competing against the joint venture company. However, as we have seen, the partners are often also competitors. In order to minimize opportunistic use of these fiduciary duties, joint venture parties routinely specify their rights and duties contractually so as to avoid excessive reliance on *ex post* adjudication of endgame and other gap-filling problems. Specific legal terms are needed for the control and management, contribution and distribution of assets and cash, and the valuation of human capital, intellectual property, and other contributed assets. Parties to a joint venture must also address the allocation and control of confidential information, trade secrets, and corporate opportunities. Generally, joint venture agreements contain provisions on reporting and disclosure of financial and non-financial statements. Should parties rely on continuing finance, the agreement must include the terms of the investment, finance contributed, priority rights, and milestones. In these cases, the contract ideally creates a mutual hostage situation by (1) conditioning the performance of a particular obligation to a prior action by one of the partners; (2) reciprocal penalties, such

----
[4] See Chapter 2.

as liquidated damages, which also create a relationship of mutual reliance; or (3) attributing rewards or attributing rights to partners that reach specifically defined goals or milestones (Fogler and Reichert 2002).

## 2.2. Dispute Resolution and Termination

The most important contractual mechanisms are directed at resolving deadlocks and other disputes. Like investors in private equity funds, joint venture parties are usually locked into their investment. The nature of the relationship and the specificity of the assets necessitates the provision of contractual 'divorce' mechanisms. *Ex ante* the parties will design a number of triggers to protect their investment when the relationship comes under strain. Voluntary winding-up provisions are intended, when a deadlock arises, to induce parties to negotiate since failure to arrive at a resolution will result in the liquidation of the venture. These provisions, however, are inherently difficult to contract for *ex ante* due to the information asymmetries regarding the assets contributed to the joint venture. When provisions are agreed, it prevents the dissenting party from frustrating the decision-making process. A continuing veto will trigger either a call or put option under which a party will have the right to exercise its buyout or expulsion rights. To be sure, buyout provisions are not entirely without difficulties. Thorny calculation issues, particularly concerning the valuation of shares and whether payment should be deferred, abound in endgame settings, since the fair value of interests is likely to be non-verifiable by courts or arbitrators.

Parties to joint venture agreements can alternatively choose to adopt 'shotgun' or 'auction' provisions in which one party proposes a price that can be accepted as either the selling or buying price of the dissolving stake. Figure 5.2 displays the Russian roulette mechanism which is often viewed as a fair solution to resolve deadlocked conflicts mostly in 50/50 joint ventures. By serving a deadlock resolution notice, either party can offer to buy the shares of the other party or to sell its own shares, thereby forcing the other party to accept or reverse the offer. The risk of reversal or receipt of counter-notice usually induces parties to value fairly the interests in the joint venture. However, a business party who has information about the other party's financial situation could act opportunistically by offering a too-low price.[5] The Texas shoot-out mechanism (see Figure 5.3) is a variation on the Russian roulette provision with a built-in auction system.[6]

A review of the above-discussed measures suggests that joint venturers can devise effective contractual arrangements that limit opportunism and encourage long-term commitments. Many of the defaults and remedies mechanisms

---

[5] It is worth noting that some commentators argue, however, that the strategic underpricing problem deters parties from using the Russian roulette mechanism.

[6] The Texas shoot-out provision provides that each party submit a secret and sealed bid to a third party who determines the outcome of the bidding process. The highest bid has to buy out the other party.

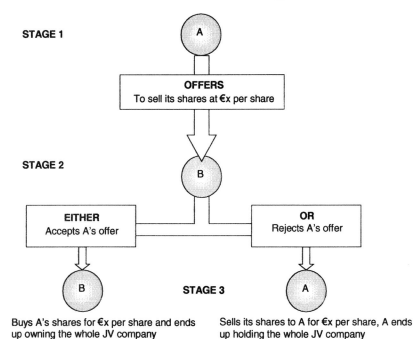

**Figure 5.2.** Russian roulette

*Source*: <www.practicallaw.com>: Deadlock and termination: international joint ventures.

that address the governance problems of these types of firms clearly specify the rights and duties of the parties involved. This conclusion rests on the premiss (common in joint ventures) that business parties, in light of the social and economic context in which they operate, are capable of organizing and managing their business in the most effective manner. Naturally, a well-thought-out contractual governance system can facilitate the development and implementation of trust norms in joint ventures, but the drafting of contractual mechanisms and techniques is no sinecure in a joint venture setting. Partly due to the tension between lawyers and managers, legal best practices tend to be kept away from the negotiation table. For instance, lawyers are usually focused on limiting risks and creating future options for their clients by recommending a majority-interest position and management control. However, this scope is considered to be narrow in the process of crafting joint venture agreements. Indeed, managers argue that lawyers' concerns about (1) a broadly defined scope; (2) a 50–50 joint venture; or (3) accepting a minority stake are often exaggerated.[7] In the managers' view,

---

[7] We can see this clearly in the context of investments in foreign markets. For example if the conditions are uncertain and risky, the investing party will tend to prefer a minority stake which is

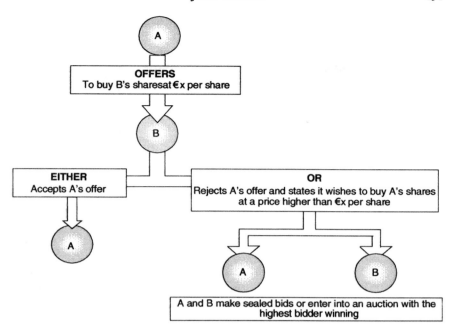

**Figure 5.3.** Texas shoot-out

*Source*: <www.practicallaw.com>: Deadlock and termination: international joint ventures.

these elements could be needed so as to stimulate the necessary trust between partners, to enhance the independence of the joint venture, or to provide growth opportunities in highly uncertain, but promising industries and countries (Ernst et al 2003; Lewis 1999).[8] However, in an era of growing emphasis on corporate governance issues, it is only to be expected that the understanding between lawyers and managers will increase and lead to well-designed and successful joint ventures. Still, the evidence suggests that unsophisticated parties or businessmen that complete agreements without legal advice may be less inclined to consider such contractual obligations and remedies in the context of creating their business obligations. Moreover, despite the commitment-enhancing effects of these provisions, contracting infirmities may persist as these mechanisms appear to favour the party with the greatest bargaining power. Finally, overconfidence,

less costly and offers a high real options value. If the project is successful, the investor has the option to increase its stake. If the project turns sour, however, it is easier for the investing party to exit with a minority stake.

[8] Lawyers who are more open to business practice could, for instance, realize that, instead of seeking a majority of the joint venture's equity, their clients could obtain future control by utilizing contractual provisions, such as buyout rights and rights of first refusal, that ensure a 'real option' of expanding or downsizing a particular venture in the future.

over-optimism, and excitement about the prospects of the venture prevent business parties from engaging in contractual planning and contemplating methods for addressing future conflicts of interest. Because parties must either trust each other or forgo the deal, they often shun tailoring their business arrangement thereby intentionally leaving gaps in their contracts. Bargaining theory in law and economics recognizes that even if the parties are willing to accept the challenge of drafting an agreement and transaction costs are marginal, information asymmetries and strategic conduct may prevent them from bargaining toward an optimal governance structure.

## 3. Family-owned Firms

In joint ventures, parties often create impressive contractual mechanisms that allow them to collaborate and share resources to reach a common goal: a successful venture. Although similar governance problems arise in the context of family businesses, the contracting circumstances are exacerbated in that a third element is added to the corporate governance discussion. In family firms the elements business and ownership are intertwined with the unpredictable factor 'family' (see Figure 5.4).

But there is more. The above three elements, which should be taken into account when devising an effective family-owned governance framework, are not static, but constantly evolve along three independent paths (Figure 5.5). Given the dynamics of and interrelation between the business cycle and family cycle, it is a daunting task to conceive of effective contractual corporate governance mechanisms that create credible commitments and mutual hostage situations.

To see this, family-owned businesses can be viewed as a nexus of oral and written agreements. Whilst such contracts can be costly and difficult to enforce, reciprocal commitments and penalties bundled together often prove effective in incentivizing parties to invest the necessary resources to achieve an optimal contractual relationship. If the relationship should threaten to break down, for instance in family businesses after the third generation (see Figure 5.6), the insertion of provisions that create 'mutual hostage' situations can encourage parties to work through their differences. The evidence shows that the most successful family-owned businesses employ a variety of contractual-based mechanisms to tie family members for generations.[9] For instance, family members who wish to exit usually face serious lock-in provisions making it virtually impossible to liquidate

---

[9] In some countries, the superior performance of family firms is usually attributed to: (1) a long-term investment horizon of the controlling family, which tends to avoid the problem of managerial myopia and; (2) more intensive monitoring of management, which reduces the main agency problem in the firm (Panunzi et al 2006). While there are some costs associated with family ownership (eg the threat of private benefit extraction), it is suggested that the two main benefits outweigh the costs. Naturally, there is concern to keep the family involved in the companies as a consequence

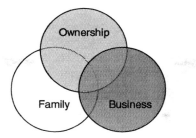

**Figure 5.4.** Three intertwined factors that influence corporate governance of family firms

*Source:* Tagiuri and Davis 1982.

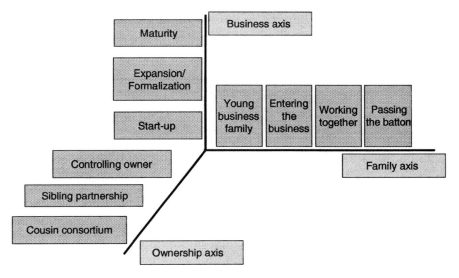

**Figure 5.5.** The changing dynamics in a family business setting

*Source:* Gersick et al 1997.

their interest in the company. Common 'penalty' mechanisms include the right of first refusal to family members on tendering shares, below-market valuations in the case of a share buyback, and restrictions on the number of shares that can be sold in a particular period. Conversely, the members will create institutions and privileges that function to foster family interests and minimize conflicts. Empirical evidence reveals that families anchor their members through large charitable organizations that offer employment to members not active currently

of their beneficial influence, although family members are not necessarily best placed to lead the company as a CEO (Bennedsen et al 2007).

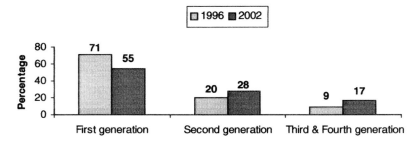

**Figure 5.6.** Proportion of ownership by generation

*Source*: Australian Institute for Social Research, Centre for Labour Research, 'Towards an understanding of the significance of family business closures in South Australia', May 2005.

in the business and include decision-making opportunities for the children of family members (Elstrod 2003).

Other contractual mechanisms in family business charters include the design of the board and the composition of its members, the voting rules and appointment procedures, the conditions for family members' participation in firm decision-making, their role in the business and succession planning, and the dissemination of information and dividends. For instance, incorporated family firms in the Netherlands often contract around company law default rules by establishing a foundation that issues depository receipts to family members to ensure the continuity of ownership. The foundation holds the voting rights, while the family members are entitled to dividend distributions. Empirical research shows that 32 per cent of the surveyed family businesses have put in place a similar governance structure.[10] Moreover, family members in need of more information and communication mechanisms rely on informal shareholders or key-issue meetings which are convened outside the statutory shareholders' meetings (see Figure 5.7).[11]

It seems that governance can be improved in family firms by treating the two life cycles—the business and family life cycle—separately. Best practice is to create separate legal institutions to permit an isolation of issues without sacrificing unity. To be sure, business decisions will be affected by certain developments within the family and vice versa. However, the establishment of, for instance, a family assembly, family council, and/or family constitution furnishes parties with the opportunity to discuss family matters, such as family values and employment policies, without directly influencing business decisions and causing deadlocked issues. Dealing with emotions in a more informal setting has the advantage that a

---

[10] See above n. 1 and accompanying text. Obviously, companies with three or more shareholders employ this structure more frequently than firms with one or two shareholders.

[11] For example, 45% of the surveyed companies convene more than one shareholders' meeting per year.

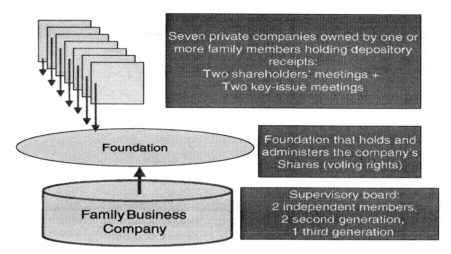

**Figure 5.7.** Governance structure of family-owned businesses

*Source*: Adapted from 'Derde generatie betrekken voor de toekomst' (Third generation involvement for the future), *Financieele Dagblad*, 23 November 2005.

much more elaborated business strategy, in which family values are maintained, can develop. Family institutions thus have a prophylactic effect in that they help avoid disputes and conflicts.

A review of the above-discussed measures suggests that family-owned firms can provide effective contractual arrangements that limit opportunism and encourage long-term commitments in much the same way as joint ventures. Many of the defaults and remedies mechanisms that address the governance problems of these types of firms clearly specify the rights and duties of the family members. Even though the combination of family ownership and a professional governance structure outperform other firms (Dorgan, Dowdy, and Ruppin 2006), there is still evidence suggesting that in particular unsophisticated parties are less inclined to consider the best practice provisions. For instance, the Family Council does not appear to be a commonly used governance mechanism in family-owned firms—approximately 5 per cent of the firms have established a family council. A supervisory board, on the other hand, can be found in 80 per cent of the larger family businesses in the Netherlands, but is rather uncommon in smaller firms.[12]

---

[12] A supervisory board is uncommon in companies with 1–9 employees. Only 2% of the companies have a supervisory board. These percentages increase with the number of employees: 8% of the companies with 10–49 employees have a supervisory board. This is approximately 30% in the category of companies with 50–99 employees (Hessels and Hooge 2006).

The corporate governance hype creates awareness and encourages parties in non-listed companies to improve the governance structure of their firm. However, as noted earlier, many of the provisions of the current corporate governance codes are less relevant for both joint ventures and family firms.[13] For instance, remuneration policies should not be a priority in family firms. Their attention should be drawn to more important issues like family member involvement and, as discussed, succession planning. The focus on succession explains why hybrid business forms play an increasingly important role in ensuring continuous family ownership of the business in the United States. For instance, the 'Family Limited Liability Company' is currently the most popular structure for family succession planning due to its legal and tax advantages. Its flexibility makes it possible to draft the most effective transfer of ownership arrangements in a non-complicated manner that is not disruptive to the continuation of the family business. In any event, the continuity of family firms may only be secured through attracting outside investors, such as venture capital and private equity funds.[14] In the next section, we turn to consider the organization and financing of venture-backed start-up companies.

## 4. Venture Capital-backed Firms

Venture capitalists are specialized intermediaries that direct capital to firms and professional services to companies that might otherwise be excluded from the corporate debt market and other sources of private finance. Venture capital financing is used to invest mainly in small and medium-size firms with good growth and exit potential. Typically, venture capital firms concentrate in industries with a great deal of uncertainty, where information gaps among entrepreneurs and venture capitalist are commonplace.[15] These ventures are identified as financially constrained. Start-up firms rely on venture capital as one of their main sources of funding. Recent empirical research has found that the effect of venture capital on the success of these ventures is considerable. The value of venture capital investment is borne out by the figures which show that venture capital-backed firms grow on average twice as fast as those not backed by venture capital firms.

---

[13] Codes, initially designed for listed-companies, could of course contain principles that are relevant for (non-listed) family firms. See, for instance, the Lebanese Code of Corporate Governance of 2006, to which an Appendix E on governance of family-owned enterprises is attached. See Chapter 7.

[14] In practice, private equity investors provide much needed capital that makes it possible to restructure and modernize operations while allowing buyout of some dissident family members that are unproductive or block productivity measures.

[15] Between 1994 and 2004, venture capitalists invested primarily in IT and health care. During the boom period of 1995–2000, there was a brief rise in media/retail investment, but the dominance of IT has remained the main source of investment (Metrick 2007).

Venture capital has been a critical component in the innovation process in the United States over the last two decades. Venture capital disbursements are more productive in generating patents, compared to corporate R&D. The strong link between venture capital and innovation is reflected in empirical research that discovered that venture-backed firms in the United States accounted for 8 per cent of US industrial innovation during the decade ending in 1992 (Kortum and Lerner 2000). Furthermore, venture funding accounted for approximately 14 per cent of US innovations for the period ending in 1998. Not surprisingly, the rapid increase in venture capital funding in continental Europe has also led to a significant rise in patent applications, particularly in Germany. The importance of venture capital for economic growth is now widely accepted. Empirical evidence from OECD countries over different time periods suggests moreover that an increase in entrepreneurial activity tends to result in subsequent higher growth rates and a reduction in unemployment (Audretsch and Thurik 2001).

In the United States, the depth of venture capital finance and private equity financing for innovative firms is large (McCahery and Reneeboog 2003a). It is commonplace that banks, insurance companies, and other investors contribute almost 50 per cent of venture capital funding. Until 2000, European pension funds contributed less than a quarter of total funding. However, European venture capitalists are now receiving an increased portion of funds from institutional investors. As in the case of Germany, 25 per cent of new capital raised is from pension funds. Moreover, European pension funds increased the level of funding to 27 per cent in 2001 (EVCA 2001). Notwithstanding the increasing amounts of institutional investment, the European market is still lagging considerably behind the US venture capital industry, as reflected in the striking difference between the United States and Europe in terms of capital invested into venture capital (see Figure 5.8). The growth in venture capital investment has been accompanied by a shift in the nature and composition of the US market. Before the 1980s, the venture capital market was dominated by small investment companies, limited partnerships, and some closed-end funds. Today, with the growth of funds flowing into the industry, the composition of the sector has been transformed with the investment adviser playing an important role in advising large pension funds and other institutions about their existing and potential investments.

In the last decade or so, venture capital has become more prominent in European countries, with investments increasing more than six times from €5.5 billion in 1995 to a record of €36.9 billion in 2004. More specifically, two-thirds of this amount was invested in buyouts and restructurings. Although the remaining amount invested in start-up companies is significantly lower, it is surprising that the number of companies receiving venture-backed finance is more than three-quarters of the companies that underwent a buyout (see Figures 5.9 and 5.10).

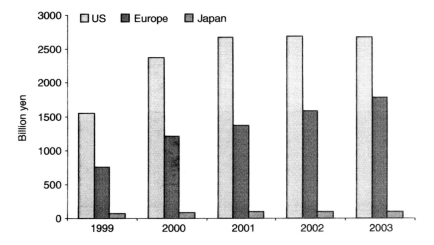

**Figure 5.8.** Venture capital investments in Japan, USA and Europe

*Source*: Graph adapted from Japan External Trade Organization (JETRO), 'Changing Environment for Japanese Venture Businesses', *Japan Economic Monthly*, May 2005.

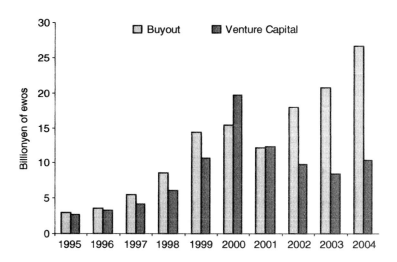

**Figure 5.9.** Amount invested by stage 1995–2004

*Source*: CEFS/EVCA, *Employment Contribution of Private Equity and Venture Capital in Europe*, November 2005.

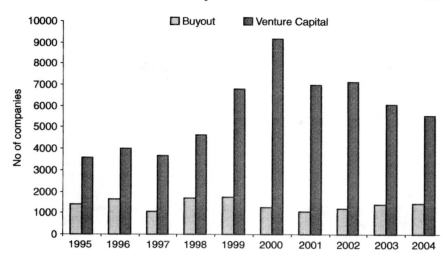

**Figure 5.10.** Number of companies invested in by stage 1995–2004
*Source*: CEFS/EVCA, 'Employment Contribution of Private Equity and Venture Capital in Europe', November 2005.

## 4.1 Governance and Screening of Venture Capital Firms

In contrast to the corporate governance structure of publicly held firms, where dispersed shareholders have disproportionately less control than equity, the governance arrangements of venture capital-backed firms tends to allocate greater control to investors. In this section, we turn to discuss how the screening techniques used by venture capitalists to evaluate business prospects serve to reduce the uncertainty and information problems associated with early stage financing. Some of the success of the portfolio company's returns will be influenced by the effort and skill expended in screening 'good' from 'bad' entrepreneurs. The basic approach to the screening of venture capital investments involves a direct and indirect component. First, direct screening serves to overcome the information problem in two important respects. Direct screening involves selecting the 'good' projects based on the examination of the prospective pool of entrepreneurs' business plans. Because venture capitalists specialize in specific technologies and markets, and evaluate many potentially good investment opportunities, the information asymmetries between portfolio firms and entrepreneurs are reduced. Portfolio companies tend to use four groups of criteria when evaluating an investment opportunity: (1) attractiveness of the project analysed in terms of market size and growth, product attractiveness, the business strategy, the likelihood of customer adoption, and the competitive position of the venture; (2) the quality of the management team and its performance to date; (3) deal terms; and (4) the financial or exit condition. Based on these analyses, the venture capitalist can make reasonable projections about the project's risks and the likelihood of success.

Venture capitalist firms also specialize by investing in companies at a specific development stage of the venture or in a particular industry (Sahlman 1990). For example, particular skills or expertise, besides financial analysis, will often lead venture capitalists to focus their activities on an industry or sector, such as biotechnology, where the critical factor for success is the optimal allocation of resources to R&D. Second, the contractual terms of venture capitalists' securities, especially in the United States, contribute to the screening process. As in the case of convertible preferred securities, the stock provides for a preference for dividends and liquidation, conversion rights and anti-dilution provisions, pre-emptive rights, go-along rights, and information rights. As a consequence of making this investment, venture capitalists will be induced to make analyses about product market competition, technology, customer and adoption, management team proficiency, financial projections, and exit strategies. The results of these findings will contribute to venture capitalists becoming ever more informed about the valuation of the company and whether to extend further financing.

Staged financing represents one of the most important contractual techniques that increase the expected value of the portfolio project and make it possible for venture capitalists to extend financing to early stage projects. In the next section, we show that staged financing provides the necessary incentives to align the interests of the entrepreneur and venture capital fund.

## 4.2  Staged Financing of Venture Capital Investment

Thus far we have argued that the venture capitalist fund's screening techniques tend to limit the problems of adverse selection and ensure that they are in a position to judge accurately the portfolio company's prospects. We address the special development technique—staged financing—which is designed to reduce the uncertainty associated with early stage, high-tech financing and supply high-powered incentives for entrepreneurs by creating performance incentives. An important advantage of staged financing is that it allows venture capitalists the real option to stop financing the venture. In most deals, the venture capitalist provides the entrepreneur with just enough capital to reach specific milestones. Specific milestones are linked to important events such as the completion of a business plan, the production of a prototype, the receipt of a patent, and the marketing of a product. The fact that when a milestone has not been reached venture capitalists can abandon the project limits the downside risk. If the initial funding runs out before the management team of the portfolio company fails satisfactorily to meet a milestone, the venture capitalist has the option either to abandon financing or reduce the level of financing by making a lower valuation of the portfolio company. As such, the staging of investment commitment performs the same function as debt in a leveraged buyout. Even though the entrepreneur can take steps to locate new financing, the first-round backers' unwillingness to fund future rounds of the project is information revealing, and may serve to deter other venture capital funds from taking on the risk. Nor will potential new investors want to extend new finance to projects where the incumbent venture capitalist fund has a contractual right of first refusal to future financing. Second, staged investment tends to limit the asymmetric information and agency problems associated with early stage investment. Accepting a contract that includes staged financing allows the entrepreneur to send a costly signal about the true quality of his project. Thus, only entrepreneurs confident about their skills and the quality of the venture will accept the incentive contract.

Staged investment also helps to attenuate the commitment problem of the entrepreneur. Given that the venture consists mainly of intangible assets at the beginning of the relationship and that the entrepreneur has the unique human capital that is critical to the success of the venture, the entrepreneur has considerable bargaining power over the claims to the venture's returns in the subsequent rounds. As a consequence, the technique of staged investing offers a potential solution to the hold-up problem. Moreover, it creates high-powered incentives for the entrepreneur to exert optimal effort to increase, for example, the speed of product development. In each stage of funding, the investors provide capital in exchange for shares of the venture. Because the entrepreneur is financially constrained, his ownership of the venture will be reduced after each round of financing. The entrepreneur can limit this effect by achieving a high valuation of the firm at each new stage of financing. The valuation determines the number of shares that will be sold. The venture capitalists and the entrepreneur fix the amounts of funds necessary to reach the next milestone. A positive correlation between high valuation and share price reduces the number of shares that must be sold. Thus, the threat of dilution supplies the entrepreneur with a high-powered incentive to exert more effort.

So far we have focused on the positive benefits of staged financing. It is important to note, however, that staged financing can give rise to opportunistic behaviour by both parties. First, staging creates incentives for the entrepreneur to focus on increasing the likelihood of the short-term positive performance of the venture ('window-dressing'). In order to increase the probability of gaining another round of financing, the entrepreneur will have an incentive to manipulate short-term performance either by emphasizing the conditions that affect the valuation more favourably or by focusing on short-term goals. Staging shifts the entrepreneur's focus from long-term goals to short-term signal manipulation, which consists of making positive news more likely to appear. Signal manipulation reduces the probability that the venture will be terminated. However, as this reduces the value of the option to abandon the project, it may become less likely that the venture capitalist will provide finance in the first place. Second, staging also puts the venture capitalist in a position to behave opportunistically. Both the initial venture capitalist and the entrepreneur know that by not investing in a future round, the initial venture capitalist sends a negative signal to other potential investors about the quality of the venture. As the signal is particularly important for early stage companies, the initial venture capitalist can misuse his bargaining power by extracting additional returns at the expense of the entrepreneur. Moreover, if the expected return is not sufficient to cover the opportunity costs of time, knowledge, and capital, the venture capitalist can choose to prematurely liquidate a venture that has economic value. Convertible preferred stock, discussed in the next section, can attenuate the window-dressing problem caused by staging. Additionally, syndicating investments can serve to alleviate the hold-up problem of the venture capitalist.

## 4.3 The Monitoring Process

In exchange for their investments, monitoring, and advice, venture capitalists usually demand control rights that are disproportionate to their shareholdings. From the perspective of the venture capitalist, monitoring of the entrepreneur and the interim performance of the venture is crucial to making the optimal continuation decision. During the post-contracting stage, the venture capitalist combines monitoring with advising activities, which are typically arranged by contract. The venture capitalist's control extends to advising management on strategic decisions, assisting in recruiting key personnel, replacing management, and providing assistance on other issues such as investment banking and legal advice. Lerner (1995) finds that venture capitalists are more likely to join or be added to the board of ventures in periods when there is a change in chief executive officer (CEO). Therefore, one would expect venture capitalists to intensify their monitoring activities at times when it is more necessary. The board mechanism also allows the venture capitalist to have access to key information about the potential profitability of the venture. In addition, most venture capitalists demand timely access to information, including detailed monthly financial statements and other operating statements. They can demand to inspect the venture's financial accounts at will. Venture capitalists spend approximately half of their time monitoring an average of nine ventures. Furthermore, one of their most frequent activities is to assist management in raising additional funds. The frequency of interaction between the entrepreneur and the venture capitalist depends on a number of factors: (a) the extent of the CEO's new venture experience; (b) the venture's stage of development; (c) the degree of technological innovation pursued by the venture; and (d) the extent of the congruence between the CEO and the venture capitalist. The result shows that the degree of management ownership has no impact on the frequency of interaction. These findings are important since they show that, even with a high degree of goal congruence, extreme levels of uncertainty may weaken signals about the appropriate course of action, therefore requiring actions to generate extra information.

## 4.4 Convertible Preferred Stock

The most suitable type of security to use in early stage ventures is convertible preferred stock (VentureOne 2008). Convertible preferred equity is considered optimal because it secures downside protection for venture capitalists by providing seniority over straight equity, while it supplies entrepreneurs with sufficient incentives to take risks in order to create higher final firm value. Convertible preferred stock gives the venture capitalist a fixed claim on the returns of the venture in the form of a dividend. The unpaid dividends accrue and must be paid to the convertible preferred equity holders before the dividend is paid out to common stockholders. Common shares provide incentives to the entrepreneur as compensation and is thus based on the performance of the venture. Using convertible preferred stock also gives venture capitalists a senior claim on cash flow and distributions in the case where the venture is liquidated. There are a number of explanations for the popularity of convertible preferred equity. One possible explanation for this pattern is that convertible preferred stock—which confers a voting right—ensures venture capitalists protection against burdensome amendments that favour other classes. Furthermore, this class voting mechanism allows holders of preferred stock to elect half or more of the board of directors, which gives the venture capitalist substantial control over the board. Recall that if the venture capitalist gains control through the board of directors, he can thus opt to replace the management team. Next, we note that with convertible preferred stock investors have the option to convert their preferred shares into common shares, which allows them to capture part of the firm's upside gains.

The conversion price is usually set equal to the purchase price of the security, insuring a one-to-one conversion. In addition, the contract contains anti-dilution protections that alter the conversion ratio thereby limiting opportunistic behaviour by entrepreneurs. Another often cited reason is that convertible preferred stock is made redeemable at the option of the venture capitalist, which ensures that they will secure some compensation for their investment (Sahlman 1990).

From a theoretical perspective, some economists argue that convertible preferred stock provides an efficient means for dealing with the double-sided moral hazard problem. Such a double-sided moral hazard problem exists when two principal–agent relationships arise between parties. This is very common in venture capital contracting since both the entrepreneur and the venture capitalist are agents as well as principals. Convertible securities can also be used to allocate cash flow rights contingent on the state of nature and the entrepreneur's efforts. As such, this contract reduces the double-sided moral hazard problem by inducing both the venture capitalist and the entrepreneur to invest optimally in the project. A critical assumption is that a positive relationship exists between the ultimate success of the project, project quality, the efforts of the entrepreneur, and the commitment of the venture capitalist. It is argued that convertible preferred stock outperforms all other mixtures of debt and equity.

The model assumes that convertible preferred stock is used only by active investors, as the venture's success is highly dependent upon their final efforts. The critical component of the convertible debt contract is the conversion ratio. It must be set at such a level that it induces the venture capitalist to invest and convert only if the entrepreneur chooses at least the efficient effort level. This in turn induces the venture capitalist to choose the right level of effort even though he loses some portion of ownership. In the event of a bad state, the venture capitalist chooses not to convert, the entrepreneur defaults on the debt, and the venture capitalist, as the holder of the debt claims, would accordingly liquidate the venture. It is widely acknowledged that convertible preferred stock is the dominant form of security used by venture capitalists in the United States. This may be due to the standardization of purchase agreements. Recently a number of empirical studies have confirmed the importance of convertible preferred stock in the United States. Table 5.2 gives a brief summary of the rights, preferences, privileges, and restrictions attached to the preferred stock.

## 4.5 The Exit Strategy of Venture Capital Firms

The exiting of the portfolio company investment is the final stage in the venture capital process. Venture capital firms have several options when considering exiting a venture. There are six ways in which a venture capital firm can exit a venture, namely: (1) the sale of a company's shares through an initial public offering; (2) the sale of shares to another company or a trade sale; (3) the repurchase of the shares by the company by leveraging the company or by buy-backs; (4) the sale of shares to another investor; (5) the reorganization of the company; and (6) corporate liquidation. The first two techniques are the most popular exit routes for US venture capitalists. The pattern in Europe presents a different picture. As data from most countries show the most common exit strategy is the sale of shares to another company and liquidation. Yet, despite the distinctive European approach to exiting, there has been a marked increase in IPO activity in recent years. The growth in listings can be largely explained by the rapid development of the new market segments created in continental Europe and the United Kingdom. It is claimed that the possibility of an exit through an IPO allows the venture capitalist to enter into an implicit contract with the entrepreneur concerning future control of the company. Clearly, this creates a strong incentive for the entrepreneur to refrain from behaving opportunistically. However, it appears that 'younger', as compared with 'older', venture capital firms have strong incentives to behave opportunistically by taking companies quicker to exit through an IPO. The reason is that a successful IPO allows the young venture capitalists to send a quality signal about their ability to potential investors. Moreover, experienced venture capital firms, with solid reputations, appear to be very good at taking companies public close to market peaks. It is worth pointing out that venture capital-backed companies have less

**Table 5.2.** Basic rights attached to preferred stock

The characteristics of the preferred shares are traditionally defined in the articles of incorporation

| | |
|---|---|
| (Cumulative) dividend right | Venture capitalists can acquire preferred shares with a cumulative dividend right. This right means that if a preferred dividend is not paid in any year, it accumulates; the accumulated arrears must be paid in full before any dividends are paid on common stock. Preferred shares can also be non-cumulative, so that the portfolio firm has no further obligation for unpaid dividends. In between those two are partially cumulative preferred shares. Furthermore, venture capitalists sometimes use participating preferred shares. In such a case, in addition to the dividend preference, they may participate with the common stock in any dividends declared on that stock. In practice, since most innovative start-ups scarcely yield any profits at the time of the venture capital financing, the parties often agree that the corporation pays no dividends at all. |
| Liquidation preference | Preferred stock usually grants the venture capitalists a liquidation preference, which provides that on liquidation a designated amount—typically, the price at which the preferred shares were issued—should be paid to the preferred shareholder before any distributions are made with respect to common stock. In the worst-case scenario, this right gives the venture capitalists a senior claim to cash flow and distributions in liquidation, through which they could retrieve at least some of their investment. It shifts the risk from the venture capitalists to the entrepreneur. |
| Voting rights | Preferred shares are normally non-voting shares. However, venture capitalists often procure convertible preferred stock that confers a right to vote. The voting rights typically correspond to the number of shares they would have after conversion. They are entitled to vote as a separate voting group on amendments that are burdensome to them as a single class and are beneficial to other classes. If the venture capitalists do not actually control the majority of the votes, this 'class voting' mechanism protects them against troublesome resolutions. In addition, the class of preferred shares is typically entitled to elect half or more of the members of the board of directors. This implies that venture capitalists may participate directly in management by serving on the board themselves. In so doing, they have substantial control over the board. It also gives them the opportunity to replace the entrepreneur as CEO if the business is in danger of failing. |
| Optimal conversion | Venture capitalists have a strong willingness to take convertible preferred stock. If the business is successful and an IPO is feasible, the venture capitalists may, at their option, convert their preferred shares into marketable common shares and sell them profitably as soon as the corporation goes public. The articles of incorporation must contain the conversion ratio at which the conversion is to take place. A favourable ratio to venture capitalists may mitigate window-dressing by the entrepreneur, since manipulating short-term signals may persuade the venture capitalists to exercise the conversion option and so dilute the ownership of the entrepreneurial team. The ratio may also depend on the performance of the business, ie 'if the company does well, the conversion price might be higher'. A contingent conversion ratio results that will increase the short-term incentive to the entrepreneurial team, as a high price due to good (short-term) results may prevent the venture capitalists from converting. In such a case, 'window-dressing' would decrease the chance of dilution of the common stock held by the entrepreneur and his key employees. |

**Table 5.2.** *(Cont.)*

| The characteristics of the preferred shares are traditionally defined in the articles of incorporation | |
| --- | --- |
| Anti-dilution provisions | The articles of incorporation normally provide for anti-dilution provisions to take into account changes that have occurred in the number of outstanding common stocks since the preferred stock was issued. They protect the venture capitalists' interests from being diluted. |
| Redemption rights | Preferred stock is often made redeemable at the option of the venture capitalist (often called a 'mandatory redemption', a 'put', or a 'buyout'). This right supplies an exit mechanism in the event that the business 'is financially viable but too small to go public.' The redemption price is typically the original purchase price increased by a reasonable rate of interest. In a few isolated instances, the entrepreneurial team has the power to redeem the preferred shares from the venture capitalists on behalf of the corporation. |
| Other rights | The venture capitalists are usually entitled to purchase new shares proposed to be issued in a *pro rata* portion of their common-stock-equivalent holdings. A pre-emptive right averts the dilution of the proportional interest of the venture capitalists in the corporation. |
| | In the event of the entrepreneur and the key employees receiving an offer to sell their stock, most preferred shareholder contracts provide that the venture capitalists can sell their shares after conversion at the same time and on the same terms. A go-along right protects the venture capitalists from the unwanted influence of a third party over the business. While they cannot prevent the third party from buying the shares, they can demand that the third party buy them out on the same terms as the entrepreneur and the key employees. This right prohibits the entrepreneurial team from selling their stock unless venture capitalists are offered the same terms. |
| | Finally, the articles of incorporation often specify that the firm must maintain and provide specific records, including financial statements and budgets. They also provide that the venture capitalists can inspect the business's financial accounts at will. |

of a positive return on their first day of trading compared with non-venture-backed IPOs. This finding supports the view that capital markets recognize the monitoring quality of venture capital firms. In other words, venture capital firms' reputational capital enables them to credibly certify the quality of the companies they take to the stock market.

This section has argued that there is a positive relationship between the venture capital market and the contractual arrangements that facilitate investment in entrepreneurial enterprises. Although the US corporation, which already began to transform into an all-purpose entity in the late nineteenth century, is still the entity of choice for fast growing companies that rely largely on venture capital in the United States, we have seen in earlier chapters that the less formal LLC is increasingly employed by these companies. A possible explanation could be that governance structure of LLCs is becoming more comparable to corporate arrangements while maintaining the possibility of avoiding corporate formalities such as meeting notice rules and other meeting formalities. A look at the fastest growing new businesses in the United States shows that a wide array of firms use the LLC in various industries.[16]

## 5. Private Equity Funds and Hedge Funds

The media has drawn attention to the confusion that private equity funds and, particularly, hedge funds, are currently causing in the world of finance and corporate governance. As we have seen, corporate governance reforms have so far focused mainly on principles to facilitate the separation of ownership and control, thereby curtailing agency costs associated with the delegation of control rights by dispersed shareholders to the self-interested board and management (De Jong 2006). In a typical publicly held corporation the shareholders are too small, dispersed, and numerous to exercise the residual rights of control. It would simply be too costly if all of them were involved in decision management. Moreover, the shareholders, who are only interested in the company's share price, lack the expertise and competency to take part in the decision-making process. As a consequence, it is recognized that delegating residual control rights is necessary to facilitate management's participation in the firm and to give management sufficient incentives to undertake relationship-specific investments as well as to act in the interest of the firm and its stakeholders.

To be sure, typical public corporations with dispersed shareholders are not common in most jurisdictions (Bratton and McCahery 1999). Controlling shareholders usually dominate listed firms through their indirect and direct influence on board decisions. Even if shareholders, ostensibly, have no majority stake in a corporation's equity, dual class shares and pyramid structures often serve the

---

[16] See <www.entrepreneur.com/hot100>.

purpose of remaining in control (Vermeulen 2006). However, the potential conflict between controlling and minority shareholders is mitigated by the fact that the controlling shareholders have strong incentives to act in the long-term interest of the firm, thereby creating shareholders'—and thus minority shareholders'—value.[17] Gatekeepers moreover play an important role in reducing information asymmetries between shareholders and in detecting fraud and other governance deficiencies.

As private equity and hedge funds are now entering the corporate governance scene with a fury, adding a new dimension to the struggle between shareholders and managers, questions arise increasingly about their proper role in relation to management and other shareholders and creditors. Unlike earlier periods, these funds are engaged in active investment management (Jaeger 2003). They not only endeavour to deliver superior returns by diligent research and insightful analysis, but also by actively reshaping a portfolio firm's business policy and strategy. Many argue that the investment style of active funds fits into the current corporate governance movement of shareholder activism.[18] Proponents urge regulators to adopt a 'hands-off' approach, pointing to the overall increase in share price and performance of firms associated with private equity and hedge funds. Others are of the opinion that it would be overly costly if activist shareholders were too involved in the daily management of the firm. They point to the fact that funds' activism is mainly directed toward short-term payoffs,[19] and argue that the transfer of effective control to a team of specialists (i.e., the board of management) will add to efficiency and long-term wealth creation.[20] Complaints by managers and shareholder groups arguably encourage policy-makers to consider increasing supervision over collective investment pools and their actions.

[17] It is worth noting, however, that there is significant blockholder heterogeneity in the USA, which may affect the policy choices of some firms and have important consequences for the economic effects of large shareholders (Cronqvist and Fahlenbrach 2007).

[18] As discussed, the corporate governance movement focuses mainly on creating mechanisms that are intended to limit the agency problem between self-interested management and dispersed shareholders. The delegation of control leads to substantial monitoring costs, as opportunistic managers may be inclined to exploit collective action problems that bar effective monitoring by shareholders. It is generally recognized that this principal–agent problem is due to managers having superior information on investment policies and the firm's prospects. Managers tend to be better informed, which allows them to pursue their own goals without significant risk. Consequently, shareholders find it difficult, due to their own limitations and priorities, to prompt managers to pursue the objectives of the firm's owners. Information and collective action problems not only prevent close monitoring of management performance, but also enable directors and managers to develop a variety of techniques to extract profits and private benefits from the firm for their own interests. Active and knowledgeable shareholders, such as private equity funds and hedge funds, that dare to intervene if corporate strategy decisions are not in the interest of investors could help overcome principal–agent problems and disputes.

[19] Some argue that hedge funds differ from private equity funds in that the hedge funds' investments are characterized by short-termism. Private equity funds typically invest for 3–5 years before they pursue an exit strategy. See Chapter 6.

[20] *Economist* (2006).

A new empirical literature, however, is emerging in the USA that shows hedge funds being long-term investors in some industries, often waiting very long periods to cash in on their investment (Bratton 2007; Brav et al 2006; Kahan and Rock 2007).

Now that the private equity and hedge fund market is under severe scrutiny by national policy-makers and regulators trying to protect domestic portfolio companies from the potential negative effects of this new form of shareholder activism, it is obvious that the governance structure of investment funds is important. It is argued here that governance issues associated with these active funds are best understood by first investigating the internal governance structure of the funds. Indeed, an analysis of the organizational and contractual features shows that business parties themselves engage in designing good governance structures so as to take advantage of investment opportunities that would otherwise never have been available. It stems from this analysis that the individual players are better capable than regulators to deal effectively with possible negative effects related to activist funds.

The next chapter will examine how the limited partnership allows the internal and external participants to reduce opportunism and agency costs. The analysis will determine which organizational and contractual features of the limited partnership make it attractive for private equity investments. The relationship between the limited partners and the general partners relies mainly on explicit contractual measures. It seems that investors employ several contractual restrictions when structuring the partnership agreement depending on the asymmetry of information and market for investment opportunities.

In typical private equity investments, i.e., long-term investments in non-listed companies, the adapted limited partnership structure works perfectly in tandem with the contractual framework that is especially designed for connecting funds with portfolio companies, such as start-ups. For instance, in contrast to the corporate governance structure of publicly held firms, the governance arrangements of private equity-backed firms tend to allocate greater control to investors. Fund managers use different screening techniques which help to evaluate business prospects and, at the same time, serve to reduce the uncertainty and information problems associated with early stage financing. The contractual terms of private equity funds' securities contribute to the screening process. As in the case of convertible preferred securities, the stock provides for a preference for dividends and liquidation, conversion rights and anti-dilution provisions, pre-emptive rights, go-along rights, and information rights. Without these contractual incentives, private equity would be unavailable for start-up firms, making their success solely dependent on funding from friends and family (Klausner and Litvak 2001). The success story of venture capital thus holds important lessons for policy-makers and regulators working on corporate governance of non-listed companies and organizational issues associated with hedge funds. History shows that contractual mechanisms are usually better suited to deal with market failures and opportunism than regulatory measures. Ad hoc regulation of private equity and hedge funds could lead to higher costs and few corresponding benefits for investors and firms, thereby limiting the beneficial effect of contracting. The next chapter will help to fill the gap in the hedge fund and private equity debate by focusing on the contractual basis of collective investment vehicles, the influence on funds' investment strategies, and the rationale for why private equity and hedge funds have chosen to play the role of activist investors in companies in which they invest.

# 6

# The Contractual Governance of Private Equity Funds and Hedge Funds: A Case Study

## 1. Introduction

Hedge funds and private equity increasingly play an important role in the financial services industry and corporate governance in both Europe and the United States. To begin, hedge funds, having first emerged in the 1950s as single fund investments, now number more than 9,000 funds globally holding more than US$1 trillion in assets.[1] They are typically structured by a team of skilled professional advisers, experts in company analysis and portfolio management, offering investors a wide range of investment styles. Fund managers employ multiple strategies as well as traditional techniques and use an array of trading instruments such as debt, equity, options, futures, and foreign currencies. In recent years, hedge fund advisers have engaged in high-risk investment strategies, including restructurings, credit derivatives, and currency trading, in order to obtain superior returns for their funds. Even though hedge funds take a variety of forms, they are characterized by a number of common features such as the pursuit of absolute returns and the use of leverage to enhance their return on investment.

In contrast, private equity fund advisers invest primarily in unregistered securities, holding long-term positions in non-listed companies. Likewise, they employ a wide range of investment strategies with varying levels of liquidity. Not only do private equity funds advance capital to new and developing companies, but they also channel investment capital for management buyouts, corporate restructurings, and leveraged buyouts. During the 1990s, the venture capital industry grew in the United States with a record amount of capital raised in 2000. With the post-boom decline in the venture capital industry, beginning in 2002, buyout funds emerged as the leading investment style with their level of investment funds increasing rapidly worldwide. In 2006, buyout funds peaked with 'mega funds' capturing the largest amount of net new capital flow. The

---

[1] HedgeFund Review (J Blanche), 'Flood of Money to Hedge Funds Swells', 19 January 2007.

emergence of the buyout fund, as the dominant investment style in this sub-sector worldwide, is attributed mainly to: (1) favourable credit market conditions; (2) robust debt supply and low interest rates; (3) changes in investor preferences; (4) a proliferation of publicly listed private equity vehicles; and (5) the increased demand by institutional investors for alternative asset classes.[2]

The existing literature on hedge fund and private equity recognizes that the two asset classes differ in terms of investments, strategies, and fundamental terms. Similarly, the underlying structural differences have clear implications for the type of investor attracted to the different investment styles. In the past, the investment decision could be made in terms of a simple set of trade-offs. However, the stepped-up competition in the hedge fund industry is the main factor driving the type of funds to operate and compete in the same investment market. Naturally it will be difficult to predict *ex ante* whether convergence between these two sectors will be sufficiently productive to promote efficiencies, spur innovation, and foster the best institutional practices. Nevertheless, convergence can be demonstrated in terms of a number of considerations, including the contractual structure of hedge funds and private equity vehicles. For instance, both private equity funds and hedge funds are typically organized as limited partnerships. However, the contractual provisions differ in a number of significant ways that are powerful enough to suggest no real trend toward convergence. In this chapter, we consider the differences by describing the terms and conditions which address fund formation and operation, fees and expenses, profit sharing and distributions, and corporate governance. The contractual features that distinguish private equity from hedge funds show that parties are perfectly capable of structuring their particular ownership and investment instruments and the exact nature of the accountability of the fund managers without being bound to regulatory requisites. The fact that private equity funds are currently engaged in a public relations offensive to overcome political resistance, thereby attributing an important role to industry groups, suggests that they have ample incentives to contract into effective information duties, stringent distribution procedures, and investor protections.

Still, no matter how appealing the prospects of convergence for some, the move toward convergence is not without major concerns. First, can both types of funds combine these different investment styles without making it more difficult for investors to obtain the same level of investment returns? Second, the transition toward financial convergence of hedge funds and private equity can be blocked if hedge fund investors object to valuations of illiquid securities based on subjective and not on actual market trading. Third, the creation of side pockets in a hedge fund to account for an illiquid security (typically capped at 15%–30% of total assets) cannot be isolated from the costs of accounting for the two streams of capital. All these criticisms suggest that convergence may not be a natural outcome.

---

[2] See *Private Equity Alert* (Weil, Gotshal, and Manges), January 2007.

However, in the medium to long run, many industry observers expect, nevertheless, that some form of hybrid structure may become an industry standard.

The chapter proceeds as follows. Section 2 examines the traditional structure and investment strategies of hedge funds and private equity and highlights the respective benefits and costs of the two types of funds. Section 3 reviews the activities of hedge funds, concentrating on the increasingly important role they play in corporate governance and corporate control. We then consider the variety of investments made by private equity partnerships. Section 4 compares the contractual structure of private equity and hedge funds, describing the terms and conditions of fund formation and operation, and the contractual features that distinguish the two types of funds. Section 5 concludes.

## 2. Hedge Funds Versus Private Equity

In this section, we begin by reviewing the differences between private equity and hedge funds. We then discuss the extent to which the two fund types are converging. We augment this discussion with an analysis of the benefits and costs of private equity and hedge fund-style investments. We conclude this section by discussing whether additional regulation is likely to meaningfully improve investor protection in relation to the industries' reliance on contractual mechanisms and best practice norms.

Note that private equity can be distinguished from hedge funds in terms of their investment strategies, lock-up periods, and the liquidity of their portfolios (see Table 6.1). Moreover, given their indefinite life, private equity fund managers have incentives to take large illiquid positions in the non-listed securities of private companies. Investments made by private equity funds take place during the first three to five years of the fund, which is followed by a holding period which averages between five and seven years in which few new investments are made. Unlike private equity, the shorter lock-in period of hedge funds and their more flexible structure explains the dominance of highly liquid, short-term investments which allow investors easier access to the withdrawal of their investment funds. Despite these differences, it is becoming more obvious that private equity and hedge funds are converging in a number of important ways.

At first glance, one noticeable incidence of convergence is the growth of hedge funds and private equity managers pursuing similar assets and investment strategies to secure superior market returns. When hedge fund advisers are dissatisfied with traditional strategies and unable to obtain their rates of return, they have moved quickly to adopt those strategies usually employed by private equity funds, such as corporate restructuring and buyouts, to achieve better value on their investments. This is partly due to the overcrowding of the hedge fund marketplace. This has led to clashes with traditional private equity funds. A noteworthy example is the bidding war between one of the largest private equity

Table 6.1.  Hedge funds v private equity funds

| | Traditional hedge fund | Traditional private equity |
|---|---|---|
| Investment strategies | • Investment in liquid securities that can be marked-to-market easily<br>• Pursue alpha generating strategies (risk arbitrage) | • Investment in illiquid equity stakes, for example stakes in private companies<br>• Add value for the fund through screening |
| Fund structure | • Typically LP | • Typically LP |
| Management Vehicle | • LLC or Corporation | • LLC or Corporation |
| Other fund terms | • Upfront investment (100% at subscription date)<br>• No lock-up periods; investors can access or exit the fund periodically<br>• Perpetual<br>• Management fees are typically 1% of NAV of the fund and paid quarterly<br>• Incentive fee: 20%, paid periodically, no clawbacks | • Commitment upfront plus drawings over time<br>• Investors typically do not have withdrawal rights and are locked up for multiple years<br>• Term<br>• Management fee is typically 2% of committed capital and paid quarterly<br>• Incentive fee: 20%, paid upon realization of profits, subject to clawbacks |

firms, Kohlberg Kravis Roberts & Co, and Cerberus Capital Management for the acquisition of Toys' R Us.

Thus, the recent emergence of hedge funds competing with private equity firms for target companies to take private is further confirmation that funds are becoming more similar and harder to distinguish. There are a number of factors that account for this trend. First, the increased number of funds and new capital flowing into private equity and hedge funds makes it harder for advisers to produce premium returns. Second, debt continues to be relatively abundant worldwide and at relatively attractive rates. Third, hedge funds and buyout funds are increasingly seeking the same cost savings and synergies that strategic buyers have always achieved to justify their higher multiples. Effectively, these trends have blurred the differences between the two fund types.

The increased convergence caused hedge funds to incorporate private equity type features in their fund structures, reducing investor flexibility through side pockets (investments in illiquid stakes, which are accounted for in terms of administrative fee and incentive fee separately from the fund), gates (caps on the amount of annual withdrawals from the fund by investor to manage the liquidity risk), and lock-ups (investors cannot withdraw from the fund within a certain period). Of course, one can cast doubt on whether these strategies can generate solutions for all the problems associated with hedge funds providing their investors with diverse investment opportunities. As long as management and performance fees are based on striking a net asset value of the fund, hedge fund investors are willing to pay the fees. However, investors are more likely to challenge performance payments to an adviser that has invested in illiquid securities that may not have an easily ascertainable market value. Private equity funds have addressed this concern through distributions based solely on realized events or the use of clawback provisions that mandate funds to return performance fees if the fund subsequently go into a loss position. These strategies to manage valuation risk have been resisted so far by the hedge fund industry.

Policy-makers and the media have drawn attention to the confusion that private equity and, particularly, hedge funds are currently causing in the world of finance and corporate governance. The recent wave of private equity-based buyouts of publicly listed companies has prompted questions and political controversy about whether private equity can perhaps be beneficial. For example, the purchase of VNU, a global information and media company, by a consortium of private equity firms triggered concerns that the advantages of taking the firm private, including cost reduction and increased operational efficiency, may not offset the costs involved when the delisting of companies entails a significant reduction in liquidity of equity markets. Moreover, the sophisticated use of financial engineering techniques, in particular the funding of acquisitions with large amounts of debt, which are subsequently loaded on the acquired businesses, raises suspicion.

Hedge funds, like private equity funds, provide markets and investors with substantial benefits. Since these funds tend to be engaged in extensive market

**Table 6.2.** Assessment of private equity

| Benefits | Costs |
| --- | --- |
| Private equity funds help large publicly held companies restructure their businesses, thereby forming a symbiotic relationship | Delisting reduces liquidity |
| Private equity deals often allow multinationals to retain a minority stake in the sold companies, thereby creating the opportunity to share in any improvements in performance | The high debt levels loaded on acquired firms as a result of leveraged buyouts may have implications in an economic downturn |
| Private equity offers publicly held firms an opportunity to circumvent the over-regulatory approach to listed companies | Private equity deals entail rather small takeover premiums |

research before taking significant trading positions, they enhance liquidity and contribute to market efficiency. Yet regulators are concerned about the lack of understanding and regulatory mechanisms to protect possible downsides of hedge funds investing strategies. Hedge funds are shrouded in nebulous mystery, and obscurity about their investors abounds. The fact that hedge funds pursue aggressive short selling techniques in order to make profit on overvalued stock just adds to the negative reputation of these funds. When they sell short, they sell borrowed shares under the expectation that they will be able to buy the shares back in the market at a lower price. Obviously, this phenomenon gives hedge funds an incentive to actively drive down the stock price by voting the borrowed shares in value-reducing ways.

This so-called 'empty voting' strategy of decoupling voting rights from economic ownership has recently added a new dimension in the corporate governance discussions (Hu and Black 2006). Questions arise increasingly about the hedge funds' role in relation to management and other shareholders and creditors. Unlike earlier periods, the new activist investors are more directly engaged in investment fund management. These funds not only endeavour to deliver superior returns by diligent research and insightful analysis, but also by actively reshaping a portfolio firm's business policy and strategy. Many argue that the investment style of these funds fits into the current corporate governance movement of shareholder activism. Proponents urge regulators to adopt a 'hands-off' approach, pointing to the overall increase in share price and performance of firms associated with hedge funds. Others are of the opinion that it would be overly costly if activist shareholders were too involved in the daily management of the firm, in particular, if they hold more votes than economic ownership. They point to the fact that funds' activism is mainly directed toward short-term payoffs, and argue that the transfer of effective control to a team of specialists (i.e., the board of management) will add to efficiency and long-term wealth creation. Complaints by managers and shareholder groups arguably encourage policy-makers to consider increasing regulation and supervision over collective investment pools and their actions.

A new empirical literature, however, is emerging in the USA that shows hedge funds being long-term investors in some industries, often, like their peers in private equity, waiting very long periods to cash in on their investment (Brav et al 2006). Indeed, this mixed picture about the costs and benefits of private equity on the one hand and hedge funds on the other hand suggests that questions remain about whether more detailed regulation and supervision of funds is required. Given the contractual mechanisms that prevail in the governance of both private equity and hedge funds, an initial hands-off approach might be warranted (Bratton 2007). What is more, private equity and hedge funds are evolving into more transparent investment vehicles. Firstly, institutional investors, demanding better risk management, encouraged equity funds to adopt better valuation techniques and controls. The UK hedge fund industry has created voluntary guidelines that seek to address regulatory and investor concerns, such as risk and transparency (Association of German Banks 2007; Hedge Fund, Working Group 2007). Secondly, buyout groups attempt to improve their reputation and image by joining respectable industry bodies, like the British Venture Capital Association, or initiating the establishment of such a group in their respective countries, such as the Private Equity Council in the United States. The purpose of these groups is to conduct research and, more importantly, provide information about the industry to policy-makers, investors, and other interested parties. Lastly, in search for more stable capital, private equity funds—and recently, hedge funds—increasingly raise money by listing funds on public markets. By floating shares or units of a fund, advisers voluntarily subject themselves to regulatory supervision. The contractual nature of private equity and hedge funds in combination with the trend towards self-regulation by industry groups suggests that the sophisticated players in the private equity are themselves capable of disciplining opportunistic behaviour by fund managers and advisers. In order to enhance capital market efficiency and transparency, policy-makers and governmental supervisors should work closely together with private industry bodies. Such an approach ensures that possible rules and regulations are in line with both best practices and standards applied in the world of private equity and hedge funds.

## 3. Hedge Funds and Private Equity Activities

### 3.1 Hedge Funds

A number of hedge funds have adopted an investment strategy to accumulate large positions in publicly listed companies, using their new ownership positions to engage in the monitoring of management. This group of activist funds diverge from traditional value investors by challenging reluctant management teams that resist their advice. Activist managers make direct interventions in corporate governance by criticizing business plans and governance practices of their target companies. Typically they confront management teams by demanding action, whether by force or persuasion, to enhance their goal of maximizing shareholder value. As a consequence, fund managers are often locked into long-term battle with a target firm's management. Depending on their response, fund managers may increase their stake in the target firm or recruit allies in order to achieve their governance goals. Once committed to a course of action, the funds form a powerful incentive for managers to increase firm value. If a target company, for example, is mismanaged or underperforming, these funds can use their capital in a focused and leveraged way so as to initiate new, different, and potentially more effective business strategies. Hedge fund activism has recently led to a large number of mergers and corporate restructurings, dividend recapitalizations, and the replacement of incumbent management and board members.

This can be seen from a typical hedge fund case in the United States where William A Ackman, founder of New York hedge fund adviser Pershing Square Capital Management LP, targeted fast-food chain Wendy's International Inc after Pershing filed a Schedule 13-D with the SEC reporting the holding of over 9 per cent of Wendy's stock. The fund claimed that their own research as depicted in a restructuring plan supported a strategy of spinning off Wendy's fastest growing business unit, Tim Hortons, in order to achieve fair value and deliver better returns for shareholders.[3] To be sure, the hedge fund's involvement and intentions gave Wendy's stock a soaring effect.[4] However, John Schuessler, Wendy's CEO and old-style manager, did not immediately give his support to the proposed reorganization and attempted to stall any progress in such a transaction.

Undeterred, Pershing lined up new Wall Street allies in their campaign against Wendy's. Ackman, in June 2005, approached the Blackstone Group LP to write a professional fairness opinion on the merits of the plans to spin off Tim Hortons, re-franchising company stores and repurchase shares with the proceeds. Blackstone's report confirmed the benefits of Ackman's proposal by concluding that Wendy's intrinsic value would increase from $48 to $60–70. In July 2005, Wendy's International Inc announced the flotation of 15–18 per cent of Tim Hortons' common shares.[5] But the plan was quickly challenged by Nelson Peltz's Trian Fund Management LP, which countered in

---

[3] Tim Hortons is the piping-hot doughnut-and-coffee sensation from Canada, based in Oakville, Ontario. The 2,597 restaurants in Canada and 288 in the United States generated 31% of Wendy's sales and 58% of profit. See *BusinessWeek* online (P Gogoi), 'A taste for Tim Hortons?', 21 March 2006.

[4] After recruiting new allies, the Blackstone Group perfected its governance goals, which eventually led to a significant increase in the stock price.

[5] For its own part, Wendy's management claimed that its decision was based on the results of earlier discussions with Goldman Sachs beginning in 2000. See *QSR Magazine* (Michael W Nuckolls), 'Big Money Talks', August 2006.

December 2005 by increasing the pressure on Wendy's management by directly contacting John Schuessler and subsequently increasing their share stake above 5 per cent when it became clear that Wendy's management was engaged in a stonewalling exercise. Trian's fund managers were of the view that Wendy's proposed reorganizations would not produce the coveted effect. In fact, the Schedule 13-D filed by Trian Fund Management clearly shows that the reason for acquiring approximately 5.5 per cent of Wendy's shares was that they believed that the shares were undervalued and hence represented an attractive investment opportunity.[6] One of the actions proposed by Peltz's fund was the immediate commencement of a 100 per cent tax-free spin-off of Tim Hortons, which was completed on 29 September 2006.[7] The activists continued their success at Wendy's when Sandell Asset Management and Trian Fund Management, in March 2006, won three board seats after they encouraged the hamburger chain to improve results and consider selling its Baja Fresh chain.[8]

There is little doubt that hedge fund pressure raised a number of questions with Wendy's management and investors, which constrained their actions initially. Nevertheless the activists' campaign proved successful in overcoming resistance partly due to passive investors deciding to be supportive and management, which held significant stock options, adopting the hedge funds' recommendations and thereby benefiting from the successful implementation of the plan.

But not all hedge fund interventions are successful (Bratton 2007). The probability of success tends to vary according to their ability to convince other shareholders, management's possibility to use defensive tactics, and the level of shareholder friendliness within a jurisdiction. For instance, investor Carl C Icahn failed to obtain the support from other shareholders to split Time Warner into four separate companies under a newly appointed management team. The disconnect between Icahn's dissident view and other investors' opinion is generally considered to be the main reason for incumbent management's victory. In comparison, Stork, a European conglomerate, has battled with two hedge funds, Centaurus Capital of the UK, and Paulson & Co, of the USA, which emerged as its largest investors holding over 31.4 per cent of the company's shares.

In 2005, the two hedge funds took up a high-profile campaign against the managers of the company, who were content to operate an old-style conglomerate structure consisting of a food systems, technical services, and aerospace

---

[6] A Schedule 13-D must be filed with the SEC when a person or group of persons acquires beneficial ownership of more than 5% of a class of a company's equity securities registered under Section 12 of the Securities Exchange Act of 1934. Schedule 13-D reports the acquisition and other information within ten days after the purchase. The SEC requires filing of an amendment when any material changes in the facts contained in the Schedule occur.

[7] Peltz proposed two additional divestitures, included in the 13-D. On 29 September 2006 Wendy's distributed 159,952,977 shares of Tim Hortons common stock to Wendy's shareholders (on record as of 15 September 2006). Wendy's International, Inc shareholders received 1.3542759 shares of Tim Horton's for every one share of Wendy's common stock.

[8] Trian was recently successful in its bid to win two seats on the board of Heinz.

division. Armed with a study of how Stork could realize shareholder value, the activist funds sought to unbundle Stork's conglomerate structure by reducing the number of unrelated divisions and concentrating solely on the high-value end of its business. Management would reject the hedge funds' advice claiming that the fund managers were merely short-term investors that care more about increasing Stork's share price through unbundling than the long-term interest of the company and its stakeholders. Responding to these allegations, the funds increased their pressure on management by calling a non-binding shareholder resolution that would ask investors to support their divestiture motion. Shareholders overwhelmingly supported the activists' non-binding resolution, which the board subsequently ignored on the grounds it was not binding legally. To further underscore its determination to neutralize the activists' threat, Stork's board continued its refusal to discuss strategy with the fund managers. The funds were ultimately forced to call an extraordinary shareholders meeting on 17 January 2007 to demand the dismissal of the members of the supervisory board on the grounds of mismanagement. Surprisingly, this action prompted the Stork Foundation, an unrelated but closely aligned entity, to trigger a poison pill device that diluted the hedge funds' interest in the Stork's equity, giving the company's board and its allies effective control of the company.

The hedge funds had no choice but to challenge the legality of the poison pill device alleging that the company was guilty of 'mismanagement' by attempting to frustrate shareholders' rights. The Enterprise Chamber, an Amsterdam court that deals with intra-corporate disputes, found that the use of the poison pill was illegal, but barred the shareholders' planned vote that called for the dismissal of the supervisory board. Instead, the Court decided to appoint three additional independent supervisory board members and to investigate the alleged mismanagement claims of shareholders. Clearly the two funds will continue their aim to restructure Stork (McCahery and Vermeulen 2007).

The Stork conflict raises important questions about the involvement of hedge funds in corporate governance. Activist funds have developed a typical pattern of engagement in which they take up an initial position in a target company, announce their holdings publicly, criticize the business strategy and governance policy of the target, and suggest management undertake value-increasing actions to benefit shareholders. Surveys show that funds will recommend that their company targets quickly undertake a major action that leads to higher short-run returns to investors and continue to be invested in target companies for two years or more.[9] Moreover, the lock-up period of hedge funds, which traditionally averaged a one-year period, but recently increased to an average of two to three years,[10] constrains hedge funds to pursuing certain types of strategies that

[9] See Chapter 5.
[10] The acceptance of the longer lock-up period is partly due to hedge funds' tendency to compete in the private equity market.

are likely to realize higher returns to investors. Still, the contrasting outcomes discussed above show that the demands made by funds do not always produce governance or strategic gains favourable to investors. That said, activist funds are not committed to short-term investments, but will remain invested in a company until they achieve their pre-investment goals. The combination of double-digit returns to investors and managerial incentives encourages funds to employ such tactics. Still, the duration of hedge fund involvement with a governance target is ultimately the result of its changing organizational structure. That is not to say that hedge funds will depict themselves as buyers of controlling equity positions in buyout transactions. The principal focus of hedge funds will remain strategies involving liquid securities.

## 3.2 Private Equity

Private equity is often associated with starting and developing companies that are unable to attract debt financing to support and finance their high-growth and often high-tech businesses. For instance, not yet revealed and unproven technologies, the lack of liquid assets, and the importance of human capital make bank finance unsuitable for these companies. Because future revenue streams are highly indefinable, access to debt financing through for instance asset-backed securitization transactions remains a major obstacle for these firms. When debt finance is unavailable, entrepreneurs have the option of starting up and financing a new business with equity or not attempting to start one up at all. Many start-ups must therefore rely on some source of private equity investment for developing and growing their business.

Private equity, which is defined as the investment of equity in non-listed companies, can take many financing forms, such as bootstrapping,[11] angel investing,[12] venture capital, management, and leveraged buyouts. In the main, there are two types of private equity funds. First of all, venture capital funds have become the main funding source for high-growth start-up businesses. These funds come in three variations in the United States: small business investment companies (SBICs),[13] traditional venture capital funds, and corporate venture

---

[11] Dell, founded with the aim to sell IBM-compatible computers directly to customers who were loath to pay computer-store prices, is a typical example of a successful bootstrap. Michael Dell started the company with his personal money and savings from friends and relatives. Yet, given the high risk involved in this method of funding, successful bootstraps are very rare in the world of venture financing.

[12] High-tech start-ups can be funded with capital from wealthy, individual investors who usually make equity investments in entrepreneurial companies at the early seed-level stage. Angel investors provide a significant amount of the financing, varying from a few tens of thousands of dollars up to hundreds of thousands of dollars, each year in the United States.

[13] Under the Small Business Administration Act of 1958, the Small Business Administration (SBA) is authorized to license SBICs to make equity and loan investments in smaller entrepreneurial firms in the United States.

capital funds. Consider Figure 6.1, which shows the amount of venture capital investment in US start-up companies. If we compare this amount to the level of venture capital investment in Europe (see Figure 6.2), it is obvious that there is a wide gap in funding, which may explain the differences in growth and innovation between the two regions.

As larger companies, such as Cisco, Intel, IBM, Kodak, Apple, and Microsoft expand the scope of their operations to invest in start-ups, entrepreneurs tend to attempt to exploit the opportunity to obtain not only financial, but also technical and managerial assistance. There may be several reasons why alliances between a start-up and a multinational may bear fruit for the venture. First,

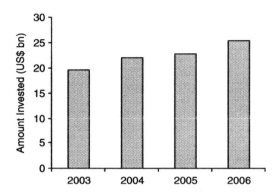

**Figure 6.1.** Venture capital investment in the United States
*Source:* Adapted from the *MoneyTree Report* by PricewaterhouseCoopers.

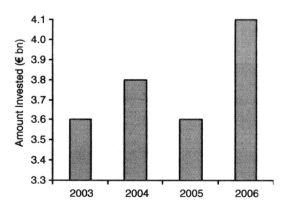

**Figure 6.2.** Venture capital investments in Europe
*Source:* Adapted from the National Venture Capital Association, VentureSource and Ernst&Young (*Global Venture Capital Insights Report* 2006).

the start-up may very well offer strategic value of synergy to the multination-al's core businesses. Second, even though a high rate of return is usually not the investor's main objective (thereby giving more stability to the venture), hav-ing a well-performing high-growth company in the portfolio may prove to be very lucrative. Third, it is generally accepted that these alliances often increase the credibility and reputation of the start-up firm. But there are also a number of disadvantages associated with the involvement of corporate venture capital funds. In particular the complexity of the transaction and the time-consuming decision-making procedures within large firms make traditional venture cap-ital funds a more accessible source of private equity capital financing for high-tech start-ups. Alliances with corporate investors require the negotiation and drafting of a multitude of ancillary agreements relating to the promoting, sell-ing, licensing and developing of technology and knowledge. More importantly, corporate investors are more inclined to carefully reconsider the investment and pull the plug in the event of a major downturn.

That is not to say that starting a business with capital from traditional venture capital pools is an easy task to accomplish. As was pointed out in Chapter 5, venture capitalists tend to monitor and protect their investments through active participation, namely by due diligence, establishing a relationship with the start-up businesses' managers and by sitting on their board of directors. As soon as venture capitalists are hooked and involved, entrepreneurs and other key employees should be ready to abdicate control over their company. To be sure, venture capitalists will not typically depose an entrepreneur by acquiring a majority of the corporation's common shares. This is usually counter-productive, as discrepancies between them and the entrepreneur, implying an increase in agency costs, would augment. Allocating a substantial equity stake in the firm to the entrepreneur and other employees, which is akin to the stock option com-pensation system, fortifies the incentive to conduct the business diligently and discourages shirking and opportunism. Instead of seeking a majority of the cor-poration's equity, venture capitalists usually obtain control by utilizing compli-cated contractual mechanisms in their relationship with the entrepreneurial team and other investors. These contractual mechanisms protect the venture capitalists extensively from adverse selection and moral hazard problems. For instance, the use of staged financing and convertible preferred stock form an optimal combin-ation which gives motivated entrepreneurs an incentive to take significant risks in order to increase firm performance while securing downside protection for venture capitalists.

It is submitted that the success of a venture capital market is mainly attrib-uted to a private ordering regime in which contractual mechanisms are prefer-ably employed to mitigate agency costs and to support the efficient structuring of staged financing and the sustained level of new entrepreneurs with high capacity to achieve their commercial aims (Gilson 2003). Governmental inter-ference and oversight appears to be counter-productive. This is especially true of the organization of venture capital funds themselves, which predominantly employ the limited partnership as the preferred vehicle to organize the venture capital fund. Recent research seems to suggest that government initiatives could crowd out the supply of venture capital. Suppose, for instance, that a tax incentive to encourage individual investors to pour money into special venture capital funds turns out, in fact, to reduce the supply of other, relatively more informed venture capital investments by institutional investors (Cumming and MacIntosh 2006).

We have seen how the main agency relationship in portfolio companies can lead to serious conflicts between the active funds and other shareholders and managers. There is a second agency relationship in the private equity market. In this context, fund managers act as agents for external investors, who choose to invest in high potential start-up firms through an intermediary rather than directly. Although this agency conflict is likely to be particularly difficult and intractable, there is inevitably a high degree of information asymmetry between the fund managers, who play an active role in the portfolio companies, and the passive investors, who are not able to monitor the prospects of each individual investment closely. To be sure, several types of sophisticated contractual governance and incentive provisions have emerged which have proved effective in limiting opportunism and controlling the level of risk.

By way of comparison, we look at buyout funds which invest mainly in mature companies. The legal structure that makes the buyout market so effective also begins with the limited partnership form by which providers of private equity investment convey money (as limited partners) to the managers (the general partners) who are running the business and actively making the investments in portfolio companies. Like venture capital funds, the relationship is governed merely by contractual provisions which allow the fund managers enough time and space to take firms private and restructure them. Note, however, that there are significant differences in the organizational structure of venture capital and buyout funds. For example, buyout funds typically invest in mature companies with fairly predictable cash flows, which causes limited partners to give less leeway to the managers and to demand a minimum rate of return before profits are shared with the managers.

Until recently, buyouts accounted for less than 10 per cent of total number of investments. By mid-April 2006, however, there were 205 buyout funds that had raised about $200 billion.[14] The statistical evidence shows the buyout business continues to boom (see *The Economist*, 10 February 2007, page 73), increasing in recent years to 20 per cent in 2005 (EVCA data 2000–5). For Europe, the total amount of private equity deals in Europe was €178 billion, 41 per cent higher than 2005.[15] Remarkably the European market is dominated

---

[14] See *Private Equity Intelligence*, cited in *FT*, Thursday, 24 April 2007.
[15] See, *Financial News* (J Mawson), 'Private Equity Levels Double in Europe', 29 January 2007.

by US-based buyout firms. Overall, more than half of the funds raised in the private equity sector are invested in MBO/MBIs. A clear pattern emerges from the many empirical studies that describe the LBO booms. It is worth noting that the 1980s LBO boom was largely a US phenomenon. Conversely, with the current LBO wave, the centre of gravity has shifted from the USA to Europe and the UK. This should come as no surprise since the European economy has performed much better than in the 1980s. What are the causes for the current expansive round in LBOs? The now-standard explanation for the highly favourable circumstances to complete deals is the easy credit terms and low interest rates which have prevailed until recently. A second explanation looks to the pressures on fund managers which prompted them to increase the allocation levels for this particular class of assets. A third explanation points to the self-interested behaviour of the managements of public companies which have responded to shareholder pressure to obtain higher prices from private equity bidders. Another key feature of the boom has been the increase in corporate governance pressures. As a result, the cost of D&O insurance has increased substantially in the wake of Sarbanes-Oxley, due to the move of making executives personally liable for the accounting practices of their companies. In addition, we have also seen more shareholder scrutiny on executive pay. Given this, talented managers usually receive more generous compensation packages when switching to a firm controlled by a private equity company. Finally, many laws, regulations and other measures are probably also responsible for the infrastructure to complete deals. One obvious message is that a favourable infrastructure is seen to be crucial for the acceleration of the private equity process.

## 4. The Pooled Investment Vehicle: Hedge Funds and Private Equity

In this section, we turn to examining the typical structures of pooled investment vehicles, namely private equity and hedge funds. We focus on the three parties: (1) the general partner; (2) the investment adviser; and (3) the limited partners. We consider the extent to which hedge funds and private equity employ similar legal forms and contractual provisions between the GP and LPs. We note that despite some overlap in fund structure and organization, private equity and hedge funds typically employ different trading strategies, compensation, and governance arrangements which are reflected in the main contract between the GP and the investors.

### 4.1 The Limited Partnership Structure

A fund of a private equity firm, hedge fund, or venture capital firm is a pooled investment. The fund can be seen as a vehicle formed to pool the capital of different

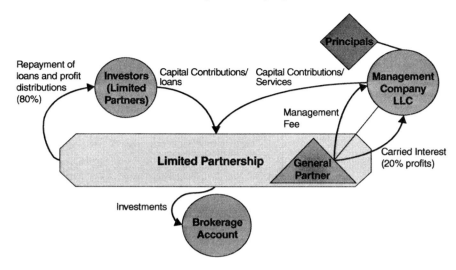

**Figure 6.3.** Typical hedge fund structure

investors. Contributors of these funds are institutional investors, pension funds, university endowments, and other wealthy individuals. They pool their money with others so that the fund can help to spread the risk of the investment and can gain access to markets where the money has the potential for significant capital growth. Professional fund managers invest the capital across a wide range of different holdings. The value of the investments can go up and down depending on the returns of the different investments. Investments of pooled investment vehicles are characterized by high expected returns and high risks.

In the United States and elsewhere, the limited partnership form is the dominant legal vehicle used in hedge funds and private equity structuring. Both fund types are usually organized as an LP, with a GP and management company, both structured as separate legal entities, and the limited partners (see Figure 6.3).

As we have seen, the popularity of this form is due to its contractual nature which allows the internal and external participants to reduce opportunism and agency costs. Indeed, the limited partnership structure permits fund managers to achieve extensive control over the operation of their funds subject to few intrusive legal obligations. Other features, such as tax benefits, the flexibility surrounding its structure and terms, and its fixed life, contribute to its continuing viability as the business form of choice for collective investment vehicles. The LP has other important advantages as well. First, it is familiar to most investors and intermediaries, which accounts for its enduring popularity. Second, there is a risk that LLCs, operating outside the USA, could be treated as a non-transparent foreign entity and taxed as a corporate body. As a consequence, some sponsors are reluctant to

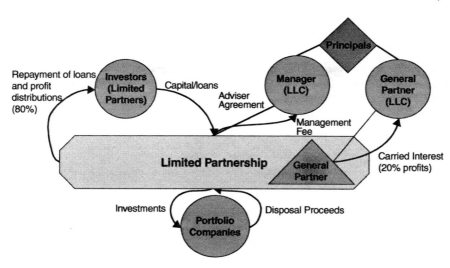

**Figure 6.4.** Simplified US private equity structure

switch to the LLC.[16] Typically the sponsor will invest between 1 and 3 per cent of the fund's total commitments. In order to obtain fees, the sponsor will create two entities: an LP and a management company, which is organized either as an LLC or corporation. Moreover, the management company is either controlled by one of the principals, or is a subsidiary of a bank or insurance company and, accordingly, will exercise effective control over the GP and fund manager.

The relationship between the limited partners and the general partners mainly relies on explicit contractual measures. For example, a key contractual technique is the compensation arrangement between the fund manager and the investors. Compensation derives from the two main sources. First, fund managers typically receive 20 per cent of the profits generated by each of the funds. The second source of compensation is the management fee. To be sure, investors attempt to ensure fund managers' performance by insisting on hurdle rates that climb upwards to 15–20 per cent, which means that profits can only be distributed after a certain threshold has been reached. Thus, from the perspective of private equity, the contractual flexibility of the limited partnership plays a central role in aligning the interests of management and investors. For instance, in order to protect the 80/20 deal, a clawback provision will be included in the agreement that provides that an overdistribution to a GP will be clawed back to the fund and then distributed to the LPs. What triggers a clawback provision?

---

[16] Nevertheless, some sponsors are now beginning to structure their funds as a Delaware LLC since it has the same organizational flexibility and tax efficiency as the LP.

In practice, clawbacks can be triggered when the preferred return or hurdle is not reached and the GP obtained carried interest, or if the GP has received more carried interest than the agreed 20 per cent of cumulative net profits. Here we can use an example to show how the clawback is intended to function. Assume that a fund has six investments: A to F were each purchased for $100. Also assume that five of these investments were sold each year for $200. As a result, the GP receives a carried interest of 20 per cent and the LP receives 80 per cent of the cumulative profits of the investments and of course the contributed capital. But, the sixth project defaults to $0. Thus, the total net profits of the fund are $400 (500–100 loss) or 67 per cent for the LPs. Yet, it was agreed that the GP would receive 20 per cent of the net profits: $80. But the GP received $100, which accordingly triggers the clawback provision.

It is noteworthy that there are also a number of approaches for structuring the clawback obligation, including the 'pay it back now' approach or the segregated reserves approach. Under the first approach, the GP will immediately provide a clawback to the LPs. This method is remarkably straightforward and requires a potentially large cash contribution by a group of individual managers who may not have the financial ability to make the required contribution. In contrast, the reserve account approach places costly constraints on managers by requiring that the cash deposited in the reserve account is invested in a safe, cash-equivalent instrument in order to satisfy eventually the clawback obligation. At the same time, there is also a limited partner clawback which is intended to protect the GP against future claims, should the GP become the subject of a lawsuit. For the most part, the clause will include limitations in the timing or amount of the judgement.

Finally, as it happens, many LP contracts will include a preferred return provision. This is a minimum return rate which ranges most of the time from 5 to 10 per cent. The idea of preferred return is that it affects the timing of the carried interest. Such a targeted return must be met before the fund manager can share in the fund profits. Preferred returns are normally required by LPs who make commitments to new funds or funds involved in buyouts. Most priority returns have a catch-up provision, which permits a reallocation of the profits to the GP after the priority return has been distributed to the LPs.

**Table 6.3.** A clawback example

|                     | GP                     | LP                                  |
|---------------------|------------------------|-------------------------------------|
| Profits             | 5 * 0.20 * 100 = $ 100 | 5 * 0.8 * 100 = $400                 |
| Contributed capital |                        | 5 * 100 = $500                      |
| Initial investment  |                        | 6 * 100 = $600                      |
| Investment return   |                        | (5 * 200–(6 * 100)) / 600 = 67%     |

## 4.2 Restrictive Covenants

In the previous section, we examined how the flexibility of the limited partnership form allows the internal and external participants to enter into contractual arrangements that align the incentives of fund managers with those of outside investors. If well structured, the limited partnership agreement can effectively reduce agency costs. In this section we turn to considering how limited partners are usually permitted, despite restrictions on their managerial rights, to vote on important issues such as amendments of the partnership agreement, dissolution of the partnership agreement, extension of the fund's life, removal of a general partner, and the valuation of the portfolio. In addition, we examine how limited partners employ several contractual restrictions when structuring the partnership agreement depending on the asymmetry of information and market for investment opportunities.

In recent years, a number of law and finance scholars have studied the role and frequency of covenants in the agreements between institutional investors and professional fund managers. An early study by Gompers and Lerner (1996) focuses on restrictive covenants imposed by institutional investors on fund managers in respect of the operation of the fund. They grouped the venture capital fund restrictive covenants into three categories: (1) restrictions on management of the fund; (2) restrictions on the activities of the GP; and (3) restrictions on the types of investment.

In terms of the first category of covenants, the first restriction in this class involves limits on the size of investment in any one firm which discourages the GP, the incentives induced by carried interest, from allocating a large portion of fund in a single investment. This is similar to the restrictions on the type of behaviour that would increase the leverage of the fund and thereby amplify the risk for institutional investors. A restriction on co-investment is designed to limit the opportunism of fund managers so as to avoid one fund artificially improving the performance of another. A second category of covenants is designed to limit the investment activities of the GP. The restriction on co-investment by fund managers is designed to limit the agency problem which might arise from selective attention to certain portfolio firms at the expense of the performance of the entire fund. The covenant is designed to limit the sale of fund interest by fund managers and that their commitment to the fund is not compromised. Further, the key person provisions and restrictions on additional partners is intended to ensure that management does not opportunistically hire new personnel to manage the fund in breach of their commitments made to the LPs. The third category of covenants is related to restrictions on types of investment that GPs can make. These covenants reduce or eliminate the potential for management to opportunistically alter the focus of the fund for their own concerns at the expense of investors. Restrictions include limitations on investments in venture capital, public securities, LBOs, foreign securities, and other asset classes.

In the context of determining the frequency of the covenants for such funds, Gompers and Lerner found that the number and type of covenant correspond to the uncertainty, information, and asymmetry and agency costs in the portfolio company. Table 6.4 shows the distribution of covenants for VC funds.

They demonstrated, moreover, that there is positive relationship between the use of restrictions and the propensity of the fund managers to behave opportunistically. As Table 6.4 shows there are a number of distinct covenants that address problems relating to the management of the fund, conflict of interests, and restrictions on the type of investment the fund can make. Other factors affecting the use of restrictions are the fund's size, the compensation system of the managers, and their reputation. In contrast, hedge funds rely less on covenants due to the shorter lock-up periods and the fund's liquidity. Finally, the public nature of the activities of hedge funds, particularly in the market for corporate control, tends to limit the principal–agent problems that might otherwise emerge.

Recently, Cumming and Johan (2006) have offered a 'quality of law' explanation for the frequency of use of investment covenants imposed by institutional investors pertaining to GP's activities relating to investment decisions, investment powers, types of investment, fund operations, and limitations on liability. An understanding of the private equity practice teaches us that the presence of legal counsel that review covenants would likely increase the probability of covenants. They find evidence, moreover, that the quality of the rule of law and other institutional and legal practice factors is positively correlated with the number of covenants relating to fund operations. In their view, the better the legal system, as measured in the increase in the Legality Index (a weighed average of the legal index variables introduced by La Porta et al (1997, 1998) as defined by Berkowitz, Pistor, and Richards (2003) from 20 to 21 (normal improvement rate for developed country), the higher the probability of an additional covenant relating to fund operation by about 1 per cent , but an increase in the Legal Index from 10–11 (normal improvement rate for developing country) increases the probability of the presence of an extra fund operation covenant by about 2 per cent.

The above studies reflect how important it is to recognize the critical role of management influence in determining the organizational and structural characteristics of a fund, the agency problems and control issues that emerge in the investment process, and the conflicts of interest that occur in times of market upheaval. LPs have high-powered incentives which greatly improve their ability to focus on addressing these problems through negotiating and implementing covenants to protect LPs and ensure the GP's incentives serve investors' interests. Further improvements in the training of legal counsel that review covenants will most likely influence positively the frequency of some covenants. A more complete solution would require increases to the quality of legal systems generally in developing and civil law jurisdictions.

**Table 6.4.** Distribution of covenants in venture capital funds

| Description | % of Covenants |
|---|---|
| **Covenants relating to the management of the fund** | |
| Restrictions on the size of investment in any one firm | 77.8 |
| Restrictions on use of debt by partnership | 95.6 |
| Restrictions on coinvestment by organization's earlier or later funds | 62.2 |
| Restrictions on reinvestment of partnership's capital gains | 35.6 |
| **Covenants relating to the activities of the general partners** | |
| Restrictions on coinvestment by general partners | 77.8 |
| Restrictions on sale of partnership interests by general partners | 51.1 |
| Restrictions on fund-raising by general partners | 84.4 |
| Restrictions on other actions by general partners | 13.3 |
| Restrictions on addition of general partners | 26.7 |
| **Covenants relating to the type of investment** | |
| Restrictions on investments in other venture funds | 62.2 |
| Restrictions on investments in public securities | 66.7 |
| Restrictions on investments in leveraged buyouts | 60.0 |
| Restrictions on investments in foreign securities | 44.4 |
| Restrictions on investments in other asset classes | 31.1 |
| **Total number of partnership agreements in sample** | 45.0 |
| **Average number of covenant classes** | 7.9 |
| **Average number of covenant classes (weighted by fund size)** | 8.4 |

*Source*: Gompers and Lerner (1996)

## 5. Conclusion: Convergence and Diversity of Hedge Funds and Private Equity

In this chapter, we have argued that private equity and hedge funds rely on similar features of the partnership form, but diverge in some important respects due to demands made by investors. For example, the partnership's duration for private equity is usually ten to twelve years, after which the profits are distributed either in cash or in shares of portfolio companies. Hedge funds, however, have shorter lock-up periods (one to three years), confirming the emphasis on short-term investments. Individuals and institutions that invest in a limited partnership can delegate investment and monitoring decisions to the fund managers, who act as the general partner. Even though the difference between private equity funds and hedge funds is not always clear, we have shown earlier (see Table 6.1) that there are various ways to distinguish the two types of funds. In fact, a clear pattern emerges. In sum, private equity funds usually invest in non-listed companies, pay management fees based on capital commitments and incentive fees only when gains are realized, maintain fixed subscription periods, grant no redemption rights but authorize distributions as investments are sold, provide for fixed fund life, establish long lock-up periods, and provide extensive contractual protections, whereas hedge funds mainly target publicly held corporations, use mark to market valuations as the basis for incentive fees, provide frequent fund openings throughout the life of the fund, provide redemption rights, participation by all investors in the same portfolio, 'high water mark' but no preferred returns, and minimum investor rights.

# 7

# The Third Pillar: Optional Guidelines

## 1. Introduction

In Chapter 6, we saw that the buyout branch of the private equity industry increasingly faces sharp criticism from regulators, labour unions and shareholders in publicly held companies. Funds are viewed as 'locusts' only interested in asset-stripping and their own enrichment. As a response, the industry, convinced of the value-increasing effect of their investments and the benefits for employment, innovation, and research and development, have established sector representatives, like the Private Equity Council in the United States, or become members of already existing associations, like the British Venture Capital Association.[1] The main reason for this may be that they need a lobby group to overcome political resistance and threatening regulations. Whatever their motives, the private equity firms' response creates an opportunity for regulatory measures to improve the transparency and accountability of buyout firms across the board.

This chapter will explain the function of soft law principles, guidelines and recommendations, specifically tailored to the governance of non-listed companies, such as private equity funds. The following questions will be addressed. Is there a credible role for best practice guidelines in improving the contractual governance arrangements of non-listed companies? Are the industry groups best placed to develop the right set of principles? Do these industry-based associations ensure the creation of optimal guidelines? What is the role of policy-makers and governmental supervisors in the creation of best practice guidelines that create integrity and awareness for the business parties and stakeholders? Answers to most of these questions can be found in practice, which already shows the emergence of distinctive guidelines and recommendations to provide greater, among other things, transparency and consistency in the valuation and reporting standards in private equity funds.

---

[1] Four of the leading US private equity funds (Blackstone, Bain Capital, Carlyle, and Kohlberg Kravis Roberts) joined the British Venture Capital Association in 2006. See *Financial Times* (P Smithin), 'Buy-out Firms Join UK Trade Group', 23 January 2007.

## 2. The Contemporary Debate on Corporate Governance

It is well documented that in reaction to the catastrophic financial collapses, US Congress promulgated the Sarbanes–Oxley Act of 2002,[2] which is designed to create improvements in governance by inducing increased oversight and monitoring of companies. The SEC followed on from Congress by promulgating new regulations needed to interpret and enforce the Act. There is no question that the recent scandals in the USA caused EU regulators also to react by devising a set of legal strategies to constrain diversions by officers, board members, and controlling shareholders of publicly listed companies (Davies 2006). Moreover, attention quickly turned to accounting and audit reforms when Parmalat collapsed with debts of €14.5 billion in December 2003. The debacle, which shattered any illusions that accounting and boardroom scandals were uniquely an American phenomenon (Enriques 2005), led regulators—who were already active on the implementation of the International Accounting Standard (IAS)—to propose additional conflicts of interest measures concerning transactions involving related parties of a company, including family controlling shareholders and key managers, and special purpose entities (SPEs).[3] At the same time, the Commission has issued a recommendation on the independence of the statutory auditor and also a directive on the duties of auditors. In Chapter 2, we discussed the recent initiatives that were announced by the EC in its May 2003 Communication on the statutory audit,[4] and will analyse in Chapter 8 the EC's efforts to increase transparency of intra-group relations and transactions with related parties and to improve disclosures about corporate practices.[5]

---

[2] Congress introduced the Sarbanes–Oxley Act of 2002 (the Act) in response to the deficiencies in the US corporate governance system exposed by Enron. The Act mandates changes in the oversight of the accounting profession and requires CEOs and CFOs to certify, on pain of criminal penalties, their firm's periodic reports and the effectiveness of internal controls, the prohibition of corporate loans to officers or directors, restrictions on stock sales by executives during certain blackout periods, and requires firms to establish an independent audit committee, of which at least one member must be a financial expert. Many of the measures are meant to deter earnings management and other forms of opportunism. For example, the certification requirement and restrictions on insider trading will certainly strengthen corporate governance, but may also create some unintended effects (diminished liquidity in company shares). Other requirements on off-balance-sheet financing and special purpose entities are crucial to limiting balance sheet manipulation. The most important changes concern independent audit committees and limitations on the provision of non-audit services.

[3] Proposal for a Directive of the European Parliament and of the Council amending Council Directives 78/660/EEC and 83/349/EEC concerning the annual accounts of certain types of companies and consolidated accounts.

[4] Communication from the Commission to the Council and the European Parliament, Reinforcing the statutory audit in the EU COM(2003) 286 final [2003] OJ C236/2.

[5] Communication from the Commission to the Council and European Parliament, On Preventing and Combating Corporate and Financial Malpractice COM(2004) 611 final 27 September 2004.

What is more, policy-makers and lawmakers have devised and adopted codes of corporate governance, which cover in varying scope and detail the protection of shareholders in publicly held corporations. In this chapter we intend to analyse the soft law measures, which we have termed here 'optional guidelines', which impose constraints on firms' conduct. Codes of conduct, of course, are designed to supplement traditional legal mechanisms, such as corporation law provisions that address the shareholders meeting, the election and removal of members of the board of management, auditing requirements, and disclosure. The attraction of codes is the greater flexibility combined with the potential to enhance the role of gatekeeper institutions who are taking steps to enforce them at the firm level. The European Corporate Governance Institute (ECGI), through its website, aims to maintain the most comprehensive and up-to-date database containing full texts of corporate governance codes from countries all over the world. This database indicates the growing popularity of corporate governance codes.

The corporate governance measures that followed the aftermath of the scandals in publicly held firms slowly but surely settle in the global business environment. Firms begin to avail themselves of corporate governance principles, codes, guidelines, and laws, thereby leaving the 'box-ticking' phase behind and turning their attention to growth and innovation (Carey and Patsalos-Fox 2006).[6] Although board members and managers of listed companies contest that there is a positive correlation between a good governance system and business performance (Chidambaran, Palia, and Zheng 2006), they nevertheless are convinced that the implementation of corporate governance measures or best practices helps to improve the accountability of the board of management and the proper supervision thereof.[7] At the same time, institutional investors and large shareholders are under a growing pressure from governmental and other official agencies, such as the World Bank, the International Monetary Fund, and the Organization of Economic Cooperation and Development (OECD) to be actively involved in a firm's decision-making process.[8] Investors increasingly tend to cast their votes at the annual general meetings of their portfolio companies. The emergence of electronic proxy and voting platforms gives the necessary impetus to solving the complex and cumbersome cross-border voting procedures. Moreover, investors that consider corporate governance a crucial factor for successful capital markets (see Figure 7.1) appear to engage with portfolio companies directly if they demand more radical changes or improvements in the governance structure of a firm. In countries with a weak corporate governance culture and regulatory framework,

---

[6] *Financial Times* (R Bruce), 'Corporate Governance: How to Make Life Both Easier and More Complex', 1 September 2006.

[7] *Financial Times* (K Burgess), 'Company Leaders Wary of Corporate Governance Rules', 17 July 2006.

[8] *Financial Times* (S Targett), 'Survey—Global Custody: Custodians are Casting Votes as They Take on a More Active Role', 6 July 2001.

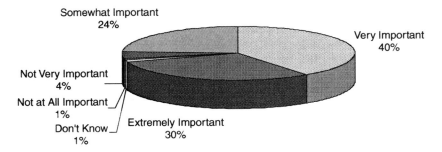

**Figure 7.1.** Importance to investors of corporate governance of portfolio companies

*Notes*: Total sample (n=322). Answers to the question: How would you describe the overall importance to your firm today of the corporate governance of portfolio companies?

*Source*: ISS 2006 Global Institutional Investor Study.

such as China, investors appear to contact a portfolio company's management directly to seek financial information or to influence decision-making and disclosure practices.[9]

Despite the antipathy to corporate governance rules and regulations, business leaders seem to recognize that corporate governance shifts from a mere compliance environment—where firms and their advisers are merely engaged in box-ticking to satisfy auditors and other financial market watchdogs—to an area in which it is viewed as an imperative for business success on a global scale. Factors like improved board structures, financial transparency and disclosure policies, and the alignment of executive pay with shareholder value play a pivotal role in the choice of investment decisions. To be sure, cumbersome and costly corporate governance measures, such as the Sarbanes–Oxley Act of 2002, spurs some directors and managers of companies to consider going private (see Figure 7.2). However, delisting is not always a pragmatic approach to the high costs attached to the implementation of corporate governance measures. Although the rules for delisting vary among stock exchanges, the exorbitant costs and regulatory restrictions prevent firms across the board from taking this step voluntarily. For instance, on the New York Stock Exchange and NASDAQ the delisting process is only set in motion when a minimum on firm size, price, publicly held shares, number of shareholders and trading volume has been reached, thereby making going private initiatives often impossible. More importantly, delisting decisions could seriously damage a firm's reputation and even cause financial difficulties if it triggers creditors to call in loans or downgrades the firm's credit rating. The upshot is that publicly held companies have no other choice but to streamline

---

[9] For instance, poor corporate governance was one of the factors that caused the decrease of the market value of Chinese listed companies (ISS 2006).

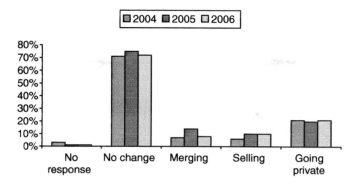

**Figure 7.2.** Strategies resulting from the implementation of the Sarbanes–Oxley Act 2002

*Notes*: Total sample 2006 (n=114). Answers to the question: As a result of the new corporate governance and public disclosure reforms implemented since the enactment of the Sarbanes–Oxley Act in 2002, is your company considering any of the following?

*Source*: Foley & Lerdner LLP, 'The Cost of Being Public in the Era of Sarbanes–Oxley', 15 June 2006.

their organizational processes according to the corporate governance rules and principles applicable in a particular jurisdiction. The fact that the compliance costs decrease indicates that firms are capable of implementing corporate governance measures effectively.[10]

There is considerable evidence that corporate governance committees across jurisdictions frequently use similar measures to address a range of common problems (Coombes and Wong 2004): (1) an active and fair protection of the rights of all shareholders; (2) an accountable management board and effective monitoring mechanisms; (3) transparent information about the financial and non-financial position of the firm; and (4) responsibility for the interests of stakeholders, including minority shareholders. It appears that the Sarbanes–Oxley Act has strongly influenced the development of corporate governance in European and Asian-Pacific markets (Ali and Gregoriou 2006). However, contrary to the mandatory force of the provisions of the Sarbanes–Oxley Act, the corporate governance codes, updates, and upgrades that arose in Europe and Asia offer a high level of flexibility by following the 'comply or explain' rule. Although firms tend to adopt and comply with the boilerplate and standardized provisions of the codes rather than explain—even though more optimal—such non-compliance (Kahan and Klausner 1997), it is submitted that the flexibility of codes prevails over the inflexible, hard law rules and regulations of the Sarbanes–Oxley Act. The development

---

[10] The average costs of being public for companies with annual revenue under $1 billion before the reform amounted to approximately $1,052,000. In 2002, the costs increased by 80% (to an estimated amount of $1,891,000). In 2005, the average costs dropped by 16% from $3,437,000 (in 2004) to $2,881,000 (in 2005). See Foley & Lardner (2006a).

of a 'comply-or-explain' practice not only gives companies the necessary room to manoeuvre, but also provides policy-makers with more leeway for adjusting the codes to the changing social and economic circumstances. Rule-based legislation tends to be overly detailed and complex. Consequently, reformers often find it difficult to make changes to existing legislation (due to standardization effects and high switching costs) (Vermeulen 2003). To be sure, principle-based codes also emphasize the need to foster standardization and awareness, but, as the standard-setting institution consists mainly of experienced individuals, the best practice principles are more accessible to customization. Table 7.1 shows that policy-makers continually review the codes' principles in light of changes in the business environment.

As indicated in Table 7.1, principle-based corporate governance codes are more responsive to economic and social change than legislative measures. Standard-setting institutions seem able to customize the existing codes in the face of demand. By doing so, companies are prepared to adopt a good governance structure despite an apparent lack of teeth of principle-based standards. Moreover, listed firms are prepared to deviate from the codes' provisions despite the fact that this could jeopardize a good corporate governance rating. A survey by the Dutch Monitoring Committee assessing the use and implementation of the corporate governance code in the Netherlands indicates that listed companies, no matter what size or nationality, explain the non-compliance with approximately 5 per cent of the best practice norms. As will be explained below, most deviations are related to the remuneration of management and supervisory board members and the term of their appointment. Furthermore, recent research on the voluntary compliance with Sarbanes–Oxley provisions clearly supports the view that companies have strong incentives to adopt or disregard governance recommendations depending on a cost-benefit assessment.[11] Initially it was argued that the 'comply or explain' approach would contribute significantly to the 'lock-in' effect in the context of rules and norms of corporate governance. The inflexibility that would result could lead to inefficiency, as the codes' provisions and mechanisms fail to respond to changes in underlying social and economic conditions. However, empirical studies are beginning to show that the implementation of codes is altering the governance practices of firms, which challenges for one thing the view that corporate governance codes involve nothing more than blueprints for box-tickers.

Indeed, consistent with the data from the Netherlands Monitoring Committee Reports (2005; 2006), we see that corporate governance practices are improving dramatically across jurisdictions in the short term. Not only is there a high overall compliance and application rate, but key characteristics of the corporate governance code in Europe have high compliance rates. It may be argued that when companies adopt good governance practices the probability of misconduct decreases and the returns on the stock are better than those with worse corporate governance (Arcot and Bruno 2006). The next subsection considers the

---

[11] *Wall Street Journal* (J Badal and P Dvorak), 'Sarbanes–Oxley Gains Adherents', 14 August 2006; Foley & Lardner (2006b).

**Table 7.1.** Customized corporate governance codes in 2005–2006 (January 2006–August 2006)

| Country | Old Code | Customized Code | Reason |
|---------|----------|-----------------|--------|
| Austria | Austrian Code of Corporate Governance November 2002 | Austrian Code of Corporate Governance (as amended on 22 February 2005) | According to the Austrian Code of Corporate Governance, the Code must be reviewed annually in the light of national and international developments and adapted, if necessary. |
| | | Austrian Code of Corporate Governance (as amended in January 2006) | |
| Cyprus | Corporate Governance Code September 2002 Addendum to the Corporate Governance Code November 2003 | Cyprus Corporate Governance Code (2nd edition, March 2006) | |
| Denmark | Recommendations for good corporate governance in Denmark (Norby Committee) December 2001 | Revised Recommendations for Corporate Governance in Denmark August 2005 | Clarification when the text is a Recommendation or a comment. This was an essential element in the process of making the Recommendations comply-or-explain proof. |
| Germany | The German Corporate Governance Code (The Cromme Code) February 2002 | Amendment to the German Corporate Governance Code ('The Cromme Code) June 2005 | Mostly text clarifications |
| | Amendment to the German Corporate Governance Code ('The Cromme Code) May 2003 | | |
| Italy | Corporate Governance Code July 2002 | Corporate Governance Code March 2006 | The structure of the Code has been profoundly changed. Each article is divided into three distinct sections (principles, application criteria, and comments) |
| Malta | Principles of Good Governance October 2001 | Principles of Good Governance for Public Interest Companies November 2005 | The 2001 Code has been reviewed and revised as a result of the experience with the former code. Moreover, there was a need to introduce a Code specifically targeted to Public Interest Companies |

Table 7.1. *(Cont.)*

| Country | Old Code | Customized Code | Reason |
|---|---|---|---|
| Norway | The Norwegian Code of Practice for Corporate Governance December 2004 | Principles of Good Governance Revised Code for Issuers of Listed Securities November 2005 The Norwegian Code of Practice for Corporate Governance (Revised 2005) December 2005 | The Norwegian Corporate Governance Board (NCGB) strives to keep the Code of Practice up to date and to promote the Code in the international corporate governance setting. |
| Portugal | Recommendation on Corporate Governance November 1999 Recommendation on Corporate Governance November 2003 (updated version) | White Book on Corporate Governance in Portugal | Update in light of international developments |
| Singapore | Code of Corporate Governance March 2001 | Code of Corporate Governance 2005 July 2005 | The Council of Corporate Disclosure and Governance reviewed and improved the 2001 Code, taking into account international developments and feedback received since the introduction of the 2001 Code |
| Slovenia | Corporate Governance Code March 2004 | Corporate Governance Code December 2005 | On the basis of a one-year experience with the Code, the initial drafters made amendments to improve the efficiency and appropriateness viewed in light of the legal and business environment. |
| United Kingdom | The Combined Code of Corporate Governance July 2003 | The Combined Code on Corporate Governance June 2006 | The changes relate in particular to remuneration committees, the treatment of votes withheld and proxy voting. |

*Source*: Adapted from ECGI (European Corporate Governance Institute)—Index of Codes (<www.ecgi.org>).

incentives of non-listed companies to adhere to corporate governance measures specifically drafted with publicly held companies in mind, thereby providing evidence that optional corporate governance principles could achieve similar effects in the area of closely held firms.

## 3. Non-listed Companies: Voluntary Compliance with Corporate Governance Measures

It is submitted that policy-makers and lawmakers, to the extent that they possess few revenue-based incentives to research the specific characteristics of non-listed companies, are inclined to recommend the application of the corporate governance structures tailored to publicly held firms. A compelling argument is advanced by policy-makers and practitioners who have indicated that the key drivers of effective corporate governance in publicly held companies also serve a similar function in their non-listed counterparts. In this view, a properly designed single set of standards for listed companies is arguably sufficient to evaluate and improve the governance structure of both listed and non-listed companies. Given the flexibility and non-binding nature of the codes and the feedback mechanisms which guarantee that firms will have the best standards available, there is little risk of negative externalities affecting either class of firms unduly.

This argument holds true for the most part. Current corporate governance measures and discussions appear to create awareness among non-listed companies about the positive impact of good governance on firm performance and value creation. Generally, corporate governance reforms have resulted in more value-creation-oriented board members in both small and large listed and non-listed companies. This suggests that there is a great appeal among non-listed companies to the utilization of existing corporate governance mechanisms. For instance, an increasing number of these companies in the United States are implementing or intend to implement parts of Sarbanes-Oxley.

While many of the corporate governance provisions are imposed on closely held firms by governmental agencies, investors, insurance companies, lenders, and other third parties, Figure 7.3 shows that non-listed companies have high-powered incentives to voluntarily comply with corporate governance provisions, even if these firms have no intention to go public or merge with a public company in the near future.[12] Firms are more convinced that Sarbanes–Oxley-type internal controls (1) reduce financial/reporting errors; (2) help firms follow their business policies and performance; (3) assist in tracking inventory; and (4) signal potential weaknesses within the firm. It might be argued that firms are willing

---

[12] Non-listed companies that (1) report to regulatory agencies; (2) rely heavily on lenders or insurers; (3) deal with disgruntled shareholders; or (4) conduct business with governmental agencies are most affected by provisions of the Sarbanes–Oxley Act (Foley & Lardner 2005).

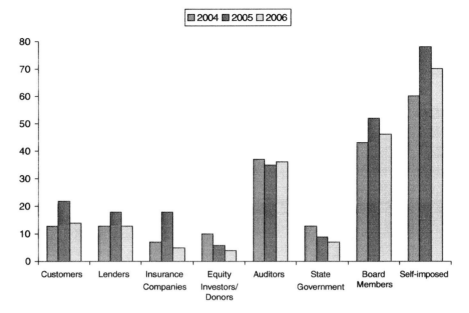

**Figure 7.3.** Who create the incentives to adopt new corporate governance measures in private and non-profit companies?

*Notes*: Total sample January 2006 (n=56—20 non-profit organizations and 36 for-profit closely held companies).

*Source*: Foley & Lardner, 2006a.

to comply with Sarbanes–Oxley provisions only to the point that the benefits exceed the compliance costs (Butler and Ribstein 2006).

Figure 7.4 contains information about both non-profit organizations and non-listed for-profit companies. We see that most pressure to comply with Sarbanes–Oxley provisions comes from inside the company (self-imposed, board members and auditors). These internal pressures are stronger in non-profit organizations (in 2006: self-imposed (80%), board members (55%), and auditors (45%)) than in non-listed companies (in 2006: self-imposed (64%), board members (31%), and auditors (42%)). This difference could partly be explained by the fact that non-profit organizations often appoint directors of publicly held firms who have more experience with the implementation and coordination of corporate governance rules. Moreover, non-profit organizations have to account to more stakeholders as compared to non-listed companies. Thus, the former organizations have stronger incentives to adopt aspects of the corporate governance regulation. Finally, this research shows that auditors tend to push larger firms (56%), which are character-ized by more complex financial statements and audits, harder to employ internal

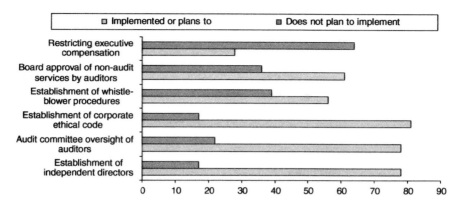

**Figure 7.4.** Implementation of corporate governance provisions

*Notes*: Total sample January 2006 (n=56—20 non-profit organizations and 36 for-profit closely held companies). Due to rounding, not all percentages add up to 100%.

*Source*: Foley & Lardner, 2006a.

governance controls than small firms (28%). Smaller firms, on the other hand, are more likely to impose corporate governance rules on themselves.

Thus there is no reason to assume that non-listed companies will only abide by corporate governance rules if a legal requirement exists to do so. Nor does the effectiveness of corporate governance principles depend on a mandatory disclosure rule, which demands an explanation of non-compliance. Policy-makers could rely more on the carrot than the stick. To the extent that corporate governance techniques add value to the organization and its performance, adoption will be the preferred strategy. At the same time, aspects that are potentially disruptive to the internal affairs of non-listed companies, leading to costly deficiencies and inconsistencies, are generally not implemented (see Figure 7.4).

The results presented in Figure 7.5 support the one-size-fits-all approach. It shows that the establishment of an audit committee, more effective board practices, and introduction of a corporate ethical code are conceived to be equally important in the area of non-listed companies. Nevertheless, non-listed firms tend to disregard some provisions that have been drafted with mainly publicly held corporations in mind. For instance, restricting executive compensation is not necessary in a firm where shareholders are supposed to be directly and actively involved in monitoring management decisions. However, even if companies are able to efficiently make these cost-benefit decisions for each aspect of the corporate governance regime, a 'one-size-fits-all' approach may nevertheless be inappropriate for some non-listed companies, significantly reducing certainty and business value. Clearly, institutions established to counter and limit the managerial agency problem, such as fully independent non-executive board members as a monitoring device, are not always a priority in family-owned businesses and joint ventures. What is more, the code provisions that apply to listed companies are often silent when it comes to conflicts between members of private firms, strategies for succession planning, and accessing outside equity capital. As already mentioned in Chapters 1 and 2 and set out in more detail in Table 7.2, there are divergent governance strategies for non-listed and listed firms which arguably call out for a separate set of recommendations.

Indeed, it becomes clear from Table 7.2 that the governance of non-listed companies like joint ventures and family firms is very complicated. Whilst the current corporate governance measures may provide an effective nexus for the arrangements between shareholders, managers, creditors, and other stakeholders, it does not, correspondingly, offer a clear solution for the problems that occur in non-listed companies. The corporate governance measures for publicly held firms are therefore poorly tailored to fit the specific needs of non-listed companies in the area of the design on the ownership structure, 'shareholder' activism, deadlock, and other conflict situations. Yet, the corporate governance hype arguably creates awareness and encourages parties in non-listed companies to improve the governance structure of their firms voluntarily. In this view, the 'gaps' in most corporate governance initiatives do not necessarily justify the introduction of distinctive guidelines for closely held companies. Indeed, as Chapter 5 describes, parties usually engage in an *ex ante* search for the contractual terms that improve their governance structure and maximize the value of their investment in a closely held business setting. Moreover, parties in a closely held business must usually deal with information asymmetries and very different expectations about the risk and return *ex ante*. This imbalance makes closely held ventures prone to conflict. Yet, the use of standard, but complex, contractual clauses and the possibility of using flexible business forms, which optimally facilitate the development of a fruitful and lasting collaboration, seem to suggest that parties often have incentives to follow good corporate governance practices without being confronted with special guidelines. Despite the commitment-enhancing effects of these provisions, contracting infirmities will often persist as these mechanisms appear to favour parties with the greatest bargaining power. Moreover, overconfidence, over-optimism, and excitement about the prospects of the venture prevent business parties from engaging in contractual planning and contemplating methods for addressing future developments.

Nevertheless, the governance failures that showed up in large, publicly held firms, have captured the political and scholarly interest. Reflection on the burgeoning corporate governance reforms in the United States and Europe has generated a growing body of research on the function and influence of legal rules and institutions that influence the performance and competitiveness of companies which must respond to rapid market and technological changes (Butler and Ribstein 2006; Armour and McCahery 2006). In the contemporary debate on corporate governance, the importance of non-listed companies has largely been ignored. Major developments on the horizon, however, could trigger a

Table 7.2. The anatomy of corporate governance: listed versus non-listed companies

| Governance in typical public companies | Additional governance challenges for joint ventures | Additional governance challenges for family-owned firms |
|---|---|---|
| **Board composition** | | |
| Board members are not employed by shareholders; represent interest of all shareholders equally. Independent directors are key to proper governance. | Board members are typically employed by one or more of the shareholders, creating potential conflicts of interest. *Better model: appoint at least one outsider director who promotes the interest of the JV business.* | Board members are typically family members. Better model: include outside directors to obtain a mixture of family views and strategic perspectives. |
| **Board roles** | | |
| Board focuses on approval of major strategic decisions, CEO succession, risk management. | Board must manage conflicts between shareholders, secure resources from shareholders, monitor transfer prices/parent transactions, manage career path of management team. | Boards must set the strategies and goals, while taking the special interest of the family into account. |
| **Decision-making** | | |
| Investors unite in desire to maximize shareholder returns, manage risks. | Key decisions (eg strategy setting, capital planning) require agreement among a few large shareholders, which may have very different interests, financial constraints, view of market. | Key decisions require the involvement of family members. It is important that all generations are directly or indirectly involved in the decision-making process. A family forum could serve as a platform for communication and consultation. |
| **Management team** | | |
| Management team members are accountable to CEO and board. | Key members of venture's management team (eg CEO, COO) are usually employees of one parent; many likely to see future career tied to returning to that parent. | Key members are often family members who are accountable to the board—which preferably consists of family members and outsiders. |
| **Resource flows** | | |
| Venture does not depend on shareholders for any operational inputs. | Venture depends (at times extensively) on one or both parents for key inputs, services, business functions (eg raw materials, administrative support, sales force). | Venture depends largely on bank and internal (family) financing. |

Table 7.2. *(Cont.)*

| Governance in typical public companies | Additional governance challenges for joint ventures | Additional governance challenges for family-owned firms |
|---|---|---|
| **Ownership structure** | | |
| Market model of corporate governance: widely dispersed shareholders. | Multi-ownership. Joint venture partners own the shares in the company. | Family members directly or indirectly hold most or all of the shares. |
| Control model of corporate governance: concentrated ownership. | The equity structure is the most important and difficult negotiating issue in joint venture agreements. | The challenge is succession planning and keeping the next generations involved. |
| Shareholders can dispose of their shares in the stock market. | Legal professionals are typically against 50–50 joint ventures, while business parties are in favour of equal joint ventures. | |
| **Shareholder activism** | | |
| Measures are advanced to encourage shareholder activism—electronic voting, proxy voting, active institutional investors. | Participants start as active shareholders. Improved governance arrangements should enable shareholders to effectively change the strategy, scope, financial arrangements and operations of the joint venture. | Corporate governance should create awareness among members of different generations. Its main objective is to supply incentives to educate family members about the ins and outs of the family business. |
| **Deadlock and other conflicts** | | |
| Board members owe fiduciary duties. Derivative and class actions. | A bundle of reciprocal commitments and penalties could prevent deadlocks and disputes. Contractual mechanisms, such as 'shogun' and 'auction' provisions, are last resort options to resolve conflicts and deadlocked issues. | Business conflicts are magnified by emotionally charged familial relationships. A family forum (and outside mediator) could be used as a bonding place which would help resolve conflicts in its initial stages. |

*Source:* Adapted from a Table published in Bamford and Ernst (2005).

transformation of the corporate governance movement, refocused on the typical problems of non-listed firms.

## 4. The Future of Corporate Governance: 'Refocus on Non-listed Companies

It is certainly reasonable to infer that rules and principles that (1) ensure the basis for an effective corporate governance framework; (2) define the rights of shareholders and the responsibilities of management; and (3) set out guidelines for enhanced disclosure and transparency, could also improve the governance of non-listed firms. In fact, many of the 'best practice' rules and principles are imposed on non-listed firms by government, investors, insurance companies, lenders, and others. This leads, however, to the question of whether such a 'one-size-fits-all' approach to corporate governance regulation is justified in economic and social terms.

For instance, under the ongoing pressure of competitive global markets, joint ventures and strategic alliances have become an important means of limiting risks, decreasing costs, and increasing economies of scale and scope. Many large firms enter into worldwide alliances and joint ventures to obtain technological know-how. Ten to twenty per cent of a large firm's revenues, income, or assets come from joint venture activities (Bamford and Ernst 2005). In addition, globalization and consumerism increasingly push small and medium-sized enterprises to get involved in international joint ventures, both among themselves and together with larger multinationals, when access to manufacturing, distribution, and other assets is either too difficult or costly to create internally. At the same time, these joint ventures and alliances encourage the further development of new technologies and the reduction of international barriers.

Even though the benefits of joint ventures are relatively straightforward, they are, for structural reasons, highly sensitive to conflict-of-interest situations. In terms of limiting these problems, parties may choose from a range of economic and legal instruments and institutions to organize their business relationships. Contractual provisions usually create a relationship of mutual reliance.[13] Relationships in joint ventures are mainly sustained by self-enforcing ingrained norms of honesty and reputation. However, in many cases, the reliance on mutual expectations and implicit norms cannot prevent the failure of a joint venture. As discussed in Chapter 5, the majority of the joint ventures break down or fail within seven years due to the lack of trust at the start and the difficulty in gaining trust midstream due to parties' conflicting interests.

[13] See Chapter 5.

Naturally a well-thought-out governance system can facilitate the development and implementation of trust norms in joint ventures, but so far these mechanisms and techniques are largely ignored. Legal best practice and organizational issues are usually kept away from the negation room. However, in an era of growing emphasis on corporate governance issues, it is only to be expected that firms interested in sustainable growth and risk management will extend the need for good governance beyond publicly held companies. In order to assist these companies to fully exploit the new investment opportunities and effectively deal with the information uncertainties and other risks, joint venture governance guidelines could assist parties in devising effective governance provisions as part of their long-term strategy to foster investment and innovation.

But there is more, the challenges confronting advanced economies, as well as emerging markets, and large conglomerates from China's cheap factors of production demands policy-makers focus on the job-creating sector of the economy. In many jurisdictions, family-owned businesses—in which a family has either significant influence or a controlling stake—are the leading force in many sectors of the economy. Family-owned businesses continue to be highly competitive, particularly in emerging markets, due to their informal structure that provides: (1) a timely and effective decision-making; (2) a deep and intimate understanding of their local market; (3) close ties with regulators and government officials; and (4) strong horizontal and vertical relations in the market. Despite these built-up competitive advantages, family-owned firms are under increased pressure as a consequence of market liberalization and competition from large multinational companies. As the market has transformed the ability of family-owned companies to compete effectively, they are less able to draw on previous strengths, which eventually leads either to bankruptcy or a change in control. Nevertheless, some family-owned businesses with clear governance rules and guidelines, a strong brand, or access to leading-edge technologies are likely to survive and remain successful. While there are a number of successful strategies for family-owned businesses, policy-makers and lawmakers should concentrate their resources on developing solutions that enable families to embrace strategies that promote their long-term success. Not only will improved governance provide a more effective means to deal with family matters that affect business, but it will also free up managerial resources that are necessary to run the business well, and thereby make possible capital-intensive work to remain in a country.

Empirical research supports the view that policy-makers and lawmakers must become more engaged in providing non-listed companies with a governance framework that will foster strong decision-making, accountability, transparency, and ultimately firm performance. An improved corporate governance framework arguably encourages private equity and venture capital investment in fast-developing, high-potential companies and hence facilitates the provision of sustainable, high-quality jobs. For example, Figure 7.5 shows that job creation of venture-backed firms over the period between 2000 and 2004 grew by an average annual rate of 5.4 per cent, which is eight times the annual growth rate of total employment in the EU. At the same time, the rapid pace of technological change and the decreasing international barriers to trade over the past decade have not only created new strategic and organizational opportunities for firms, but have also made them more vulnerable to risks.

Thus, a shift in the focus from publicly held companies to non-listed companies is important, because, as we have argued earlier, the preponderance of firms worldwide are non-listed and ownership and control are usually not completely severed. Even though governance is but one of many determinants of investment and expansion decisions by firm owners and investors, there is little doubt that the core considerations affecting these decisions are operational and macroeconomic. Still, the changed economic environment in which firms operate makes them increasingly sensitive to governance issues. It is, therefore, necessary to obtain a better appreciation of the design and content of the legal governance framework of non-listed companies.

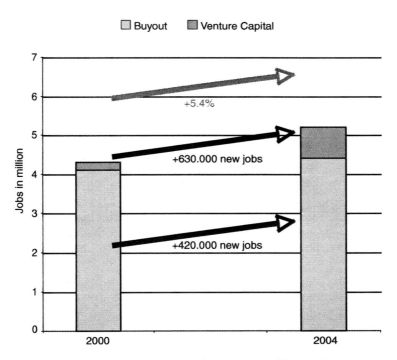

**Figure 7.5.** Job creation by private equity and venture capital financed companies

Source: CEFS/EVCA, 'Employment Contribution of Private Equity and Venture Capital in Europe', November 2005.

This is confirmed by the Basel II accord, which aims to govern risk for financial service organizations and embraces a comprehensive approach to bank supervision. Basel II demands that banks and other financial firms have internal monitoring systems and processes in place that make them Basel II compliant. This process may very well speed up the awareness and demand for corporate governance principles in non-listed companies across the board, as it arguably induces non-listed companies to comply with best practice principles as part of the process of credit rating and risk assessment. If we look, for instance, at the corporate governance progression matrix developed by the International Finance Corporation—an organization that provides debt and equity to the private sector in developing countries—we see that corporate governance issues already play an important role in making investment decisions.

That said, it is predicted that the developments that are described here will slowly but surely induce policy-makers to refocus their attention to the governance needs of non-listed companies. In fact, we can already foresee a pattern of demand for and supply of corporate governance institutions that prompts policy-makers to devise and introduce corporate governance rules and best practice principles that are better equipped to tackle difficult problems and challenges typical to family businesses, joint ventures, and venture capital-backed firms. In the next section, the role guidelines are currently playing is discussed.

## 5. Optional Guidelines for Non-listed Companies

This section will explain the function of soft law principles, guidelines and recommendations, specifically tailored to non-listed companies, in assisting firms to overcome contractual bargaining problems and the uncertainties connected with the formation and operation of the business. The following questions will be addressed. Is there a credible role for best practice guidelines in improving the contractual governance arrangements of non-listed firms? Why are guidelines drafted for the benefit of listed companies not sufficiently robust or even remotely appropriate for advising legal practitioners when serving the needs of their non-listed sector clients? Does each industry segment require the introduction of governance guidelines specific to the industry and its business model? Which institution or group is best placed to develop the right set of principles? Do governmental corporate governance committees or industry-based associations ensure the creation of optimal guidelines? Having seen that the procedures involved for the creation of best practice guidelines create integrity and awareness for the business parties and stakeholders, the question is whether what matters most is the substantive variation in guidelines across the industry sector or the standardization achieved by a general code that focuses on non-listed companies across the board.

Answers to most of these questions can be found in practice which already shows the emergence of distinctive guidelines and recommendations for private, non-listed, companies (see Table 7.3). For instance, a separate corporate governance code for non-listed companies was introduced in Belgium in September 2005. Experts immediately praised the code for its fresh perspective and educative value to firms (OECD 2005). However, there were some doubts about the willingness of non-listed and family-owned companies to even consider incorporating these recommendations in their organizational structure. The lack of substantive guidance and potential for enforcement made firms question the value added to adopting it. Nevertheless, the core recommendations were created by a well-seasoned governance committee represented by top business leaders and legal practitioners, under the chairmanship of Baron Buysse, which were sensitive to the dynamics of the environment in which these firms compete.

In January 2006, the Central Chamber of Commerce of Finland published an official statement to encourage larger non-listed companies to adopt the corporate governance recommendations of the listed firms by following the 'comply-or-explain' principle. At the same time, it was recognized that the general corporate governance recommendations were badly suited to most closely held businesses. For that purpose, the Board of Directors of the Chamber of Commerce issued a so-called 'Agenda for Improving Corporate Governance of Unlisted Companies' (based on proposals from a working group that was established on 18 October 2004 to study corporate governance practices in unlisted companies). Like the Buysse Code, the compliance with the agenda items is not mandatory, nor are firms obliged to explain any deviations. Its main purpose is to provide companies with guidelines that help them evaluate their business policy and strategy. The voluntary nature of the recommendations is important in preventing an environment in which legal exposure hampers the effectiveness and willingness of, for instance, independent board members, to help improve firm performance.[14] Although both initiatives have the same goal, the topics that the codes address differ in some important areas. As we can see in Table 7.3, the Buysse Code draws attention to the relationship with third parties outside the firm, whereas the Finnish recommendations follow a more traditional framework which could help improve the internal governance structure of non-listed companies across the board.[15]

---

[14] See *Het Financieele Dagblad* (P Couwenbergh and F Rolvink), 'Commissaris vreest risico's van het werk', 6 October 2006 (referring to a KPMG global survey of approximately 1,200 audit committee members). Regulatory measures that are mandatory in nature intensify the workload of audit committee members and, consequently, increase the legal exposure.

[15] Although it is argued in this chapter that non-listed companies have incentives to voluntarily comply with corporate governance measures that improve the internal organization of the firm (including the protection of the minority), such incentives may not be present in the case of creditor protection and the openness to third parties. Non-listed companies, in particular smaller firms, seem to be reluctant to open their books to the public (see Chapters 2 and 3). The unfamiliarity of firms with the provisions that address the relationship with third parties in the Buysse Code evinces

**Table 7.3.** Corporate governance guidelines for non-listed firms

| Country | Code | Introduction | Topics |
|---|---|---|---|
| Belgium | Code Buysse (Corporate Governance for Non-listed Companies) | September 2005 | Judicious use of outside advisers<br>An active board of directors<br>A high-performance management<br>Involved shareholders<br>External audit<br>The shareholders' agreement<br>Publication of the corporate governance rule<br>The family forum<br>The family charter<br>Consultation with the shareholders<br>Succession<br>Resolving conflicts<br>The relationship with banks and financial institutions<br>The relationship with suppliers<br>The relationship with customers<br>The relationship with personnel<br>The government as partner |
| Finland | Improving Corporate Governance of Unlisted Companies | January 2006 | General meeting of shareholders<br>The board of directors<br>The managing director<br>Compensation systems<br>Internal control and risk management<br>Audit<br>The articles of association<br>Shareholders' agreements<br>Redemption and approval clauses<br>Communication and information<br>Change-of-generation in family enterprises |

| | | | |
|---|---|---|---|
| Lebanon | The Lebanese Code of Corporate Governance | June 2006 | Shareholders' rights and obligations<br>Board of directors, structures, responsibilities and prerogatives<br>Auditing and related aspects of corporate transparency<br>Appendices:<br>List of shareholders' rights<br>Shareholders' rights to information<br>The rights of shareholders with regard to shareholders' meetings<br>Board composition and minority shareholders<br>Governance of family-owned enterprises<br>The board committees<br>Directors' charter and duties<br>Related party transactions |
| Switzerland | Governance in Family Firms | December 2006 | Family governance<br>• Family forum<br>• Information and communication<br>• Succession<br>Corporate governance<br>• Structure and organization<br>• Culture and incentives<br>• Key persons<br>• Succession<br>Public governance<br>• Customers<br>• Employees<br>• Investors<br>• Partners<br>• Government |

In June 2006 and December 2006 respectively, Lebanon and Switzerland followed suit. With the introduction of the Code, the Lebanese Transparency Association aims at professionalizing family-owned firms by encouraging the adoption of family adapted governance structures, such as a family council or family assembly, to enhance sustainability, while at the same time reducing the dependence on family relationships in the firm's decision-making process. In Switzerland, the *Vereinigung der Privaten Aktiengesellschaften* (VPAG), Prager Dreifuss, and Continuum AG drafted guidelines for family firms with three aspects in mind: the belief that (1) self-regulation provides family firms with the much-needed flexibility; (2) the guidelines should be complementary to the Swiss corporate governance code for listed companies; and (3) the members of family business should be involved in the drafting process. By following these drafting principles, the draftsmen were able to provide companies with well-conceived and well-drafted guidelines that encourage clarity and stability to the critical governance issues in family businesses.

Another 'soft law' example is the launch of the European Venture Capital Association (EVCA) Corporate Governance Guidelines for the Management of Privately Held Companies in 2005 (European Venture Capital Association 2005). Designed in consultation with industry experts, the EVCA guidelines provide a set of optional measures that focus on the staged investment decisions of venture capital and private equity funds and the contractual circumstances surrounding these investments. In contrast to family-owned firms, these guidelines focus on meeting the governance concerns of venture capital-backed firms. For example provisions that enunciate the duties and responsibilities in relation to the design and execution of corporate strategy are a core feature of the recommendations. These corporate governance recommendations work in tandem with other standards and guidelines in order to provide greater transparency and consistency in the private equity and venture capital industry. The EVCA members should follow reporting guidelines, valuation guidelines, governing principles, a code of conduct, and corporate governance recommendations. (European Venture Capital Association 2003; 2006a; 2006b) Each of these documents addresses issues that occur on a different level of the investment process. The code of conduct obviously applies to the general partners as fund managers. The reporting and valuation guidelines set out recommendations intended to represent common practice on the content of reports to limited partners. The governing guidelines also aim at streamlining the relationship between investors and fund managers. As noted the corporate governance recommendations play a role in the actual investment decisions.

that non-listed companies are to a large extent unaware of the importance of corporate governance mechanisms designed to protect creditors and other third parties. The survey by UNIZO (Dossier Corporate Governance: De Code Buysse 1 year later) shows that less than 30% of the non-listed companies in Belgium are aware of the code's recommendations to improve third party relations.

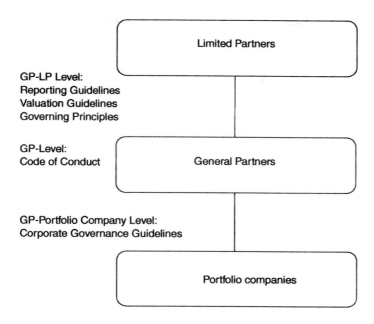

GP-LP Level:
Reporting Guidelines
Valuation Guidelines
Governing Principles

GP-Level:
Code of Conduct

GP-Portfolio Company Level:
Corporate Governance Guidelines

**Figure 7.6.** Interaction among the EVCA guidelines
*Source:* Adapted from EVCA, 2003, 2005, 2006a, 2006b.

We can thus distinguish between the two types of recommendations (industry-based versus national-oriented) for non-listed companies. The question naturally arises: which approach is the best alternative? Although industry-based guidelines are theoretically better able to address some industry-specific problems and issues, thereby promoting performance and professionalism in firms, national-oriented codes can ensure that the principles are more suitably designed to interact with the economic and social environment as well as the legal rules and institutions in a particular jurisdiction. Both sets of guidelines contain provisions—on the different ownership and control structures of non-listed companies, the composition of the board of management, transparency requirements, accessing outside capital, and strategies for conflict resolution—that arguably educate and train board members and shareholders on becoming competent and reliable business parties in both growing and mature non-listed companies. It goes without saying that a special set of guidelines induces companies to pay increasing attention to the importance of strong and professional governance structures in thriving and surviving in a rapidly changing and internationalizing world.

**Table 7.4.** Adoption of the Buysse Code recommendations after one year

| | | | |
|---|---|---|---|
| Are you prepared to appoint outside directors? | Yes: 39% | No: 44% | No Answer: 17% |
| How many board meetings are convened on a yearly basis? | Yearly: 40% | Less than 4 times a year: 12% | Quarterly 26% or Monthly 22% |
| Do you make a judicious use of outsider advisers? | Yes: 68% | No: 29% | No Answer: 3% |
| Have you set up a consultative committee? | Yes: 8% | No: 88% | No Answer: 4% |

*Source*: Data from Foley & Lardner 2006a.

Besides the enhancing effect on the adoption of the concepts of good governance, optional industry guidelines could serve another important goal. These guidelines could be used as a self-regulatory mechanism in response to increased political pressures for greater disclosure requirements and the openness of the market. Although voluntary by nature, guidelines could form a code of conduct that could be used by the industry as a 'sword of Damocles' in the event of non-compliance. If non-compliers were expelled from the industry's association or appear on some kind of blacklist which is publicly available, the voluntary guidelines would arguably have a mandatory effect. The advantage of this approach over legislative measures is the flexibility and adaptability of the regulations.

Of course, there are also several advantages in putting the responsibility of the design of optional guidelines in the hands of national-oriented committees, groups, and other associations. In addition to economies of scale, the publicity of the drafting process reduces the information costs for potential users of the guidelines. Moreover, new networks are more likely to arise around these national-oriented products. Indeed, the first results of a survey by UNIZO (*Unie van Zelfstandige Ondernemers*) in Belgium on the application of the Buysse Code (one year after its introduction) among 308 Flemish small and medium-sized enterprises indicate that its recommendations became as widely known as any corporate governance code for listed companies. Approximately 70 per cent of the Flemish companies are aware of the existence of a separate set of corporate governance recommendations and 20 per cent comply with some of its provisions. Even though critics and opponents of the Buysse Code rightly cast doubt on its success (pointing to the disappointing implementation rate), the project will arguably generate network benefits, such as customs and practices, that assist in interpreting and adopting the code's recommendations. In fact, UNIZO—supported by the Flemish Ministry of Social Economy and Belgium's largest employers' organization and trade association Agoria—introduced measures to further improve the corporate governance of non-listed companies by drawing attention to Buysse's recommendations in May 2007. The most important aspect is the publication and dissemination of a checklist that helps to assess a firm's need to implement the corporate governance recommendations. Such a checklist was requested by 68 per cent of the surveyed companies. As expected, this demand is higher in smaller companies with 10–49 employees (89%).[16]

To give an indication of the impact of the Buysse Code one year after its introduction, the survey by UNIZO supplies us with information on four important recommendations in the Buysse Code (see Table 7.4). First, even though in non-listed companies a manager's competence is more important than his or her independence from other managers and controlling shareholders, the Code advises the appointment of outside directors. Second, the Code emphasizes the importance of having at least four board meetings. Third, the Code recommends that entrepreneurs should make judicious use of outside advisers. Finally, it is advisable to set up a consultative committee that could support the board of management in its decision-making and governance responsibilities. To be sure, the survey shows mixed results on the implementation of the corporate governance recommendations and guidelines that are reflected in the Buysse Code. However, it is only to be expected that the 2007 measures will lead to a broader acceptance and wider application of the corporate governance recommendations. For instance, 30 per cent of the surveyed companies were interested in establishing a consultative committee if they received more information and guidance on this topic.

If we accept the idea that corporate governance guidelines for non-listed companies could create awareness and provide for stronger governance structures, then a proliferation of codes, whether industry based or national oriented, is likely to further stimulate discussion and feedback leading to the cross-fertilization and refinement in the code-making processes. Parallel work by standard-setting institutions, such as corporate governance committees and industry associations, could be viewed as effective and appropriate because they arguably produce clearer and more defined norms that allow a firm to be better able to identify and address key factors for its long-term success on the one hand, while introducing standards that reflect the ever-changing conditions of the business environment on the other. Moreover, this process serves to limit the effects of lock-in obsolescence when code-producing institutions are engaged in the continuous revision of the governance guidelines against the background of economic and social change so as to draft up-to-date and successful recommendations.

---

[16] The checklist, which is available at <www.behoorlijkbestuur.be> (in Dutch), enables firms to assess their own governance against the code's provisons.

## 6. Conclusion

It is difficult to resist the conclusion that 'corporate governance' has become an integral part of the day-to-day decision-making processes of listed companies. Even though many corporate governance measures are principle based, providing firms with the necessary leeway and discretion to decide to comply with or explain deviations from best practice norms, firms are aware of the importance of an effective and improved governance structure. The fact that policy-makers keep the codes up-to-date contributes to firms' willingness to take a corporate governance project seriously and adopt its recommendations.

This trend is exemplified by the increasing number of non-listed companies voluntarily complying with cumbersome Sarbanes–Oxley provisions. To be sure, the application of corporate governance norms devised for listed companies could very well lead to some undesired spill-over effects on non-listed companies. However, these companies are to a large extent capable of drafting and adopting contractual mechanisms to create credible commitments that help to protect investors and others against the abusive tactics of a firm's agents. Indeed, examples in the area of private equity funds, joint ventures and family businesses portrayed a range of contractual arrangements through which business parties could be encouraged to resolve their differences and conflicts before resorting to a more costly and uncertain judicial process.

In this respect, 'new company law' developments, which offer the contracting parties more flexibility and accessibility, are likely to occur more rapidly and with higher-quality results. Increasingly, legislatures in many jurisdictions are realizing the importance of the role of hybrid business forms in transaction planning and organizing optimal corporate governance structures. Yet, we have shown that even if new company law rules are sufficiently flexible to enable business parties to contract into the desired organizational structure, some of the parties, in particular family firms, may not be aware of specific measures that could improve a firm's performance.

Thus, an optional set of recommendations could play a pivotal role in the awareness creation of the importance of good governance practices. Such a set could, for instance, contain provisions about the benefits of educating and training board members and shareholders to become competent and reliable players in non-listed companies. Although the first empirical results arising from a survey conducted in Belgium show a mixed picture on the impact of voluntary-based corporate governance measures for non-listed companies, the network-creating capabilities of these initiatives confirm the anticipated productivity effects for non-listed companies overall.

In this chapter, we have set out six important conclusions for improving the corporate governance framework of non-listed companies and for developing incentives for these firms to adopt a variety of corporate governance measures:

(1) There is no reason to assume that non-listed companies will only abide by corporate governance rules and principles if they are required to do so. Moreover, the effectiveness of corporate governance measures does not depend on a mandatory disclosure rule, which demands an explanation of non-compliance. Policy-makers should therefore rely more on the carrot than the stick. It seems that non-listed companies are willing to comply with corporate governance norms to the point that benefits exceed the compliance costs.

(2) The use of standard, but complicated, contractual clauses and the employment of new flexible business forms, which optimally facilitate the development of a fruitful and lasting collaboration, suggest that parties have ample incentives to follow good corporate governance practices without being confronted with special guidelines.

(3) However, transaction costs and information asymmetries may prevent the emergence of effective and optimal governance solutions. It is argued that an optional set of corporate governance recommendations could contribute to the education of non-listed companies and assure the steady and healthy growth of these businesses.

(4) Indeed, non-listed companies implement or intend to implement mechanisms that ensure that (a) financial statements fairly present the performance of the business; (b) independent and knowledgeable directors and/or supervisors are appointed; (c) audit committees are established; and (d) strong internal control systems and processes reduce business risks and lower costs.

(5) Industry guidelines, such as the array of standards introduced by the European Venture Capital Association, could head off legislative pressures not only by imposing greater disclosure requirements, but also by codifying and publicizing best practice standards. The latter could temper third party concerns about concealed investment practices. The upshot is that policy-makers can reduce the uncertainties they face by relying on the information that industry groups convey through best practice guidelines and other sources (Grossman and Helpman 2001).

(6) Finally, national-oriented initiatives, which already emerged in Belgium and Finland, hold out the prospects of creating a dynamic and sustainable network of business practices and advice tailored to the needs of non-listed companies. In order to be effective, however, policy-makers should draft coherent standards that are flexible, but specific enough to provide meaningful guidance and practical solutions to a variety of non-listed companies. Moreover, the corporate governance recommendations should ideally contain guidelines as to when and how to use them.

# 8

# Hybrid Business Forms and the Regulation of Illicit Transactions

## 1. Introduction

As we have seen earlier, flexible corporate forms and hybrid business vehicles are diverse and serve a range of complex needs for business parties. At their core, they allow business people to carry on important commercial activities. Organizing commercial activities through these vehicles solves a number of contracting problems while contributing to the development of a sophisticated and complex commercial environment. We have seen that the flexibility and adaptability of these business entities to accommodate the financial and organizational needs of entrepreneurs and investors could contribute to the deepening of financial markets. Irrespective of how effective these forms might be for meeting the needs of a broad range of businesses and investors, there have been increasing concerns about the degree to which these forms are used for fraud, tax evasion, money laundering, and other illegal or abusive transactions. For quite some time, many developed countries' financial and banking systems have become more international and, in important respects, encouraged the development of nearby off-shore financial centres. Now that these centres have become well established and accessible for most business people, a number of individuals and opportunistic investors, criminal organizations, and others have taken advantage of insufficient regulation and gate-keeping in these jurisdictions to perpetrate a wide range of illegal or illicit activities.[1]

It is clear, however, that the success of these suspicious activities depends not only on inadequate supervision, bank secrecy laws, and other facilitating mechanisms, but equally on the misuse of the limited liability vehicles. Some of the major offshore jurisdictions have encouraged investors to move capital and use their financial institutions by creating legislation that effectively restricts the

---

[1] *Financial Times* (M Peel) 'Corruption Claims Taint Island Tax Haven', 8 August 2007 (corruption in Bermuda could benefit Cayman Islands and other offshore jurisdictions in attracting new and existing businesses that wish to avoid any reputational damage that could arise from a recent scandal involving questionable accounting practices and fraudulent deals attributed to the Prime Minister).

identity of the beneficial owner of the company. There are a number of company law rules that make it difficult to establish the true ownership of a company: (1) bearer shares; (2) nominee shareholders; (3) nominee directors; (4) chains of corporate vehicles; and (5) intermediaries. Along with these instruments for achieving anonymity, there are also a variety of legal measures, such as restrictions on gatekeepers to assist regulators with determining the true identity of parties, that allow money launderers and other pursuing criminal schemes to invest with minimal scrutiny.

In the *Enron* case, for example, the underlying problem was the prevalence of significant related party transactions involving high-ranking officers of the company.[2] Since independent parties would not provide economic hedges for its merchant investments, Enron engaged in hedging transactions with related entities that in theory allowed Enron to accomplish its temporary accounting objectives of not reporting any decline in the value of the investments. Since the hedges lacked economic substance, the temporary accounting results were unsustainable and eventually required the reporting of significant losses that surprised the marketplace. These transactions not only furnished these officers with the possibility to enrich themselves at the expense of the company, but also provided short-term accounting benefits that enabled Enron to materially overstate its earnings. Enron exploited accounting benefits that would not have been available in arm's length transactions with third parties.

Likewise, Parmalat's underlying problems were due to the massive fraud that was facilitated by the prevalence of special purpose entities (SPEs) and offshore subsidiaries that were used by the managers and officers to carry out illicit related party transactions (Bratton 2002; Coffee 2005; Schwarcz 2002). But, unlike Enron, it was Parmalat's family-controlled management and advisers that structured the group's various financial arrangements to enrich members of the Tanzi family at the expense of the shareholders and creditors (Ferrarini and Giudici 2006). While extreme, the *Parmalat* case is hardly unique. A number of similar cases, employing complex and opaque strategies, have emerged within continental Europe exploiting regulatory weaknesses at both the member state and the European Union level. There are both industry and market reasons that explain the appearance of this form of financial transaction and complex fraud. Evidence suggests that private benefits extraction is higher in European groups of companies, particularly those organized in a pyramid structure (Friedman, Johnson, and Mitton 2003; Holmén and Högfeldt 2005). Inefficient controlling shareholders

[2] See FASB, Consolidation of Certain Special Purpose Entities: An Interpretation of ARB No 51 (proposed 1 July 2002). The proposal deals with SPEs and would have caused the consolidation of Enron's LJM 1 and 2 partnerships. It also increases the outside equity requirement to 10% for a residual class of SPEs that would have included those in question. A second initiative addresses disclosures of guarantees, on the grounds that the present rules lack clarity. FASB, Interpretation No 45, Guarantor's Accounting Disclosure Requirements for Guarantees, Including Indirect Guarantees of Indebtedness of Others (25 November 2002).

have given rise to a huge variety of sophisticated techniques to tunnel assets, profits, and corporate opportunities. The investigations into the Parmalat scandal showed that management used a virtual hydra head of offshore subsidiaries and special purpose entities to cover up their losses and prop up the financial situation of the group.[3]

Early attempts to locate effective solutions to the arrangements that led to the collapse of Parmalat have run up against interest group pressures in Italy. Despite these barriers, the need is apparent and urgent for new mechanisms to address the regulatory problems triggered by the use of these vehicles. While there are numerous conventional legal strategies available to curtail management's capacity to carry out self-dealing transactions (Kraakman et al 2004), the post-scandal debate revealed significant differences of opinion regarding the extent to which mandatory disclosure, director's fiduciary duties, and audit control can prove effective in discouraging illicit, related party transactions. In many jurisdictions, lawmakers have strengthened regulation in the core areas of audit and auditors, non-executive directors, and board structure. Yet legal protections and organizational change are not the whole story.

Perhaps the most important change lies on the enforcement side, where the private and public institutions are notably weak in Europe compared to the USA. In circumstances where legal regulation would otherwise be justified, market mechanisms can be of considerable practical significance in imposing costs on self-dealing transactions (Klausner 2004). This is not to say that market mechanisms are the most important factor in curtailing self-dealing, but there is much to be said for a regulatory framework that would employ a diversity of legal rules and standards to govern related party transactions.

This chapter focuses on the regulation of related party transactions by corporate managers and transactions by controlling shareholders which conflict with the interests of minority shareholders. We will consider the EU-level reforms designed to deter these transactions. Attention will also be given to the variety of other mechanisms, such as industry standards,[4] for dealing with these issues.

The chapter is divided into six sections. The next section analyses the significance of diverse patterns of ownership and control for regulating the conflicts between majority and minority shareholders. Section 3 explores the arguments for and against the regulation of related party transactions. This section also examines the Parmalat scandal and explores the mechanisms employed by the

---

[3] *Securities and Exchange Commission v Parmalat Finanziaria SpA* Case no 03 CV 10266 (PKC) Complaint, United States District Court (SDNY) 29 December 2003, available at < www. sec.gov/litigation/complaints/comp18527.htm> (30 June 2005); Enrico Bondi, Extraordinary Commissioner of Parmalat Finanziaria Spa, Parmalat Spa and Other Affiliated Entities in *Extraordinary Administration v Citigroup Inc, Citibank NA, Vialattea LLC, Buconero LLC and Eureka Plc* No BER-L-10902–04 (NJ Super Ct Law Div) (unpublished decision on motion to dismiss).
[4] See Chapter 7.

family-controlling shareholder to extract private benefits at the expense of minority shareholders and creditors. Section 4 examines legal mechanisms designed by EU lawmakers to regulate related party transactions. Whilst the problem of related party transactions is closely connected to the disclosure of beneficial ownership, we argue in section 5 that it is important to recognize that legal structures used to regulate conflicted transactions may not have a direct effect in obtaining information on beneficial ownership and control. However, the reporting obligations of financial intermediaries that could lead to the detection of common ownership structures may have the effect of revealing the presence of related party transactions. We examine the mechanisms to hide the identity of the beneficial owner and critically assess the efforts by international bodies to pierce through the corporate veil. We conclude by suggesting how the insights explored here may serve to overcome the difficulties in the regulation of related party transactions and beneficial ownership.

## 2. Controlling Shareholdings

European company law regimes have traditionally included a number of mechanisms that constrain shareholders from extracting resources from enterprises they control. Such disparity between ownership and control is characteristic of

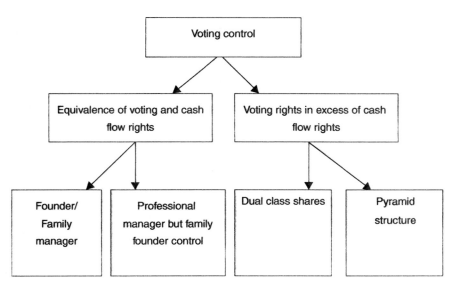

**Figure 8.1.** Voting control within the firm
*Source*: Halpern 1999.

countries that permit the exploitation of corporate opportunities.[5] Figure 8.1 depicts some instances in which shareholders may assume voting control, even if they, ostensibly, have no majority stake in the firm. Dual class shares and pyramid structures often serve the purpose of remaining in control.

The most widely used mechanism to accumulate control power with a limited investment is ownership pyramids or cascades which can enable a shareholder to maintain control throughout multiple layers of ownership while at the same time sharing the investment with other (minority) shareholders at each intermediate ownership tier. Some European countries have traditionally allowed companies to design a pyramidal structure, which is one of the mechanisms that reduces the liquidity constraints of large shareholders while it allows those shareholders to retain substantial voting power (Panunzi et al 2006). There is significant evidence about the availability of pyramid structures in Europe (ISS 2007).

In a similar vein, the issuance of dual-class voting shares to separate ownership and control allows a large shareholder to transfer resources from the company. The private benefits of control are non-transferable benefits beyond the financial return on investment. The large shareholder is usually allowed a seat on the board of directors and will thus receive non-public information on the firm's cost structure or on supply contracts of the competitors. The large shareholder could, for example, after obtaining such strategic information, renew negotiations about the subcontractor's price. Consequently, such transactions can lead to the creation of an agency conflict, namely the oppression of minority shareholders' rights.

Some economists have shown that dual class shares are also widely used by listed family companies in Western Europe (Faccio and Lang 2002). There is widespread use of dual class shares in Scandinavia, France, Spain, Italy, and the USA. Dual-class shares are thus commonly employed by European firms, but with large differences across EU member states. In Finland, Italy, Denmark, Switzerland, and Sweden, the proportion of firms with outstanding dual-class stocks ranges from around 35 to 65 per cent. For Norway, Germany, UK, Austria, and Ireland, the range varies from 13 to 24 per cent. In Portugal and Spain, the proportions are almost negligible.

The negative effect of concentrated ownership is reflected in the size of the control premium. This is the difference between the market value of shares, and how much someone is willing to pay for those shares if they confer (or maintain) control over a company. The existence of a control premium reflects the gains that majority shareholders can make at the expense of outside, minority shareholders. The size of the control premium depends on a number of factors, including the competition in the market for corporate control, the size of the block sold, the distribution of shares in the target firm, the inequality of voting power, the

---

[5]  See Chapter 2.

nationality of the buyer, and the financial condition of the firm involved (Berglöf and Burkart 2003). The existence of large private benefits of control suggests that blockholders may be able to obtain a large share of the rents. In some European countries, the size of private benefits appears to be significant (Dyck and Zingales 2004; McCahery and Renneboog 2003).

Recent studies have attempted to show more directly the influence of controlling shareholders' non *pro rata* distributions on the shares of the company. Claessens and others (2002) study the implication of greater control rights versus greater cash-flow rights on firm value. It is assumed that the lower the cash-flow rights of controlling shareholders, the greater the incentive for dominant insiders to divert firms assets for their own benefit. Evidently, these studies support calls for new legal rules and other reform strategies that offer a better chance to limit the effects of managerial self-dealing and transactions involving controlling shareholders. In response to the weaknesses of established company law frameworks, policy-makers have attempted to address these agency problems by providing more effective courts, better mechanisms to enforce shareholders' rights, and increased transparency. Certainly, in some continental European jurisdictions with poor quality law, the question is what combination of measures will suffice. More particularly, if self-dealing is the mainstay of blockholder returns, then the introduction of a tougher reform package may be necessary to constrain self-dealing transactions. The experience in other jurisdictions has shown that strong legal rules and institutions can place constraints on the potential for insiders to tunnel resources out of firms.

## 3. Related Party Transactions

As noted above, the Enron and Parmalat scandals illustrate the difficulty that auditors and regulators face in identifying related party relationships and transactions that are motivated by fraud or illicit earnings management. While there is widespread agreement on the need to regulate related party transactions, there is much less convergence on what transactions should be subject to deterrent regulation. To be sure, the nature of the problem varies: in companies with controlling shareholders and with corporate groups, the measures need to be different from those situations where ownership is spread and where the board and management is effectively entrenched.

### 3.1 Why Should One Care About Related Party Transactions?

The received wisdom is that related party transactions play an important and legitimate role in a market economy. For firms, trade and foreign investment are often facilitated by inter-company financing transactions. Lower costs of capital and tax savings provide a strong incentive for engaging in these transactions. Indeed, there are many examples of related party transactions that yield benefits for companies. By far the most popular transactions include (1) inter-company loans or guarantees from parent to foreign subsidiary; (2) the sale of receivables to a special purpose entity; and (3) a leasing or licensing agreement between a parent and a foreign subsidiary. A key concern about related party transactions is that they might not be undertaken at market prices but can be influenced by the relationship between the two sides of a transaction: there is a conflict of interest for some persons in the company. For both controlling shareholders and insiders such as management, related party transactions can be the mechanism for extracting private benefits of control at the cost of other shareholders. There are a broad array of legal strategies to regulate disclosure of related party transactions and conflicts of interests. Before proceeding, we will begin in the next section with a summary of the competing strategies for dealing with these transactions. The US debate provides a good summary of the lack of consensus around conflicted transactions.

## 3.2 Understanding the Competing Regulatory Visions

A large body of literature has considered these issues by referring to the American experience with conflicted transactions by management and controlling shareholders (Henry et al 2007). It is important to recognize that US law once prohibited interested transactions involving managers and directors (Clark 1986). But the strategy for prohibiting self-dealing transactions underscores a particular political-legal tradition rather than a credible means to protect private investors and foster a more equitable distribution of wealth in society. Accordingly, the prohibition strategy failed to deter reallocations of wealth. In fact, aside from providing little protection against a single undetected transaction, the prohibition of self-dealing may have left many companies worse off as a consequence of preventing many efficient transactions.

This prompted the need for regulators to allow companies to pursue certain related party transactions not leading to conflicts of interest. The shift in self-dealing rules reflected the view that some non-abusive transactions are valuable and that parties should have incentives to pursue these transactions. US company law rules provide that self-dealing transactions are permitted subject to legal controls (Klein, Ramseyer, and Bainbridge 2003). To protect outside investors from abusive transactions, state and federal laws regulate self-dealing, corporate opportunities, insider trading, and the compensation agreements with executives.

However, there are suggestions that the modern regulation of self-dealing transactions is misguided (Easterbrook and Fischel 1991). Thus, where managerial value diversion does not raise fairness and distributional concerns, there is no obvious need to protect shareholders against expropriation. Moreover, to the extent that value diversion is an alternative form of compensation, it probably makes little sense to subject conflicted transactions to restrictive legal rules.

Another approach, inspired in part by these views, stresses that the benign view of value diversion is misleading (Bebchuk and Jolls 1999). Managerial value diversion creates significant agency costs by eviscerating the incentive effects of performance-based pay. To be sure, there is evidence that extra-legal mechanisms, such as trust and loss of reputation, can lessen but not eliminate the inefficient subtraction of firm earnings. Notwithstanding these constraints, if the gains of opportunism are very large, legal standards may be insufficient to limit management from engaging in opportunistic behaviour. This is an argument for encouraging more protective measures of minority investors, increased transparency, and stronger shareholder involvement in decisions involving transactions that could implicate a conflict of interest with management or a controlling shareholder.

## 3.3 Identifying Related Party Transactions

Various terminology and definitions are employed to define related parties and related party transactions across jurisdictions. In the USA, the Financial Accounting Standards Board's (FASB) Statement no 57[6] provides that related party transactions involve transactions between a parent company and subsidiary; subsidiaries of a common parent; an enterprise and trusts for the benefit of employees; an enterprise and its principal owners, management, or members of their immediate families; and affiliates.[7] It is unlikely, however, that there is a simple definition that is sufficient for identifying all the transactions with related parties. A second ground for eliminating this approach is that certain complex transactions, which fail to meet the relevant criteria, may be too easily excluded on these grounds. Ruling out this approach is an important step for developing a basis to identify these transactions.

Seen in this light, the attempt to identify related party transactions raises complex issues. That said, the nature of related party transactions is best highlighted by general principles such as those of the International Accounting Standards Board rather than listing categories of people and entities. According to IAS 24, parties are considered to be related if one party has the ability to control the other party or exercise significant influence over the other party in making financial and operating decisions. Related party transactions are defined as a transfer of resources or obligations between related parties, regardless of whether or not a market price is charged. The OECD Principles take a similar approach and state

---

[6] FASB Statement No 57, Related Party Disclosures.
[7] See also the revised version of IAS 24 9 (2003).

that related parties can include entities that control or are under common control with the company, board members, and significant shareholders, including members of families and key management personnel.

Transactions involving major shareholders or their close family either directly or indirectly are potentially the most difficult types of transactions to identify.[8] Again, the Enron and Parmalat scandals illustrate the difficulty that regulators face identifying related party relationships and transactions that are motivated by fraud. The complications arise not only from the complexity of many of these transactions, but also involve auditors' problems of detecting material misstatements in financial statements due to a related party transaction.

There is no question that the American Institute of Certified Public Accountants' (AICPA) Statement of Auditing Standard No 45, AU Sec 334 (2001) has supplied a feasible approach for identifying material transactions, such as interest-free borrowing, asset sales that diverge from appraisal value, in-kind transactions, and loans made without scheduled terms. Other indicators can be used as well to detect potential opportunism. One possibility is to have auditors obtain information about management responsibilities to run the company, controls over management activities, and management arrangements with various components of the entity. At the same time, AU Sec 334 can be used to identify the existence of related party transactions. Company auditors can employ a range of audit procedures, from the review of non-recurring transactions to the invoices of regular services, to evaluate conflicted transactions.

The next section shows that it is hard to distinguish legitimate related party transactions from the illicit ones. This is particularly the case for controlling shareholders that are able to conceal control through mechanisms, such as dual class shares, pyramidal ownership, and cross-holdings, and can use, without risk of punishment, a variety of non-arm's-length transactions for their own benefit. The section below discusses the *Parmalat* case which is an important illustration of a family-controlling blockholder diverting private benefits for their own use.

## 3.4 Parmalat

Often described as the European Enron, Parmalat collapsed with debts of €14.5 billion in December 2003. To begin, the Parmalat Group raised more than €13.2 billion in debt and equity from investors in Europe and the United States. Even though the company was highly successful in raising new sources of funding, the Parmalat Group was forced, due to its loss-making operations, to divert many of its proceeds from these issues to cover expiring bonds. It turns out that Calisto

---

[8] IAS 24.9 provides 'that a related party transaction is a transfer of resources, services, or obligations between related parties, regardless of whether a price is charged'.

Tanzi, Parmalat's chairman and CEO, employed a range of fraudulent schemes to enrich family members and private companies controlled by the family trust. Not only were the company's top directors and family-controlled managers involved in perpetuating the scheme, but the gatekeepers and lawyers allegedly facilitated the fraud by manipulating balance sheets and financial disclosures to regulators. The deceit was pursued successfully over a number of years until the group's eventual collapse in December 2003. It is hard to imagine a more devastating critique of the controlling shareholder system of governance in Europe. For these reasons, the basic element of the fraud is discussed below.

Until its collapse, the Parmalat Group was one of the world's largest leading dairy and food products groups with operations in more than thirty countries worldwide. The company, which was controlled by the Tanzi family and operated out of Collecchio, Parma, was formed in the 1960s as a classic food trading concern. The family-controlled business was rapidly transformed, as a consequence of innovations in the processing of milk (UHT), into a dairy company, and thereafter quickly extended its operations into foreign and food-related markets. By the 1980s, the group had diversified into non-food-related markets. However, these ventures were unsuccessful, which eventually led to financial problems. In order to redress these financial problems, Coloniale restructured the group, and Parmalat Finanziaria, the listed holding company, emerged.

In the 1990s, Parmalat continued its expansion of its dairy and food services and diversified into tourism and the professional sports sector through the sponsorship of a number of domestic Italian and foreign football teams. For Parmalat, most of these investments were loss making from their inception. Having extended its reach to North and South America to more than fifty companies by the end of the decade, Parmalat derived most of its income internationally. Parmalat financed its ambitious growth expansion strategy by a combination of national and international debt issues and equity.

In 2001, Parmalat suffered financial difficulties with its operations in Latin America, which, if known to the market, would have led to higher costs of capital. In order to appear investor-friendly, Parmalat artificially enhanced its consolidated income statements and balance sheets while taking actions to conceal its ever-increasing debt mountain. This led to top management and officers, in turn, undertaking a series of paper-trail transactions designed to systematically mislead investors regarding certain assets and liabilities. For example, Parmalat's management created false documentation and bank accounts to improve their cash position. As part of this effort, a letter from the Bank of America was created confirming a €3.9 billion bank account of Bonlat Financing Corporation, a Parmalat subsidiary incorporated in the Cayman Islands.[9] This

---

[9] *In re Parmalat Securities Litigation*: Master Docket 04 Civ 0030 (LAK) ECF Case, First Amended Consolidated Class Action Complaint for Violation of the Federal Securities Laws, United States District Court (SDNY).

false confirmation letter was used by Bonlat's auditors to certify its 2002 financial statement. Moreover, as part of its fraudulent effort, Parmalat supported its 2003 offerings of unsecured notes to US investors by disclosing Bonlat's 2002 certification and its 2002 audited financial statement, which included references to a non-existent bank account.[10]

During the years 2002 and 2003, the Parmalat Group encountered questions from supervisory authorities and gatekeepers about the quality of its financial statements and disclosures. For example, a February 2003 bond issue was cancelled due to concerns over debt sustainability and accounting problems. Subsequently the placement of private bonds in July 2003 led to regulatory pressures from Consob, the Italian financial regulator, when Parmalat Finanziaria's statutory auditor, Deloitte, cast doubt on financial statements. On 8 December 2003 the Parmalat Group was unable to make payment on a bond expiry, which led Standard and Poors to downgrade its debt to junk status. Meanwhile, Tanzi resigned as CEO on 15 December after acknowledging that company records were false, which the Bank of America confirmed on 19 December 2003. The company filed for bankruptcy on 23 December and was declared insolvent on 27 December 2003.

In the end, between 1990 and 2003, the Parmalat Group increased its total debt by €13.2 billion, while generating €1 billion from operations. But it spent €5.4 billion on unproductive acquisitions, €5.3 billion in bank charges and commissions, and €2.3 billion in financial diversions. From this perspective, then, the behaviour of the Parmalat Group is immediately apparent. The expansion strategy was a costly failure that led to huge losses. The financial structure of the group needed to be expanded in order to support significant diversions of private benefits, the rapidly deteriorating balance sheet, and the costly arranging and borrowing fees. The architects of the fraud had anticipated that their strategy of foreign expansion and corresponding exploitation of weak foreign and Italian governance systems would allow them to exploit minority shareholders and creditors for a reasonably long period. If nothing else, the detailed investigations into Parmalat's collapse revealed the extent to which the same gatekeepers who did a poor job with Enron were prone to a sobering list of failures in their role of securing investors against fraud and improper disclosure. In several important areas, the gatekeepers provided little monitoring help and, in some cases, may have made accurate certification of the financials more difficult. In an environment with these characteristics, crises will persist unless regulators have an incentive to alter the regulatory monitoring environment. The next section will assess the various measures designed to regulate related party transactions.

---

[10]  *SEC v Parmalat Finanziaria SpA* Complaint p 4.

## 4. Regulation of Related Party Transactions

### 4.1 Information and Transparency

Minority shareholders must have means to detect opportunistic behaviour by the controlling shareholders. Minority shareholders may gather public information and private information. The main source of public information is the periodic publication of the company's financial disclosures and audited annual report. In Europe, public companies are obliged to publish their annual reports under the Fourth Directive. However, as discussed in Chapter 2, the disclosure rules often disclose timely information about possible expropriation of the company's benefit. It is obvious that direct and indirect transactions between the company and controlling shareholders can negatively affect the accuracy of the annual reports.

There is satisfactory transparency regarding such transactions for all listed companies with the European Union under IAS 24 and under the national codes.[11] In terms of disclosure of related party transactions, regardless of whether there have been transactions between a parent and a subsidiary, an entity must disclose the name of its parent and, if different, the ultimate controlling party. If neither the entity's parent nor the ultimate controlling party produces financial statements available for public use, the name of the next most senior parent that does so must also be disclosed (see IAS 24.12). Furthermore, IAS 24 mandates that for each category of related parties, companies should disclose the nature of the related party relationship as well as information about the transactions and outstanding balances necessary for an understanding of the potential effect of the relationship on the financial statements (see IAS 17–18). Such disclosure should include the amount of the transactions, the amount of outstanding balances, provisions for doubtful debts related to the amount of outstanding balances, and expenses recognized during the period in respect of bad or doubtful debts due from related parties.

Recently, the EU extended the disclosure of related party transactions for non-listed companies beyond affiliated undertaking in order to restore public confidence in companies' financial statements and contribute to integrated capital markets.[12] EC regulators defend the requirement on the grounds that (1) related party transactions are very often material for non-listed companies;

---

[11] In the chapter, we discuss the revised (2003) version of IAS 24, which became effective on 1 January 2005. In February 2007 a draft of proposed amendments to IAS 24 were released. This proposal particularly attempts to reduce the disclosure requirements in IAS 24 for some state-owned or state-influenced entities.

[12] Directive 2007/36/EC of the European Parliament and of the Council of 11 July amending Council Directives 78/660/EEC and 83/349/EEC concerning the annual accounts of certain types of companies and consolidated accounts.

**Table 8.1.** IAS 24 (after the December 2003 revision)

Objective: ensuring that a firm discloses the existence of related parties and related party transactions, which may affect its financial position.

Related Parties

IAS 24.9   A party is related to an entity if:
- (a) directly, or indirectly through one or more intermediaries, the party:
- (i) controls, is controlled by, or is under common control with, the entity (this includes parents, subsidiaries, and fellow subsidiaries);
- (ii) has an interest in the entity that gives it significant influence over the entity; or
- (iii) has joint control over the entity;
- (b) the party is an associate (as defined in IAS 28 Investments in Associates) of the entity;
- (c) the party is a joint venture in which the entity is a venturer (see IAS 31 Interests in Joint Ventures);
- (d) the party is a member of the key management personnel of the entity or its parent;
- (e) the party is a close member of the family of any individual referred to in (a) or (d);
- (f) the party is an entity that is controlled, jointly controlled, or significantly influenced by or for which significant voting power in such entity resides with, directly or indirectly, any individual referred to in (d) or (e); or
- (g) the party is a post-employment benefit plan for the benefit of employees of the entity, or of any entity that is a related party of the entity.

IAS 24.11   Not related are:
- two enterprises simply because they have a director or key manager in common;
- two venturers who share joint control over a joint venture;
- providers of finance, trade unions, public utilities, government departments, and agencies in the course of their normal dealings with an enterprise;
- a single customer, supplier, franchiser, distributor, or general agent with whom an enterprise transacts a significant volume of business merely by virtue of the resulting economic dependence.

Related Party Transaction

IAS 24.9   A related party transaction is a transfer of resources, services, or obligations between related parties, regardless of whether a price is charged.

Disclosure

IAS 24.12   Relationships between parents and subsidiaries (irrespective of transactions)
IAS 24.16   Key management compensation
IAS 24.17-18   Related party transactions:
- the amount of the transactions;
- the amount of outstanding balances, including terms and conditions and guarantees;
- provisions for doubtful debts related to the amount of outstanding balances;
- expense recognized during the period in respect of bad and doubtful debts due from related parties

IAS 24.21   The firm must provide proof if it states that related party transactions were made on terms that are common in arm's length transactions.

*Source*: <www.iasplus.com>.

and (2) disclosure would not be too cumbersome, as these firms usually do not have complicated off-balance-sheet arrangements.

Nevertheless, there are numerous techniques that parties use to avoid the IAS 24.[13] As we have seen earlier, the controlling shareholder is able to obtain non-public information and use it for personal financial benefit or tip other family members—who might then make an investment decision on the basis of the information. The inaccuracy of public information is less pressing if a minority shareholder is also a director in a company. In that case, he will be able to influence and monitor management decisions directly. Legally requiring shareholder approval may have the same effect. However, if minority shareholders are not in a managerial capacity or involved in the decision-making process, they are unlikely to gather the information without relying on a legal mandate.

Thus, even though enhanced financial statement transparency should be encouraged, regulators must not underestimate the higher costs of disclosure for those non-listed companies. If the idea is to increase the accountability of non-listed companies, the EC may need to subject disclosure of related party transactions on an aggregate basis.

## 4.2 Special Purpose Entities

Typically, SPEs are employed by financial intermediaries and companies to facilitate arm's length financial transfers. As noted above, Parmalat and former CEO Fausto Tonna used an array of off-balance-sheet arrangements in pursuit of this scheme to artificially inflate assets on the group's consolidated balance sheet and preserve its access to external funding, particularly in the USA. The preferred method was to transfer assets, falsely, from Parmalat to an SPE in exchange for consideration, which the SPEs would raise from loans from Parmalat. Subsequently, management of Parmalat would remove the asset from its own books and then record the loan as an asset. Since these off-balance-sheet arrangements played a central role in the Parmalat fraud and accounting scandal, the Commission has improved disclosure by amending the Fourth and Seventh Directive, mandating that companies must disclose all off-balance-sheet arrangements that have a material impact on the company. Companies below the small and medium-sized thresholds are not required to satisfy these requirements.[14]

The new SPE rules are arguably likely to improve the source of information to investors. The complex and obscure transactions designed by Parmalat's executive and professional advisers ensured that investors would have little accurate and

---

[13] The Draft IFRS for SMEs also provide for the disclosure of related party transactions. Sections 33.7–33.12 contain the definition of a related party transaction as well as a minimum of disclosures.
[14] See Chapter 2 for discussion of the thresholds.

timely information to assess the company's performance. To the extent the rules are likely to have an impact on companies, it should be clear that the new measures will likely cause most difficulties for groups of companies, such as Parmalat, that have been able to successfully prevent disclosure of these type of conflicts.[15]

## 5. Legal Business Entities and their Potential for Misuse

Off-balance-sheet vehicles played an important role in the Enron scandal and the build-up to Parmalat's troubles. In this context, it is important to evaluate their purpose and function in light of the growing popularity of hybrid business entities and their multitude of uses in financial transactions. Thus, we begin in this section with a review of the legitimate aims of legal vehicles and their potential for misuse by parties to engage in illicit activities. The primary objective is to describe and analyse the competing methods for identifying beneficial ownership and control. In this context, we examine the UK Treasury and DTI assessment on beneficial disclosure of unlisted companies to consider the various regulatory options available to enhance enforcement of people who use private vehicles for criminal purposes. We then move on to discuss the EU regulatory framework governing money laundering with a view to assessing its potential for curbing illegal activities.

While there have always been a number of techniques that make it difficult to establish the true ownership of a company, such as bearer shares and nominee shareholders, modern legal business forms, which are even less regulated than traditional corporate form, are even more apt to establish a chains of SPEs. Lighter regulation provides these entities with a more flexible structure. More importantly, they can be established cheaply and often within twenty-four hours. These characteristics make these types of business forms vulnerable to misuse for illicit purposes. A number of individuals and opportunistic investors, criminal organizations, and others could take advantage of the light regulation of these modern business forms to perpetrate a wide range of illegal or illicit activities.

Whilst misuse of company law vehicles is difficult to discover, there is ample reason to believe that the illicit use of private and public entities is widespread. These forms are used in a variety of contexts, from money laundering to the diversion of corporate assets. Corporations, trusts, foundations, limited partnerships, and now hybrid business forms, such as the LLC and LLP are the vehicles most commonly associated with misuse. The OECD (2001), which is concerned to combat corruption and money laundering, has articulated a number of policy objectives in respect of preventing the misuse of company law vehicles.

---

[15] Department of Trade and Industry (UK) European Company Law and Corporate Governance, Directive Proposals on Company Reporting, Capital Maintenance and Transfer of the Registered Office of a Company, A Consultative Document (DTI, London, 2005).

The emphasis on restricting their misuse is in line with other international initiatives that seek to establish the appropriate standards to assist law authorities and financial institutions that could effectively stem cross-border crime.

As far as jurisdictions have mechanisms that make it possible to obtain access to beneficial ownership, it is emphasized that proper oversight and high integrity of the system is also necessary to ensure the adequacy and accuracy of the information. It is submitted that the misuse of legal entities can be limited by the maintenance and sharing information on beneficial ownership and control through a number of mechanisms. These alternative mechanisms include: (1) an up-front disclosure system; (2) mandating corporate service providers to maintain beneficial ownership information; and (3) primary reliance on an investigative system.

The OECD approach is based on the insight that the most effective technique to identify the beneficial owner is to, when necessary, pierce through the legal form of corporate or hybrid vehicles in order to obtain information about the legal owner of the shares or the party that exercises effective control over the corporate vehicle. The argument for pursuing this strategy is largely pragmatic, namely there are an array of effective legal techniques available that permit regulators and other parties to obtain such information.[16] The supervisory authorities,

Table 8.2. OECD menu of possible options for obtaining and sharing beneficial ownership and control information

| *"upfront" disclosure to public authorities* | |
|---|---|
| Advantages | Disadvantages |
| • improves transparency | • imposes significant costs on |
| • beneficial ownership and control information available at all times | business vehicles (especially small and medium-sized enterprises) |
| • strong deterrent effect | |
| *the holding of information by intermediaries* | |
| Advantages | Disadvantages |
| • implementation is cheap | • potential for delays in the provision of information |
| *the use of an investigative system to obtain information* | |
| Advantages | Disadvantages |
| • may avoid unnecessary costs and burdens on business vehicles, which may stifle legitimate business formation | • potential for delays in the provision of information |
| • maintain a reasonable balance between ensuring proper monitoring / regulation of business vehicles and protecting legitimate privacy interests | |

*Source*: OECD 2001.

[16] There are obviously a range of techniques, including subpoenas and other court orders to obtain information about the legal owner of the company.

in some markets, subject financial intermediaries involved in the creation of such corporate vehicles to obtain a written declaration of the identity of the beneficial owner and renew verification of the identity of the contracting party or beneficial owner during the course of the business relationship. Not only must financial intermediaries obtain the identification of the beneficial owner, they are bound to establish documents, make the information available to supervisors, and retain the information long after the business relationship has ended. At a fundamental level, we see that the misuse of corporate vehicles can be controlled by a combination of mechanisms. Thus the choice between the particular mechanisms will be influenced by the efficacy of the legal system and the enforcement history and level of cooperation in the market. Differences in the legal traditions and culture will complicate agreement on standards, much less effectively enforcing them.

In principle, the solution, however, to the problem of disclosure of beneficial ownership is straightforward: introduce a strong up-front disclosure system and investigative system. Indeed, the elements of a sound system of disclosure of beneficial ownership are well known by policy-makers. For instance, the Financial Action Task Force (FATF), which is charged with promoting the development of and compliance with standards to efficiently curtail the effects of money laundering, has already moved in this direction, in the context of the review process of the Forty Recommendations, by extending the scope of its regime applicable to financial intermediaries to non-financial professions and the treatment of bearer shares and trusts. That the standards to combat money laundering converge with the OECD Report confirms the desirability of reaching agreement on standards and devising effective techniques to implement them. Subsequently, the FATF issued nine special recommendations on Terrorist Financing which, together with the forty recommendations that were already published in 2003, provide a complete set of principles against money laundering which can be flexibly adopted by countries.

Promoting greater disclosure of beneficial ownership of shares in non-listed companies was also the subject of the UK Treasury and the Department of Trade and Industry's (2002) consultation document on the Regulatory Impact Assessment on Disclosure of Beneficial Ownership of Unlisted Companies.[17] For some time, the UK government has pursued an ambitious reform agenda in its fight against international organized crime, terrorism, and other illegal activities. That it requires rigorous disclosure requirements of beneficial ownership of unlisted companies and effective enforcement is now agreed upon. The Regulatory Impact Assessment (RIA) sought, in light of the report by the UK Cabinet Office Performance and Innovation Unit on Recovering the Proceeds of Crime, to evaluate the benefits and costs of registering beneficial owners, by reference to five cumulative options, from the duty of the owners of private

---

[17] HM Treasury and DTI, Consultation Document, Regulatory Impact Assessment on Disclosure of Beneficial Ownership of Unlisted Companies, July 2002.

companies to identify themselves to the company to the disclosure of ownerships and directorships on a searchable database. However, analysts were split about the beneficial aspects of direct legislative follow up from the RIA, which may explain the apparent reluctance of Parliament to take up new legislative measures subsequently.[18]

Indeed, the failure to make early legislative progress in the area arguably reflects a change in direction by UK lawmakers away from mandating the disclosure of beneficial ownership by private companies. In this context, The Companies Act 2006 includes a provision that allows directors to file a service address rather than their residential address. The apparent effect of this requirement is to make it extremely burdensome and complicated for regulated persons to carry out their function under the money laundering regulations. In any event, despite the loss of initiative on some fronts, reformers have been able to step up efforts in constraining abusive actions of directors in private limited companies by virtue of the new provision in the Companies Act 2006 that at least one actual person—and not just another company—act as a director in a private limited company. Clearly this change will make the private limited company a less attractive vehicle for illicit use by parties' criminal activities. In the next section we turn to examine the mechanisms for achieving anonymity and the action taken by policy-makers to stem the abusive conduct of perpetrators.

## 5.1 Chain of Legal Vehicles

There are many techniques available to move money swiftly and effectively to evade tax authorities and other enforcement officials. Specialists on financial crime and money laundering frequently note that perpetrators will seek to avoid detection by creating a chain of company law vehicles in separate jurisdictions. Such a structure is simple and cost efficient to set up. For example, an offshore company acts as nominee for an offshore principal. In this construction, the nominee company represents the offshore company, and transacts all the contracts and business on its behalf, including invoicing and accounting. The advantages are clear, namely no invoices or other papers will appear in the file of the offshore principal. Such a construction, moreover, assumes that the nominee company will not trade in its country of incorporation, buy or sell goods in its own name, and sign contracts with the nominee company outside its home jurisdiction. In order to develop the chain, parties will go on to establish companies in a third jurisdiction and so forth.

---

[18] As far as UK public listed companies are concerned, all listed companies are required to disclose all interests including beneficial ownership to the UK Listing Authority. Because UK company law has developed its own comprehensive set of disclosure rules which places considerable information on the public record, the need for further regulation may be undesirable and costly.

While critics warn that a chain of company law vehicles is an effective solution for a number of commercial parties, officials claim that the anonymity created by these structures serves to benefit those involved in criminal activities. To be sure, some jurisdictions have moved to introduce measures that would make information on beneficial owners more readily available. In the previous section, we saw that UK officials are beginning to discuss reform strategies along these lines in order to create the conditions for effective enforcement. In addition, the use of a chain of company vehicles to engage in illicit conduct is vulnerable to the disclosure obligations, which require financial intermediaries and other non-financial professionals to declare related-party transactions and the connection between the ownership of the onshore and offshore companies. While more comprehensive efforts may be needed, it is suggested that the banking industry and other self-regulatory organizations can fill in the gap to combat these practices.

## 5.2 Disclosure of Beneficial Interest

Supervisors and policy-makers have long recognized that unlisted companies are being used to facilitate money laundering and other illicit activities. In order to stem these activities, the RIA looked at a number of legal approaches that would reduce the incidence of serious and organized crime. The main question addressed concerned whether any system of disclosure should place an obligation on the beneficial owner or the legal, registered owner, or both. To this end, the Consultation document weighted the costs and benefits of five cumulative options ranging from imposing a duty on owners of private companies to identifying themselves to the company involved through the disclosure of ownership and directorships on a searchable database of legal and beneficial ownership.[19] A number of significant benefits were identified, including higher recovery rates along with more effective deterrence and enforcement. That said, Option 3,

---

[19] The five options include: (1a) an individual should be required to inform a private company if they have a beneficial interest in the company's shares which is not more than 3%; 1(b) in addition to the above, persons holding a beneficial interest above the 3% threshold should disclose to the company the percentage of the company's shares that they have a beneficial interest in, and should be disclosed on an annual basis; 1(c) in addition to the above, persons holding a beneficial interest above 3% should disclose to the company, with a specified period, each time their holding changes by one percentage point; (2) in addition to the above, information on persons holding a beneficial interest above the 3% threshold should be disclosed by unlisted and private companies to Companies House via annual returns; (3) in addition to the above, all changes in beneficial interests exceeding the 3% threshold should be disclosed to Companies House via annual returns; (4) in addition to the above, the Companies House should establish a modern database which allows the names of the persons to be inputted and then reveal which shareholdings and beneficial interests that person holds; and (5) in addition to the above, such a database would allow the names of the person to be inputted and then reveal what directors and shadow directors that person holds. (Treasury/DTI 2003: 7–8).

which recommended a duty to report changes in ownership to Companies House as they occur and placing details on a public register, was considered the most cost-effective alternative for disclosure of beneficial ownership.

Nevertheless, critics observed that there were a number of problems with the RIA approach generally. First, the 3 per cent threshold for basic disclosure under option 1(b) or the subsequent 1 per cent threshold increase under option 1(c) are arguably immaterial in the context of a private firm. In addition, the proposed recommendation to report changes in beneficial ownership as they occur is not proportionate in the private company setting. Despite these limitations, the RIA approach can serve as a good example of regulators undertaking steps to understand the relevance of identifying ultimate beneficial owners. We can expect in the future that other regulatory bodies, in their efforts to curb illegal activities carried out by controllers of legal business vehicles, will likely benefit from the first generation efforts in this area.

Having seen the potentially crucial role that disclosure requirements can play in limiting criminal activities of perpetrators who use a chain of legal vehicles, we now turn to consider the regulatory framework governing financial and non-financial intermediaries. It is well known that these intermediaries sometimes assist their clients in devising structures that obscure the identity of the beneficial owners of legal entities. We consider the various legal measures to limit such conduct in the next section.

## 5.3 Combating Money Laundering and the Role of Intermediaries

Over the last decade or so, the European Union has undertaken to implement uniform rules in order to curb the misuse of financial centres by criminal organizations and to contain money laundering. Money laundering is defined as the process by which a party conceals the illegal existence, illegal source, or illegal application of income and then disguises it in order to make it appear legitimate. Money laundering typically involves a three-step process: placement, layering, and integration. There is little disagreement that steps are needed to minimize the incidence of money laundering. However, because money laundering involves numerous forms of corruption, it is difficult to identify, let alone prosecute successfully. Given the harm that money laundering causes to financial markets and the effect that it has in undermining confidence in government and public officials, we argue that strengthening the weak links in regulation is needed, especially with regard to the supervision of the financial intermediaries who have knowledge of the assets implicated in these transactions and a relationship with parties and company law vehicles connected to these illicit activities.

In terms of initiatives, the EU adopted, in 1991, a directive to combat money laundering in order to protect the integrity and soundness of the financial system.[20] The central aim of the Directive is to mandate that financial institutions satisfy specific reporting obligations intended to aid in the detection of money laundering. The effect of implementing the Directive is to move to criminalize money laundering. At the same time, the preamble of the Directive allows member states to extend the prohibition to drug-related criminal activities and the proceeds of other criminal activities. In terms of regulating financial institutions, the Directive requires compliance with reporting requirements designed to identify the contracting party, for any transaction amounting to ECU 15,000 or more, on the basis of conclusive documentary evidence. Equally, financial institutions are required to undertake all efforts to identify contracting parties engaged in money laundering transactions, even if such schemes fall below the monetary threshold. In order to enhance and strengthen the investigations by the supervisory authority, the financial institution is required to retain documents concerning the transactions undertaken for a period of five years.

Despite the implementation of the directive at the member state level, there have been few convictions for money laundering.[21] It is unclear why these measures have failed to prevent money laundering generally. Recent experience has demonstrated that money launderers, faced with new regulations designed to discover and prevent their schemes, will rely on alternative techniques and institutions that avoid supervisors' oversight and regulation of those practices. There are also many questions about the absence in the directive of imposed requirements on professionals, such as lawyers and accountants, which are involved in establishing the corporate vehicles and other schemes needed to conceal the illicit origins of their funds. As a consequence of these deficiencies, the European Parliament and the Council amended the Directive on the Prevention of the Use of the Financial System for the Purpose of Money Laundering.[22]

With regard to the amended directive, the EU extended the scope of those occupations and enterprises that are likely to be involved, directly or indirectly, in money laundering to non-financial intermediaries, such as auditors, accountants, tax advisers, and real estate agents; dealers in high-value goods; and casinos.[23] These professional and other intermediaries will be subject to the Directive's

---

[20] EC Council Directive 91/308 on Prevention of the Use of Financial Systems for the Purpose of Money Laundering, 1991 OJ (L 166) 77.

[21] Explanatory Statement of the Report on the Proposal for a European Parliament and Council Directive amending Council Directive 91/308/EEC on Prevention of the Use of the Financial System for the Purpose of Money Laundering, Eur Parl Doc (COM(99) 352-C5-0065/ 1999-1999/0152 (COD)) (1 June 2000).

[22] EC Council Directive 2001/97 of the European Parliament and of the Council amending Council Directive 91/308 on Prevention of the Use of the Financial System for the Purpose of Money Laundering, 2001 OJ (L344) 28/12/2001.

[23] Member states had to bring into force the laws, regulations, and administrative provisions necessary to comply with the Directive by 15 June 2003 at the latest.

required reporting requirements. The controversy over the inclusion of lawyers and accountants in the reporting requirements led to a compromise in the Council that permits derogation from the reporting obligation. In this regard, lawyers and accountants are not obliged to inform the authorities of any fact which might lead to an inference of money laundering in respect of information that they obtain from their client in connection with the determination of the legal position for their client, or when performing their task of defending their client in legal proceedings.

EU policy-makers responded also to earlier criticism providing, in the amended Directive, a more accurate definition of financial credit institutions. Arguably, the failure to effectively enforce the Directive was not so much due to the failure of member states to implement the measures, as they were poorly designed. By providing a comprehensive definition of credit institutions,[24] the EU has stepped up efforts to curtail the opportunities of money launderers to wash their funds. The Directive's coverage of financial institutions went well beyond banks to include: bureaux of exchange, money remittance offices, investment firms, and insurance companies.

Despite the increased scrutiny of financial institutions, there remained a number of important difficulties. First, even though in the Annex to the amended Directive there was a Code of Conduct that provided a basis for imposing reporting requirements in non-face-to-face operations, it was of little consequence. Imposing face-to-face reporting obligations on financial institutions was undermined when the Directive exempted non-face-to-face interactions with attorneys and accountants. In order to regulate this form of conduct, it made no sense to promulgate halfway measures. Second, enforcement was also complicated by the reporting exemption for bank-to-bank transactions. Significantly, illicit activities are facilitated by the use of bank-to-bank transactions involving a domestic bank with offshore financial institutions. This difficulty highlights more complicated problems in areas which the amended Directive had yet to address, such as corresponding banks and shell banks. The truth of the matter is a significant amount of money laundering activities are facilitated by these institutions and consequently more work has to be done in this area in order to limit these activities.

It is clear that the amended Directive, despite the above-mentioned shortcomings, introduced a number of important modifications which were necessary to redress the Directive's earlier shortcomings and to ensure that a wider group of financial and non-financial institutions are subject to reporting obligations and supervision by regulators. The EU has been committed to ensuring effective enforcement of the amended Directive, which was a sticking point. The point about effective enforcement is that relying on measures and sanctions against financial institutions must be supplemented with other mechanisms, such as

[24] Ibid at Art 1(a).

reputation and the activities of self-organizing bodies like the Wolfsberg Group, to assist in the compliance exercise whenever possible.[25]

In 2005, the European Commission welcomed the adoption of the Third Directive on the prevention of the use of the financial system for the purposes of money laundering or terrorist financing, effective from 15 December 2007.[26] This Directive builds on existing EU legislation and incorporates the June 2003 revision of the Forty Recommendations of the FATF. For the sake of clarity, it repealed and replaced the 1991 Directive, as amended in 2001, with the difference that it introduces additional requirements and safeguards for situations of higher risks, such as trading with banks located outside the European Union. Significantly, the European Commission published, in December 2006, two Commission Staff Working Documents on the application of the anti-money laundering obligations to the legal profession and the identification of clients in non-face-to-face transactions. In the context of the formation and operation of non-listed companies, the first document is of paramount importance. The working document stated that the application of the obligations has not produced the coveted impact and concluded that: (1) the quality of national legislation should be improved; (2) effort to create awareness should be undertaken; and (3) further research should reveal additional tools to facilitate compliance. It goes without saying that the implementation of the Third Directive provides member states with a new opportunity to improve the quality of the implementation.

In practice, the upfront identification of a client who wants to set up a legal entity is not without practical difficulties. Firstly, the identification of residents of other member states could severely hamper and delay the formation process. In particular, it is difficult to identify corporate clients that are located outside the European Union. Besides the cultural resistance of some countries to deliver supporting evidence for their residents' identification, clients often provide incorrect or uncertified copies of supporting documents, which increases the transaction costs regarding the formation and operation of legal entities. Despite these extra costs, professional organizations representing notaries in several member states are of the opinion that the identification procedures have a positive impact on the prevention of money laundering and illicit use of legal vehicles. However, if we recall the earlier chapters of this book, we can observe that the company law reforms increasingly enable business parties to set up companies without the intervention of professionals. It could be argued that this trend would only simplify the money laundering process. However, one must bear in mind that legal entities, in order to conduct activities, often have to open bank accounts which require the submission of VAT and corporate ID numbers. Financial institutions are thus the most suitable parties to prevent and combat money laundering.

---

[25] Swiss Confederation (2003: 27).
[26] Directive 2005/60/EC, 26 October 2005.

In this view, lawyers and other legal professionals provide an extra layer that serves as safety net in the prevention of the financial system for the purpose of money laundering. It should be noted that the Third Directive explicitly acknowledges this role by stating in Article 14 that member states may permit that legal professionals rely on client due diligence performed by trusted third parties.

In the conclusion, we will assess the important insights from previous sections and discuss the various reforms that policy-makers may wish to consider when approaching the regulation of related party transactions and beneficial ownership.

## 6. Conclusion

At the beginning of this chapter, we pointed out that there is a trade-off between the relative ease to establish new business entities and the illicit use of these vehicles. On this basis, this chapter has provided an overview of the actions taken by policy-makers to ameliorate the problem of related party transactions and beneficial ownership and control.

We commenced with a description of the contrasting ownership structures in Europe and argued that the problems created by majority and minority shareholder relationships are complex and that, given the variety of circumstances in which problems can arise, the balance of strategies needed to provide an effective regulatory framework to protect minority shareholders will be determined by different factors in each system and policy debate in each jurisdiction. We then asked why, given concentrated ownership, regulators should be concerned to stem the flow of illicit related party transactions. It was pointed out that, in some cases, related party transactions can play a positive role for firms. But to the extent that illicit related party transactions are detrimental to firm performance, we argued that they can be identified and prevented by a range of techniques. We argued the newly proposed audit reforms in the EU, which are designed to restore and enhance investor confidence through increased disclosure and transparency of related party transactions and SPEs, could prove effective in preventing the recurrence of Parmalat-style irregularities.

In section 5, we turned to discuss a closely related question, namely the disclosure of beneficial ownership and control. In this section we reported on multilateral and domestic initiatives to combat the misuse of corporate vehicles for illicit purposes. There is clear evidence of an association between the ability to obscure the identity of the beneficial owners from the authorities and the use of legal entities to carry out illegal activities. The incidence of illegal activity carried out through legal entities suggests that this type of problem cannot be ignored and may require a comprehensive solution, which as we have seen, may not rise immediately to the top of lawmakers' reform agendas. In order to obtain information about beneficial ownership, a variety of steps must be taken to facilitate effective disclosure. The most promising initiative focuses on the option of three possible disclosure systems for obtaining extensive disclosure of information in order to identify the beneficial owner. There are a number of factors that affect the selection of disclosure system for a jurisdiction. While we agree with this view, it is difficult to resist the conclusion that there may not be one efficient solution and that the appropriate system for a particular jurisdiction may change over time to conform to local conditions and company law traditions. We moved on to analyse the way anonymity is obtained and critically examined the possible legal strategies designed to induce disclosure. Since many of these strategies are new and untested, it is difficult to be confident about their effectiveness for curbing the abuse of legal entities. It should be noted, however, that the 'illicit-use' bias by regulators does not seem to hamper company law reforms that simplify the formation and operation of legal business forms to enable firms to organize and manage their business in the most effective manner. Although flexible and cheap business forms could surely stimulate the misuse of these entities, it is impossible to predict beforehand which ones will be engaged in illicit activities. Therefore, if the adoption of clear and simple company law rules is to be encouraged, the pain associated with the illegal use of these modern business forms must be regulated outside the realm of company law.

Naturally, the optional guidelines that were discussed in Chapter 7 could supplement the existing legal frameworks. Such guidelines do not enshrine principles and norms that are a 'must' for adoption by all firms. These guidelines should be in the form of advice. In that respect, they serve three purposes: (1) they provide the business participants with recommended solutions to complement the contractual flexibility of the company law rules; (2) they provide focal point solutions to corporate governance problems among business participants; and (3) they are meant to assist business participants in the interpretation and implementation of good governance practices. The guidelines should arguably contain recommendations on the different ownership and control structures of companies, the composition of the board of directors, and the best practice regarding related party transactions.

# 9

# Governance of Non-listed Companies: The Way Forward

## 1. A New Corporate Governance Debate

At the end of the twentieth century, the corporate governance movement captured the imagination of policy-makers, lawmakers, and company executives worldwide. Sceptics might have argued that it all started as merely a fashion trend among corporate law professors who were inspired by Berle and Means's book *The Modern Corporation and Private Property* (1933). In the modern corporation, characterized by the separation of ownership and control, the shareholders have lost their direct influence and involvement in the firm. As a consequence, managers and insider control groups are encouraged to pursue their own personal goals without taking the interests of the shareholders, other stakeholders, and society into account. Scholars have written extensively on the managerial agency problem, and have recommended the introduction of both market mechanisms and legal strategies that mitigate opportunism and shirking in listed companies (Klein and Coffee 2007).

The finance-ridden scandals in Europe and the USA further brought attention to the importance of governance and provided new momentum for introducing important legal and regulatory reforms. Certainly the scandals were not only instrumental in moving corporate governance up the policy-making agenda, but also in making corporate governance an integral part of the day-to-day decision-making process of public firms. Corporate governance is currently a major political issue, attracting considerable attention from policy-makers, lawmakers, company executives, shareholders, banks and other investors, the media, and legal and financial professionals. To be sure, managerial abuses have been around for as long as minority investors poured their money into risky ventures (such as the Dutch East India Company), and, as always, policy-makers and lawmakers have attempted to mitigate the underlying governance failures and errors. However, some argue that the current corporate governance movement has tended to over-react by creating too many rules and attempt to overprotect shareholders and other stakeholders. Unchecked, this trend could jeopardize entrepreneurship and longer-term economic growth. This prompts questions about the 'one-size-fits-all' mentality of policy-makers, lawmakers, and gatekeeper institutions and the success of ready-made strategies that can be detrimental to the operation and development of non-listed companies.

In this book, we have explored four developments that could usher in a new movement towards corporate governance initiatives focused on non-listed companies. First, the 'one-size-fits-all' and regulatory mentality of policy-makers arguably led to some undesired spill-over effects to non-listed companies. In this respect, separate corporate governance projects could mitigate the ambiguity and spill-over effects related to these issues. Second, since firms cannot afford to ignore the rewards of joint venturing any longer, it is important that business parties, both large and smaller enterprises, be made aware of the benefits of improved and stronger corporate governance structures for these joint operations. The refocusing of corporate governance on typical problems in these non-listed companies could help promote the economic performance of countries. Third, it is widely acknowledged that family-owned businesses and start-ups are the backbone of a country's economy. The typical life cycle of family-owned firms, however, indicates that where the first generation establishes the business, the second generation develops it and the third generation destroys it. Only companies with strong and professional governance structures are able to survive beyond the third generation. It is submitted that education and training of family-owned firms is of utmost importance to assure the steady and healthy growth of these businesses, while ensuring the continued participation of family members. Finally, it is only to be expected that non-listed firms, which rely heavily on bank finance and venture capital, would be required to have a professional governance structure in place. Separate corporate governance discussions could well contribute to the awareness creation regarding the beneficial effects of such measures.

## 2. The Corporate Governance Framework of Non-listed Companies

Why have policy-makers repeatedly chosen to provide governance structures for non-listed companies that are derived mainly from the framework designed for the public corporation? This book tested three theories that seek to explain the pattern of legal reform measures in this area. First, there are those who argue that the predominance of a particular legal structure tends to thwart the evolution of the law rather than enhancing its development. It is no surprise that this view, which argues that standardization of governance measures confers increasing returns on business parties, helps to explain the persistence and continuous use of the dominant business form, namely the corporate form, even if not ideally suited to some firms. A second theory, which builds on the economic theory of legislation, assumes that legal rules are demanded and supplied in much the same way as other products. Typically, interest groups will seek to influence key policy-makers and legislators to supply legal products in order to satisfy the outstanding demand for these changes. We expect the effectiveness of lobby groups corresponds not only to their size, organization, and ability, but to the height of the barriers they face when intervening to realize gains for the parties they represent. Third, those governments with sufficient resources may choose to ignore existing interest group pressures and instead officials may be encouraged to undertake innovations themselves. Besides traditional governance measures, policy-makers sometimes look to develop a variety of reforms to support their indigenous industries to successfully compete in this new environment.

The three views on the implication of legal reform give insights into the variations of corporate governance frameworks across countries, from the introduction of hybrid business forms to the emergence of codes of conduct for non-listed companies. In order to understand the variations, we look at the specific legal and contractual components of the corporate governance framework and focus on domestic debates to explain the domination of specific arrangements. We introduce a common approach for discussing a variety of corporate governance issues for non-listed firms. The common approach, which explains the three-way interaction among controlling shareholders, minority shareholders, and management, employs a three-pillar framework that consists of company law, contractual arrangements, and optional guidelines.

One of the key pillars, of course, is company law which could be viewed as the most important source of corporate governance techniques in the context of non-listed companies. The company law systems across jurisdictions contain rules on management control and disclosure and transparency, which are designed to enable shareholders to employ legal techniques that secure accurate and timely information on the financial affairs and performance of the company. In general, company law also provides for basic techniques that protect minority shareholders' interests through participation rights and legal restrictions on managers' power to act in response to directions given by controlling shareholders. More effective lock-in rules, moreover, should ensure both continued investment and minority protection. Fiduciary duties, for instance, should play an important role in preventing non *pro rata* distributions. The open-ended duty of loyalty arguably provides a safety mechanism to protect investors against the abusive tactics of controlling shareholders. In this view, courts and other conflict resolution bodies are crucial to fill the gaps in the corporate governance framework *ex post*.

However, the *ex post* gap-filling function of courts arguably resolves some issues only to raise others. In many cases, judicial intervention leads to costly and time-consuming procedures without making their outcome any more predictable. It is therefore not surprising that business parties often prefer to bargain for contractual provisions that deal with possible dissension and deadlocks *ex ante*. Examples from the area of family businesses and joint ventures portrayed a range of contractual arrangements through which business parties could be encouraged to resolve their differences and conflicts before resorting to the more costly and uncertain judicial process. Policy-makers and lawmakers appear to have picked up on this by either modernizing their company laws or introducing contractual entities that combine the best of traditional corporation and partnership forms. Indeed, pass-through taxation and the freedom to contractually establish the rights and obligations within the organizational structure economize on transaction costs such as drafting, information, and enforcement costs. The flexible provisions give business parties the opportunity not only to contract around the company law default rules, but also permit them to contract into additional protective measures that reflect their preferences.

Yet even when company law rules are sufficiently flexible to enable business parties to contract into the desired organizational structure, transaction costs and information asymmetries may prevent the emergence of effective and optimal governance solutions. While there could be a great appeal to the utilization of existing corporate governance mechanisms (designed for listed companies) to address, among other things, the ownership and control structures, the composition and operation of the board of management, transparency requirements, accessing outside capital, and strategies for succession planning and conflict resolution, this book has advocated the introduction of a separate approach to the creation of corporate governance guidelines. It is important, particularly in view of the need for more professionally managed non-listed businesses, to produce measures that are sufficiently attractive and coherent from a cost-benefit perspective to persuade non-listed companies to opt into a well-tailored framework of legal mechanisms and norms.

Thus, an optional set of recommendations could not only play a pivotal role in the awareness creation of the importance of good corporate governance practices, but also contain provisions about the benefits of educating and training board members and shareholders to become competent and reliable players in non-listed companies. Despite the prospective benefits of these guidelines, empirical research is needed to confirm the anticipated productivity effects for non-listed companies overall. In this regard, an important starting point for such work would be to analyse the implementation of the recent recommendations introduced by standard-setting institutions, such as the Belgian Buysse Committee and the European Venture Capital Association. Clearly, non-listed companies that operate under a well-designed and effective governance structure are likely to perform better and consequently will be more attractive to external investors. All in all, the flexibility and informality of company law and the introduction of optional guidelines have proved beneficial in the European venture capital industry. Yet, as is always the case, government regulation, such as restrictions on foreign direct investment and rules governing public offerings, may influence the structure of ownership in non-listed companies. Surely the real amount of regulation needed for non-listed firms is a crucial issue that should not be ignored in the corporate governance discussions.

Three important directions for the future, which lie in the relationship between the firm and the government are outlined in the following subsections.

## 2.1 Company Law Restrictions on Foreign Direct Investment

In the context of foreign direct investment (FDI), countries over the years have with increasing frequency sought to liberalize their foreign direct investment rules and the array of restrictions that affect the flow of capital across borders. We can clearly observe the changes that are taking place in the areas of foreign ownership and foreign participation. Still the evidence suggests that many countries, like China, Thailand, and surprisingly Canada, are found to have highly restrictive measures to protect their domestic industries, primarily in the services sectors including transportation, electricity, financial services, and insurance. In particular, the rules on management and the composition of the board of directors add another layer to the regulatory costs for foreign investors. For instance, should a foreign investor undertake to establish a subsidiary in a country with restrictive measures on FDI, we typically see at work the implementation of draconian restrictions (i.e., mandatory screening and approval by the government of the foreign direct investor, restriction of ownership, etc) that effectively undermine all efforts to attract FDI.

This is an important issue, for emerging market economies that have been found to create legislation that promotes FDI were unable to ensure implementation and effective enforcement of such measures. Naturally, this situation creates complications for foreign firms that are, regardless of circumstances, obliged to employ directors and carry out their operations according to standards set by their investors. If, for example, a parent company is required to appoint one or more local directors to the board of its subsidiary, it should be expected, given the incentives, that protective measures are in place to oversee the performance of these directors. Equally important, governments continue to use ownership restrictions that make it difficult for investors to maximize their returns on investment.

There are alternatives to this situation. Consider the free trade agreements (FTAs) that are entered into by investor countries to liberalize the restrictions on investment and trade. While the potential for this approach is high, empirical work that has already been conducted indicates that there are numerous restrictions that continue to hamper investment across the board (Urata and Sasuya 2007). In addition, there is another strand of empirical work conducted under similar lines which asks how the corporate governance framework in emerging markets can be influenced by the entry of foreign firms (Loungani and Razin 2001). Since the emerging markets with their relatively small number of listed companies have a particular interest in seeking to understand the corporate governance challenges for non-listed companies, we clearly need more empirical research to show the most effective measures to increase transparency and control and to facilitate the conditions for effective business contracting while limiting corruption.

## 2.2 The Development of an Equity-oriented Market

Smaller firms are sometimes foreclosed from raising capital from banking institutions because they are unable to commit collateral and have a limited track record of success. The implementation of the Basel II Accords is likely to reduce further the availability of funds for small and medium-sized enterprises. At the same time, we expect more closely held firms, like family-controlled companies, to access the public capital markets for their financing needs, particularly as Europe moves towards the adoption of an equity-oriented system.

It is noteworthy that the New Markets in Europe were launched already in the late 1990s. They were conceived to facilitate the financing of innovative companies with low capitalizations and high growth potentials that would ordinarily have been excluded earlier. As with United States-based NASDAQ, the alternative markets adopted a combination of stricter disclosure rules and less stringent entry requirements (regarding size, age, and minimum profitability requirements) than companies on first-tier markets. Lower regulatory barriers and ideal market conditions together led to the development of a very active IPO market in Europe until 2001, when a wide-ranging market shake-up occurred leading to the rapid consolidation of this market segment. Ultimately, the Alternative Investment Market (AIM) emerged as the market leader due largely to having succeeded in diversifying the mix of companies seeking a listing, and ensuring effective disclosure for investors.

Throughout the recent period, AIM consolidated its position as the market leader in listings based primarily on admissions rules that are not very stringent for firms with low market capitalization. As such, AIM functions as an alternative to the private equity market for many classes of companies. We clearly see that AIM has succeeded in attracting US firms which have attempted to flee the higher regulatory costs introduced in the wake of the Enron scandal. AIM serves as a model for other jurisdictions, such as Brazil, in developing a platform for facilitating alternative sources of financing for SMEs and family firms. Still, we believe it would be worthwhile to carry out a more systematic exploration of the implications of establishing AIM-style exchanges that can be seen as substitutes for private equity financing. That said, we also would like to explore whether the AIM model is likely to emerge as the dominant approach for public listings or will the tighter regulated NASDAQ prove superior in the longer run (Doidge et al 27; Committee on Capital Markets Regulation 2006).

## 2.3 The Going Private Decision and the Listing of Private Equity Firms

Despite the extra costs of complying with the tougher corporate governance regulations, the corporate form arguably remains the dominant form of structuring a business. In most western jurisdictions, the majority of firms are organized under the provisions of corporate statute. Such statutes confer substantial learning and network effects on its users, including statutory provisions and case law. These effects, which come from the use of the corporate form, for instance, explain why most of the parties that originally opted into this form have an incentive to continue to use the regime. Factors that arguably add to the value of the corporation include avoidance of formulation errors, ease in drafting the articles of association, availability of case law on the interpretation of the statute, and the familiarity to business participants. The consequence of network and learning effects is the continuous use of the dominant business form, even if it is not ideally suited to some types of firms. Indeed, the recent corporate governance reforms are of course no impediment to ending the dominance of the corporate form. On the one hand, the listed firms have no other choice but to comply with the new regulations or to explain why they take a different route. Other firms may even be attracted to applying these tougher corporate governance rules voluntarily. They use compliance with rigorous corporate governance principles as a marketing tool to demonstrate to potential investors their trustworthiness and transparent status.

On the other hand, however, a large number of publicly held firms view the corporate governance reforms as too cumbersome and costly. They look to escape the application of corporate governance regulations by delisting their shares from the stock exchange. In addition, firms that are planning an IPO may very well reconsider their intention.

From these firms' perspective, the exorbitantly high compliance costs (lawyers fees, director's liability, hiring independent directors or supervisors) exceed the network and learning benefits of the corporate form. They are not persuaded that the new regulations will be effective in promoting better corporate governance and may even lead to unintended results. They are of the opinion that the corporate governance reforms have gone too far. The new developments may even hamper enterpreneurship. In this view, the costs of complying with the new rules and standards only exhaust the firm's resources. The only winners are the accountants and other company advisers, and the firm's competitors to which the extensive transparency requirements are a welcome opportunity to adjust their business policies.

Given the rising regulatory burden, a large number of firms have chosen to delist. Some have even been taken private by large private equity firms, such as Carlyle, Blackstone, and Kohlberg Kravis Roberts. It is perhaps an irony that a number of the leading private equity firms have taken a radical step to go public through listings on the New York Stock Exchange, London Stock Exchange, and the Euronext respectively. There will be surely those commentators who argue that these new-style offerings involving private equity partnerships may lead to a different type of firm. To see this, the private equity firms taken public have employed, for example, a limited partnership structure in which the public investors own units. In this construction, investors are deprived of the normal complement of rights, such as fiduciary duties and voting powers, that accompany the corporate form. While the decision-making authority rests solely with the general partners in these constructions, investors enjoy few privileges as a consequence of contracting into this arrangement. Clearly this trend raises a number of important policy questions. First, can we identify the consequence of the trade-off investors make between the package of rights that they typically receive when purchasing shares in a public corporation, and the normal distributions and incentive structure that characterize the private equity-based partnership structure used in this industry? Second, do we need a separate governance structure that offers investors in these limited partnerships a direct right to influence the decision-making procedure in portfolio companies? It has become apparent that the private equity partnership has chosen to continue operating non-listed companies to avoid excessive state and federal regulation that now threatens the public corporation. If this trend were to succeed, it could very well become a blueprint for a new type of firm.

## 3. Where We Stand

In the end, the central reason for analysing the corporate governance of non-listed companies is that this subject should begin to play a pivotal role in policy discussions around the world. If we recall the dominant position of the public corporation in mainstream discussions on corporate governance, we understand why non-listed companies receive less attention than their public counterparts. But there is no excuse for neglecting the needs of closely held companies. In this book, we have encouraged an expansive approach to corporate governance, notably by bringing into proper focus the realm of the closely held company, as a legitimate and important perspective for policy-makers and lawmakers to think about when undertaking legislative reforms.

# References

Abd Ghadas, Z.A. (2007), 'Limited Liability and its Potential for Malaysian SME Entrepreneurs', *IIUM Law Journal*, 14/1.

Alchian, AA, and Demsetz, H (1972), 'Production, Information, and Economic Organization', *American Economic Review* 62: 777–85.

Ali, PU, and Gregoriou GN, (eds) (2006), *International Corporate Governance after Sarbanes-Oxley*, Hoboken, NJ: Wiley Finance.

Arcot, SR, and Bruno, VG (2006), 'One Size Does Not Fit All, After All: Evidence from Corporate Governance', Working Paper (available at SSRN: http://ssrn.com/abstract=887947).

Arlen, J (1998), 'The Future of Behavioral Economic Analysis of Law', *Vanderbilt Law Review* 51: 1765–88.

Armour, J (2006), 'Legal Capital: an Outdated Concept?', *European Business Organization Law Review* 7: 5–27.

—— and McCahery, J (eds) (2006), *After Enron: Improving Corporate Law and Modernising Securities Regulation in Europe and the US*, Oxford: Hart Publishing.

Arthur, WB (1994), *Increasing Returns and Path Dependence in the Economy*, Ann Arbor: University of Michigan Press.

—— (1996), 'Increasing Returns and the New World of Business', *Harvard Business Review* 72: 100–9.

Association of German Banks (2007), 'Making Hedge Funds More Transparent', 15 May (available at: <www.bdb.de>).

Audretsch, DB, and Thurik R (2001), 'Linking Entrepreneurship to Growth', OECD Science, Technology and Industry Working Paper, 2001/2, OECD Publishing, doi:10.1787/736170038056.

Ayres, I (1992), 'Judging Close Corporations in the Age of Statutes', *Washington University Law Quarterly* 70: 365–97.

—— (1998), 'Default Rules for Incomplete Contracts', in P Newman (ed), *The New Palgrave Dictionary of Economics and the Law*, London: Macmillan Reference Limited, i. 585–90.

Bainbridge, SM (2005), 'Abolishing LLC Veil Piercing', *University of Illinois Law Review* 77–106.

Bamford, J and Ernst, D (2005), 'Governing Joint Ventures', *The McKinsey Quarterly* special edition: *Value and Performance*.

Bankman, J (1994), 'The Structure of Silicon Valley Start-ups', *UCLA Law Review* 41: 1737–68.

—— and Gilson, RJ (1999), 'Why Start-ups?', *Stanford Law Review* 51: 289–308.

Banoff, BA (2001), 'Company Governance under Florida's New Limited Liability Company Act', Florida State University College of Law Public Law and Legal Theory Working Paper No 43.

Bebchuk, LA and Jolls, C (1999), 'Managerial Value Diversion and Shareholder Wealth', *Journal of Law, Economics and Organization* 15: 487.

—— and Roe, MJ (1999), 'A Theory of Path Dependency in Corporate Ownership and Governance', *Stanford Law Review* 52: 127–70.

Becht, M, Mayer, C, and Wagner, HF (2007), 'Where Do Firms Incorporate?' ECGI Law Working Paper No 70/2006, September 2007.

Becker, GS (1983), 'A Theory of Competition among Pressure Groups for Political Influence', *Quarterly Journal of Economics* 98: 371–400.

Bennedsen, M, Nielsen, K, Perez-Gonzales, F, and Wolfenzon, D (2007), 'Inside the Family Firm: The Role of Families in Succession Decisions and Performance', *Quarterly Journal of Economics*, 647–91.

—— (2003), 'The Transplant Effect', *American Journal of Comparative Law* 51: 163–203.

Berglöf, E, and Burkart, M (2003), 'EU Takeover Regulation', *Economic Policy* 173–213.

Berglöf, E, and Claessens, S (2004), 'Enforcement and Corporate Governance', World Bank Research Policy Working Paper No 3409, September.

Berkowitz, D, Pistor, K, and Richard, J-F (2002), 'Economic Development, Legality and the Transplant Effect', *European Economic Review* 32: 221–39.

Berle, AA, and Means, GC (1933), *The Modern Corporation and Private Property* (rev edn 1991).

Berman, HJ (1983), *Law and Revolution: The Formation of the Western Legal Tradition*, Cambridge, Mass.: Harvard University Press.

Bernardo, AE and Welch, I (2001), 'On the Evolution of Overconfidence and Entrepreneurs', *Journal of Economics & Management Strategy* 10/3: 301–30.

Blashek, RD, and McLean, SA (2006), 'Investments in "Pass-Through" Portfolio Companies by Private Equity Partnerships: Tax Strategies and Structuring', PLI Order No 9068.

Blumberg, PI (1986), 'Limited Liability and Corporate Groups', *Journal of Corporation Law* 11: 573–631.

Bolton, P, and Dewatripont, M (2005), *Contract Theory*, Cambridge, Mass.: MIT Press.

Bourdieu, P (1987), 'The Force of Law: Toward a Sociology of the Juridical Field', *Hastings Law Journal* 38: 805–53 (Translator's Introduction by R Terdiman).

Bratton, WW (2002), 'Venture Capital on the Downside: Preferred Stock and Corporate Control', *Michigan Law Review* 100: 891–945.

—— (2007), 'Hedge Funds and Governance Targets', *Georgetown Law Journal* 95: 1375–433.

—— and McCahery, JA (1995), 'Regulatory Competition, Regulatory Capture, and Corporate Self-Regulation', *North Carolina Law Review* 73: 1861–947.

—— (1997), 'An Inquiry into the Efficiency of the Limited Liability Company: Of Theory of the Firm and Regulatory Competition', *Washington and Lee Law Review* 54: 629–86.

—— (1999), 'Comparative Corporate Governance and the Theory of the Firm: The Case against Global Cross Reference', *Columbia Journal of Transnational Law* 38: 213–97.

—— (2001), 'Tax Coordination and Tax Competition in the European Union: Evaluating the Code of Conduct on Business Taxation', *Common Market Law Review* 38: 677–718.

—— (2006), 'The Equilibrium Content of Corporate Federalism', *Wake Forest Law Review* 41: 619–96.

Brav, A, Jiang, W, Partnoy, F, and Thomas, RS (2006), 'Hedge Fund Activism, Corporate Governance, and Firm Performance', Working Paper.

Butler, HN and Ribstein, LE (2006), *The Sarbanes-Oxley Debacle: What We've Learned; How to Fix It*, Washington, DC: AEI Press.

Buxbaum, RM, and Hopt, KJ (1988), *Legal Harmonization and the Business Enterprise*, Berlin: de Gruyter.

Callison, WJ (2001), *LLC: State by State Guide to Law and Practice*, St Paul, Minn.: West Publishing.

Carey, DC, and Patsalos-Fox, M (2006), 'Shaping Strategy from the Boardroom', <www.mckinseyquarterly.com>.

Carney, WJ (1997), 'The Political Economy of Competition for Corporate Charters', *Journal of Legal Studies* 26: 303–29.

Cary, WL, and Eisenberg, MA (1988), *Corporations, Cases and Materials*, Westbury: The Foundation Press.

Charkham, J (2005), *Keeping Better Company, Corporate Governance Ten Years On*, Oxford: Oxford University Press.

Charny, D (1991), 'Competition among Jurisdictions in Formulating Corporate Law Rules: An American Perspective on the "Race to the Bottom" in the European Communities', *Harvard International Law Journal* 32: 423–56.

Cheffins, BR (1997), *Company Law: Theory, Structure, and Operation*, Oxford: Clarendon Press.

Chidambaran, NK, Palia, D, and Zheng, Y (2006), 'Does Better Corporate Governance "Cause" Better Firm Performance', Working Paper.

Claessens, S, Djankov, S, Fan, J, and Long, L (2002), 'Separation of Ownership and Control in East Asian Corporations', *Journal of Financial Economics* 57: 2741–71.

Clark, R (1986), *Corporate Law*, Boston: Little & Brown.

——(1989), 'Contracts, Elites, and Traditions in the Making of Corporate Law', *Columbia Law Review* 89: 1703–47.

Coase, RH (1988), *The Firm, the Market, and the Law*, Chicago: University of Chicago Press.

Coffee, JC Jr (2005), 'A Theory of Corporate Scandals: Why the US and Europe Differ', *Oxford Review of Economic Policy* 21.

Committee on Capital Markets Regulation (2006), 'Interim Report of the Committee on Capital Markets Regulation', 30 November (available at: <http://crapo.senate.gov/documents/committee_copmarkets_reg.pdf>).

Coombes, P, and Chiu-Yin Wong, S (2004), 'Why Codes of Governance Work', (available at <www.mckinseyquarterly.com>).

Cronqvist, H, and Fahlenbrach, R (2007), 'Large Shareholders and Corporate Policies', Fisher College of Business Working Paper.

Cumming, DJ, and Johan, SA (2006), 'Is it the Law or the Lawyers? Investment Fund Covenants across Countries', *European Financial Management* 12: 535–74.

——and MacIntosh, JG (2006), 'Crowding out Private Equity: Canadian Evidence', *Journal of Business Venturing* 21: 569–609.

Davies, PJ (2006), 'Enron and Corporate Law Reform in the UK and the European Community in Armour' in J Armour and JA McCahery (eds), *After Enron: Improving Corporate Law and Modernising Securities Regulation in Europe and the US*, Oxford: Hart Publishing.

De Figueiredo, JM (2002), 'Lobbying and Information in Politics', Harvard John M Olin Discussion Paper no 369.

——and Tiller, EH (2001), 'The Structure and Conduct of Corporate Lobbying: How Firms Lobby the Federal Communication Commission', *Journal of Economics & Management Strategy* 10: 91–122.

De Jong, A (2006), 'De Ratio van Corporate Governance', Inaugural Lecture Erasmus University Rotterdam, 6 October 2006.

De Jong, A, and Röell, A (2005), 'Financing and Control in the Netherlands: A Historical Perspective', in R Morck (ed), *A History of Corporate Ownership around the World: Family Business Groups to Professional Managers*, Chicago: University of Chicago Press, 341–64.

De Jong, B, and Nieuwe Weme, M (2006), *Publicatie van de jaarrekening*, Deventer: Kluwer.

Department of Finance Canada (2005) *Canada's Tax and Other Issues Related to Publicly Listed Flow-through Entities (Income Trusts and Limited Partnerships)*.

Dixit, AK (2004), *Lawlessness and Economics: Alternative Modes of Governance*, Princeton: Princeton University Press.

Djankov, S, La Porta, R, Lopez-de-Silanes, F, Shleifer, A (2002), 'The Regulation of Entry', *Quarterly Journal of Economics* 117: 1–37.

Doidge, C, Karolyi, GA, and Stulz, R (2007), 'Has New York Become Less Competitive in Global Markets? Evaluating Foreign Listing Choices over Time', ECGI-Finance Working Paper No 173/2007 (available at: <SSRN: http://SSRN.com/abstract=982193>).

Dorgan, SJ, Dowdy, JJ, and Rippin, TM (2006), 'Who Should and Shouldn't Run the Family Business', (available at: <www.mckinseyquarterly.com>).

DTI (1999), *Modern Company Law for a Competitive Economy: The Strategic Framework*, UK Consultation Document from the Company Law Review Steering Group (available at: www.dti.gov.uk/bbf/co-act-2006/clr-review/page22794.html>).

——— (2001), *The Company Law Review Steering Group's Final Report 2001* (available at: <www.dit.gov.uk/cld/review.htm>).

Dyck, A, and Zingales, L (2004), 'Private Benefits of Control: An International Comparison', *Journal of Finance* 59: 537–600.

Easterbrook, FH, and Fischel, DR (1986), 'Close Corporations and Agency Costs', *Stanford Law Review* 38: 271–301.

——— (1991), *The Economic Structure of Corporate Law*, Cambridge, Mass.: Harvard University Press.

Ebke, WF (2000), '*Centros*: Some Realities and Some Mysteries', *American Journal of Comparative Law* 48: 623–60.

*Economist* (2006), 'Battling for Corporate America', 9 March.

Edwards, V (1999), *EC Company Law*, Oxford: Clarendon Press.

Elstrod, H-P (2003), 'Keeping the Family in Business', (available at: <www.mckinseyquarterly.com>).

Enriques, L. (2004), 'Silence is Golden: The European Company Statute as a Catalyst for Company Law Arbitrage', *Journal of Corporate Law Studies* 4: 77–95.

——— (2005), 'Bad Apples, Bad Oranges: A Comment from Old Europe on Post-Enron Corporate Governance Reforms', *Wake Forest Law Review* 38: 911–34.

——— and Macey, JR (2001), 'Creditors versus Capital Formation: The Case against the European Legal Capital Rules', *Cornell Law Review* 86: 1165–204.

Ernst, D et al (2003), 'Crafting the Agreement: Lawyers and Managers', in JD Bamford et al, *Mastering Alliance Strategy: A Comprehensive Guide to Design, Management, and Organization*, San Francisco: Jossey-Bass, 88–106.

European Venture Capital Association (2001), *Corporate Venturing European Activity Report Update 2001*, Brussels: EVCA.

—— (2003), 'EVCA Governing Principles' (available at: <www.evca.com>).

—— (2005), 'EVCA Corporate Governance Guidelines' (available at: <www.evca.com>).

—— (2006a), 'EVCA Reporting Guidelines' (available at: <www.evca.com>).

—— (2006b), 'International Private Equity and Venture Capital Valuation Guidelines' (available at: <www.evca.com>).

Faccio, M, and Lang, L (2002), 'The Ultimative Ownership of Western European Companies', *Journal of Financial Economics* 65(3): 365–95.

Fama, EF, and Jensen, MC (1983a), 'Separation of Ownership and Control', *Journal of Law and Economics* 26: 301–25.

—— (1983b), 'Agency Problems and Residual Claims', *Journal of Law and Economics* 26: 327–49.

Fanto, JA (2002), 'Persuasion and Resistance: The Use of Psychology by Anglo-American Corporate Governance Advocates in France', Working Paper, 7 May.

Feldman, S (2005), *Principles of Private Firm Valuation*, London: Wiley.

Ferrarini, GA (2005), 'Origins of Limited Liability Companies and Company Law Modernisation in Italy: A Historical Outline', in E Gepken-Jager et al, *VOC 1602–2002: 400 Years of Company Law*, Deventer: Kluwer Legal Publishers, 187–215.

—— and Giudici, P (2006), 'Financial Scandals and the Role of Private Enforcement: The Parmalat Case', in J Armour and JA McCahery (eds), *After Enron: Improving Corporate Law and Modernising Securities Regulation in Europe and the US*, Oxford: Hart Publishing, 159–213.

Fleischer, V (2003) 'The Rational Exuberance of Structuring Venture Capital Startups', UCLA School of Law, Law & Econ. Research Paper no 20–03.

Foley and Lardner, LLP (2005), '2005 Private Cost Study', (available at: <www.Foley.com>).

—— (2006a), The Impact of Sarbanes-Oxley on Private & Non-Profit Companies (March 2006)

—— (2006b) The Cost of Being Public in the Era of Sarbanes-Oxley (June 2006).

Freedman, J (1999), 'The Quest for an Ideal Form for Small Businesses: A Misconceived Enterprise?', in BAK Rider and M Andenas (eds), *Developments in European Company Law*, ii: *The Quest for an Ideal Legal Form for Small Businesses*, London: Kluwer Law International, 5–34.

—— (2004), 'Limited Liability Partnerships in the United Kingdom: Do They Have a Role for Small Firms?', in JA McCahery, MJGC Raaijmakers, and EPM Vermeulen (eds), *The Governance of Close Corporations and Partnerships: US and European Perspectives*, Oxford: Oxford University Press, 293–316.

Friedman, E, Johnson, S, and Mitton, T (2003), 'Propping and Tunneling', *Journal of Comparative Economics* 31: 732–50.

Gaastra, FS (1991), *De geschiedenis van de VOC*, Zutphen: Walburg Press.

Gammie, M (2003), 'The Role of the European Court of Justice in the Development of Direct Taxation in the European Union', *Bulletin for International Fiscal Documentation* 57: 86–98.

Gersick, K, Davis, J, Hampton, M, and Lansberg, I (1997), *Generation to Generation: Life Cycles of the Family Business*, Cambridge, Mass.: Harvard Business School.

Gillette, CP (1998), 'Lock-in Effects in Law and Norms', *Boston University Law Review* 78: 813–42.

Gilson, RJ (2001), 'Globalizing Corporate Governance: Convergence of Form or Function', *American Journal of Comparative Law* 49: 329–58.

Gilson, R (2003), 'Engineering a Venture Capital Market: Lessons from the American Experience', *Stanford Law Review* 55: 1067–1104.

Goetz, ChJ, and Scott, RE (1985), 'The Limits of Expanded Choice: An Analysis of the Interactions between Express and Implied Contract Terms', *California Law Review* 73: 261–322.

Gompers, PA (1995), 'Optimal Investment and Staging of Venture Capital', *Journal of Finance* 50: 1461–89.

——and Lerner, J (1996), 'The Use of Covenants: An Empirical Analysis of Venture Capital Partnership Agreements', *Journal of Law and Economics* 39: 463–98.

Grossman, G, and Helpman E (2001), *Special Interest Politics*, Cambridge, Mass.: MIT Press.

Halbhuber, H (2001), 'National Doctrinal Structures and European Company Law', *Common Market Law Review* 38: 1385–420.

Halpern, P (1999), 'Systemic Perspectives on Corporate Governance Systems', Working Paper.

Hamilton, RW (2001), 'Professional Partnerships in the United States', *Journal of Corporation Law* 26: 1045–60.

Hansmann, H, and Kraakman, R (2000), 'The Essential Role of Organizational Law', *Yale Law Journal* 110: 387–440.

Hart, O (1995), *Firms, Contracts, and Financial Structure*, Oxford: Clarendon Press.

Hedge Fund Working Group (2007), 'Consultation Paper, Part I: Approach to Best Practice Context', 9 October.

Henry, E, Gordon, EA, Reed, B, and Louwers, T (2007), 'The Role of Related Party Transactions in Fraudulent Financial Reporting', Working Paper.

Hessels, SJA, and Hooge, EH (2006) 'Small Business Governance', Een verkenning naar de betekenis en de praktijk van corporate governance in het MKB, Zoetermeer, 14 February.

Hochstetler, WS, and Svejda, MD (1985), 'Statutory Needs of Close Corporations—An Empirical Study: Special Close Corporation Legislation or Flexible General Corporation Law?', *Journal of Corporation Law* 10: 849–1049.

Holmen, M, and Högfeldt, P (2005), 'Pyramidal Discounts: Tunneling or Agency Costs', ECGI Working Paper (available at: <SSRN: http://SSRN/com/Abstract=667743>).

Hopt, K (2007), 'Concluding Remarks 1st ECFR Symposium in Milan, 2006', *European Company and Financial Law Review* 4: 169–72.

Horowitz, DL (1994), 'The Qur'an and the Common Law: Islamic Law Reform and the Theory of Legal Chance', *American Journal of Comparative Law* 42: 233–93; 543–80.

Hu, HTC, and Black, B (2006), 'The New Vote Buying: Empty Voting and Hidden (Morphable) Ownership', *Southern California Law Review* 79: 811–908.

Inman, RP, and Rubinfeld, DL (1997), 'Rethinking Federalism', *Journal of Economic Perspectives* 11: 43–64.

IASB (2007), 'Exposure Draft for Small and Medium-sized Entities' (available at: <www.iasb.org>).

ISS (2006), 'Corporate Governance Assessment Report of the 100 Top Chinese Listed Companies in 2006', (available at: <www.issproxy.com>).

——Shearman & Sterling and ECGI (2007), 'Report on the Proportionality Principle in the European Union, Brussels: ISS Europe, Shearman & Sterling and ECGI (available at: <http://www.ecgi.org/osov/documents/final-report_en.pdf>).

Jaeger, RA (2003), *All about Hedge Funds*, New York: McGraw-Hill.

Jensen, C, and Meckling, WH (1976), 'Theory of the Firm: Managerial Behavior, Agency Costs and Ownership Structure', *Journal of Financial Economics* 3: 305–60.

Kahan, M, and Klausner, M (1996), 'Path Dependence in Corporate Contracting: Increasing Returns, Herd Behavior and Cognitive Biases', *Washington University Law Quarterly* 74: 347–66.

——(1997), 'Standardization and Innovation in Corporate Contracting (or "The Economics of Boilerplate")', *Virginia Law Review* 83: 713–70.

——and Rock, EB (2007), 'Hedge Funds in Corporate Governance and Corporate Control', *University of Pennsylvania Law Review* 155: 1021–91.

Kamar, E, Karaca-Mandic, P, and Talley, E (2006), 'Going Private Decisions and the Sarbanes Oxley Act of 2002: A Cross-Country Analysis', Rand Institute of Civil Justice Reviewed Working Paper, WR-300-ICJ and USC Center in Law Economics and Organization Research Paper, No 005–12.

Katz, ML, and Shapiro, C (1986), 'Technology Adoption in the Presence of Network Externalities', *Journal of Political Economy* 94: 822–41.

Kelsen, H (1967), *Pure Theory of Law*, Berkeley: University of California Press.

Kirchner, C, Painter, RW, and Kaal, W (2005), 'Regulatory Competition in EU Corporate Law after Inspire Art: Unbundling Delaware's Product for Europe', *European Company and Financial Law Review* 2: 159–206.

Klausner, M (1995), 'Corporations, Corporate Law, and Networks of Contracts', *Virginia Law Review* 81: 757–852.

——(2005), 'Limitations of Corporate Law in Promoting Good Corporate Governance', in JW Lorsch, L Berkowitz, and A Zelleke (eds), *Restoring Trust in American Business*, Cambridge, Mass.: MIT Press.

——and Litvak, K (2001), 'What Economists Have Taught Us about Venture Capital Contracting', in MJ Whincop (ed), *Linking Government with Regulatory Policy*, Aldershot: Ashgate.

Klein, WA, and Coffee, JC jr (2007), *Business Organization and Finance*, New York: Foundation Press.

——Ramseyer, JM, and Bainbridge, SM (2003), *Cases and Materials on Business Associations: Agency, Partnership, and Corporations*, New York: Foundation Press.

Kobayashi, BH, and Ribstein, LE (2007), 'The Non-uniformity of Uniform Laws', Working Paper.

Kortum, S, and Lerner, J (2000), 'Assessing the Contribution of Venture Capital to Innovation', *RAND Journal of Economics*, 31: 674–92.

Kraakman R, Davies, P, Hansmann, H, Hertig, G, Hopt, KJ, Kanda, H, and Rock, EB (2004), *The Anatomy of Corporate Law: A Comparative and Functional Approach*, Oxford: Oxford University Press.

Laffont, J-J, and Tirole, J, (1993), *A Theory of Incentives in Procurement and Regulation*, Cambridge, Mass.: MIT Press.

Lamoreaux, NR (1998), 'Partnerships, Corporations, and the Theory of the Firm', *American Economic Review* 88: 66–71.

La Porta, R, Lopez-de-Silanes, F, Shleifer, A, and Vishny, RW (1997), 'Legal Determinants of External Finance', *Journal of Finance* 52: 1131–50.

—— (1998), 'Law and Finance', *Journal of Political Economy* 106: 1113–221.

Leleux, P (1968), 'Corporation Law in the United States and in the E.E.C.: Some Comments on the Present Situation and the Future Prospects', *Common Market Law Review* 6: 133–76.

Lemley, MA, and McGowan, D (1998), 'Legal Implications of Network Economic Effects', *California Law Review* 86: 479–611.

Lerner, J (1995), 'Venture Capitalists and the Oversight of Private Firms', *Journal of Finance* 50: 301–18.

Lewis, JD (1999), *Trusted Partners: How Companies Build Mutual Trust and Win Together*, New York: The Free Press.

Liebowitz, SJ, and Margolis, SE (1995), 'Path Dependence, Lock-in and History', *Journal of Law, Economics and Organization* 11/1: 205–26.

—— (1998), 'Network Effects and Externalities', in P Newman (ed), *The New Palgrave Dictionary of Economics and the Law*, London: Macmillan Reference Limited, ii: 671–5.

Loss, L (1998), *Fundamentals of Securities Regulation*, Boston: Little, Brown and Company.

Loungani, P, and Razin, A (2001), 'An Analysis of the Restrictions on Foreign Direct Investment in Free Trade Agreements', RIETI Discussion Paper 07-E018.

Lutter, M (1998), 'Limited Liability Companies and Private Companies', in D Vagts (ed), *International Encyclopedia of Comparative Law*, xiii: Business and Private Organizations, Tübingen: Mohr Siebeck.

McCahery, JA, and Renneboog, L (2003a), *The Economics of the Proposed European Takeover Directive*, Brussels: Center for European Policy Studies.

—— (2003b), 'Venture Capital and the Financing of High Tech Firms: An Introduction', in JA McCahery and L Renneboog (eds), *Venture Capital and the Valuation of High Tech Firms*, Oxford: Oxford University Press, 1–26.

—— and Vermeulen, EPM (2007), 'Corporate Governance, Investor Protection and Performance in The Netherlands', *Revue Trimestrielle de Droit Financier* 95–108.

McCormick, RE and Tollison, RD (1981), *Politicians, Legislation, and the Economy: An Inquiry into the Interest-Group Theory of Government*, Boston: Martinus Nijhoff Publishing.

McCubbins, MD, Noll, RG, Weingast, BR (1989), 'Structures and Process, Politics and Policy: Administrative Arrangements and the Political Control of Agencies', *Virginia Law Review* 75: 431–82.

—— and Schwartz, T (1984), 'Congressional Oversight Overlooked: Police Patrols versus Fire Alarms', *American Journal of Political Science* 28: 165–79.

Macey, JR (1998), 'Public Choice and the Law', in P Newman (ed), *The New Palgrave Dictionary of Economics and the Law*, London: Macmillan Reference Limited, iii. 171–7.

Mahoney, PG (1998), 'Trust and Opportunism in Close Corporations', National Bureau of Economic Research (NBER) Working Paper 6819 (available at: <SSRN: http://SSRN.com/Abstract=141122>).

Mattei, U (1994), 'Efficiency in Legal Transplants: An Essay in Comparative Law and Economics', *International Review of Law and Economics* 14: 3–19.

Mendoza, JM (2007), 'Securities Regulation in Low-Tier Listing Venues: The Rise of the Alternative Investment Market', (available at: <www.SSRN.com>).

Metrick, A (2007), *Venture Capital and the Finance of Innovation*, Hoboken, WJ: John Wiley & Sons.

Milgrom, PR, North, DC, and Weingast, BR (1990), 'The Role of Institutions in the Revival of Trade: The Law Merchant, Private Judges, and the Champagne Fairs', *Economics and Politics* 2: 1–23.

Milhaupt, CJ (2005), 'In the Shadow of Delaware? The Rise of Hostile Takeovers in Japan', *Columbia Law Review* 105: 2171–216.

Miller, SK (1997), 'Minority Shareholder Oppression in the Private Company in the European Community: A Comparative Analysis of the German, United Kingdom, and French "Close Corporation Problem"', *Cornell International Law Journal* 30: 381–427.

Miller, R, Glen, J, Jaspersen, F, and Karmokolias, Y (1997), 'International Joint Ventures in Developing Countries', *Finance & Development* (March): 26–9.

Monateri, PG, and Sacco, R (1998), 'Legal Formants', in P Newman (ed), *The New Palgrave Dictionary of Economics and the Law*, London: Macmillan Reference Limited, ii. 531–3.

Murdoch, CW (2001), 'Limited Liability Companies in the Decade of the 1990s: Legislative and Case Law Developments and their Implications for the Future'. *Business Lawyer* 56: 499–571.

Nam, SM and Nam, JE (2004), *Corporate Governance in Asia, Recent Evidence from Indonesia, Republic of Korea, Malaysia, and Thailand*, Asian Development Bank Institute (available at: <www.krsi.org>).

Niemeier, W (2006), GmbH und Limited im Markt der Unternehmensrechtsträger, *Zeitschrift für Wirtschaftsrecht (ZIP)* 37:1794-1801.

—— (2007), 'Die "Mini-GmbH" (UG) trotz Marktwende bei der Limited: *Zeitschrift für Wirtschaftsrecht (ZIP)* 38: 2237-50.

OECD (2001), *Behind the Corporate Veil: Using Corporate Entities for Illicit Purposes*, Paris: OECD.

—— (2004), *Principles of Corporate Governance*, Paris: OECD.

—— (2005), *Corporate Governance of Non-listed Companies in Emerging Markets* Paris: OECD.

Oesterle, DA (1995), 'Subcurrents in LLC Statutes: Limiting the Discretion of State Courts to Restructure the Internal Affairs of Small Business', *University of Colorado Law Review* 66: 881–920.

Ogus, AI (1998), 'Law-and-Economics from the Perspective of Law', in P Newman (ed), *The New Palgrave Dictionary of Economics and the Law*, London: Macmillan Reference Limited, ii. 486–91.

O'Kelley, CR jr (1992a), 'Opting in and out of Fiduciary Duties in Cooperative Ventures: Refining the So-called Coasean Contract Theory', *Washington University Law Quarterly* 70: 353–64.

—— (1992b), 'Filling Gaps in the Close Corporation Contract: A Transaction Cost Analysis', *Northwestern University Law Review* 87: 216–53.

Olson, M (1965), *The Logic of Collective Action*, Cambridge, Mass.: Harvard University Press.

O'Neill, TA (1998), 'Reasonable Expectations in Families, Businesses, and Family Businesses: A Comment on Rollock', *Indiana Law Journal* 73: 589–99.

Panunzi, F, Favero, CA, Giglio, SW, and Honorati, M (2006), 'The Performance of Italian Family Firms', ECGI—Finance Working Paper No 127/2006 (available at: <SSRN: http//SSRN.com/Abstract=918181>).

Paredes, TA (2004), 'A Systems Approach to Corporate Governance Reform: Why Importing U.S. Corporate Law isn't the Answer', *William and Mary Law Review* 45: 1055.

Parisi, F, Fon, V, and Ghei, N (2001), 'The Value of Waiting in Lawmaking', *European Journal of Law and Economics* 18: 131–48.

Partnoy, F and Thomas, RS (2007), 'Gap Filling, Hedge Funds, and Financial Innovation', in Y Fuchita and RE Litan (eds), *Brookings—Nomura Papers on Financial Services*, Washington D.C.: Brookings Institution Press.

Petska, T, Parisi, M, Luttrell, K, Davitian, L, and Scoffic, M (2005), *An Analysis of Business Organizational Structure and Activity from Tax Data*, Internal Revenue Service.

Pistor, K, and Xu, C (2003), 'Fiduciary Duty in Transitional Civil Law Jurisdictions: Lessons from the Incomplete Law Theory', in C Milhaupt (ed), *Global Markets, Domestic Institutions*, New York: Columbia University Press.

Pollack, MA (2003), *The Engines of European Integration: Delegation, Agency and Agenda Setting in the EU*, New York: Oxford University Press.

Posner, RA (1982), 'Economics, Politics, and the Reading of Statutes and the Constitution', *University of Chicago Law Review* 49: 263–91.

Rajan, RG and Zingales, L (2003), *The Great Reversal*, Chicago: University of Chicago Press.

Ramsay, I (1992), 'Corporate Law in the Age of Statutes', *Sydney Law Review* 14: 474–94.

Rasmussen, E (1994), 'Judicial Legitimacy as a Repeated Game', *Journal of Law, Economics, and Organization* 10: 63–82.

Ribstein, LE (1995), 'Statutory Forms for Closely Held Firms: Theories and Evidence from LLCs', *Washington University Law Quarterly* 73: 369–432.

—— (2001), 'The Evolving Partnership', *Journal of Corporation Law* 26: 819–54.

—— (2002), 'Lawyer Licensing and State Law Efficiency', Working Paper (Draft of March 2002).

—— (2004), 'Why Corporations?', *Berkeley Business Law Journal* 1: 183.

—— (2007), 'An Analysis of the Revised Uniform Limited Liability Company Act', Illinois Law and Economics Research Papers Series Research Paper No LE07-027.

—— and Kobayashi, BH (2001), 'Choice of Form and Network Externalities', *William and Mary Law Review* 43: 79–140.

—— (2007), 'The Non-Uniformity of Uniform Laws', University of Illinois Law and Economics Research Paper no LE07-030 (available at: <SSRN: http://ssrn.com/Abstract998281>).

Rock, EB, and Wachter, ML (1999), 'Waiting for the Omelet to Set: Match-Specific Assets and Minority Oppression in Close Corporations', *Journal of Corporation Law* 24: 913–48.

—— 'Corporate Law as a Facilitator of Self Governance', *Georgia Law Review* 34: 529–45.

Roe, MJ (2006), 'Legal Origins and Modern Stock Markets', ECGI Working Paper (available at: <SSRN: http://ssrn.com/Abstract908972>).

Sacco, R (1991), 'Legal Formants: A Dynamic Approach to Comparative Law', *American Journal of Comparative Law* 39: 1–34; 343–402.

Sahlman, WA (1990), 'The Structure and Governance of Venture-Capital Organizations', *Journal of Financial Economics* 27: 473–521.

Schlesinger, RB, Baade, HW, Herzog, PE, Wise, EM (1998), *Comparative Law: Cases-Text-Materials*, New York: Foundation Press.

Schön, W (2007), 'The Mobility of Companies in Europe and the Organizational Freedom of Company Founders', *European Company and Financial Law Review* 4: 122–46.

Schwarcz, S (2002), 'Lessons from Enron: The Use and Abuse of Special Purpose Entities in Corporate Structures', Working Paper Duke University Global Capital Markets Center.

Schwartz, A and Scott, RE (1995), 'The Political Economy of Private Legislatures', *University of Pennsylvania Law Review* 143: 595–654.

—— (2003), 'Contract Theory and the Limits of Contract Law' *Yale Law Journal* 113: 541–620.

Seibert, U (2006), 'Close Corporations—Reforming Private Company Law: European and International Perspectives', *European Business Organization Law Review* 8: 83–92.

Stevenson, SW (2001), 'The Venture Capital Solution to the Problem of Close Corporation Shareholder Fiduciary Duties', *Duke Law Journal* 51: 1139–78.

Stone Sweet, A, and McCown, M (2001), 'Path Dependence, Precedent, and Judicial Power', Paper prepared for delivery at the 2001 Annual Meeting of the American Political Science Association, San Francisco, California, 30 August–2 September.

Swiss Confederation (2003), 'Combating Money Laundering in Switzerland', (available at: <http://www.ebk.admin.ch/d/archiv/2003/20031030/m031030_02e.pdf.>).

Tagiuri, R, and Davis, J (1982), 'Bivalent Attributes of Family Firms', *Family Business Review* 9: 199–208.

Terra, B, and Wattel, P (2005), *European Tax Law*, The Hague: Kluwer Law International.

Thomas, RL (ed) (1992), *Company Law in Europe*, London: Butterworths.

Thompson, RB (1995), 'The Taming of Limited Liability Companies', *University of Colorado Law Review* 66: 921–46.

Tollison, RD (1988), 'Public Choice and Legislation', *Virginia Law Review* 74: 339–71.

Treasury/DTI (2003), *RIA on Disclosure of Beneficial Ownership of Unlisted Companies*, Consultation Document, July 2002, London: DTI (available at: <www.hm-treasury.gov.uk/mǒdia/E/O/beneficial_condoc.pdf>).

Urata, S, and Sasuya, I (2007), 'How Beneficial is Foreign Direct Investment for Developing Countries Finances and Development', Working Paper, June.

Van Duuren, TP, Portengen, HJ, Vermeulen EPM, and Bier, B (2006), *De vereenvoudigde BV: Preadvies van de Vereeniging 'Handelsrecht' 2006*, Deventer: Kluwer.

Ventoruzzo, M (2007), 'Cross-border Mergers, Change of Applicable Corporate Laws and Protection of Dissenting Shareholders: Withdrawal Rights under Italian Law', *European Company and Financial Law Review* 4: 47–75.

VentureOne (2008), *Outlook 2008* (available at: <www.ventureoneoutlook.dowjones.com/>).

Vermeulen, EPM (2003), *The Evolution of Legal Business Forms in Europe and the United States*, *Venture Capital, Joint Venture and Partnership Structures*, The Hague Kluwer Law International.

—— (2006), 'The Role of the Law in Developing Efficient Corporate Governance Frameworks', in OECD, *Corporate Governance of Non-listed Companies in Emerging Markets*, Paris: OECD Publishing.

Vestal, AW (1993), 'Fundamental Contractarian Error in the Revised Uniform Partnership Act of 1992', *Boston University Law Review* 73: 523–79.

Villalonga, B and Amit, R (2006), 'How Do Family Ownership, Control and Management Affect Firm Value?', *Journal of Financial Economics* 80: 385–41.

—— (2008, forthcoming), 'How Are US Family Firms Controlled?', *Review of Financial Studies*.

Villiers, C (1998), *European Company Law: Towards Democracy?*, Aldershot: Ashgate Dartmouth.

Ward, JL (2005), 'Governing Family Businesses', *E Journal USA*, (available at <http://usinfo.state.gov/journals/ites/0205/ijee/ward.htm>).

Watson, A (1974), *Legal Transplants: An Approach to Comparative Law*, Edinburgh: Scottisch Academic Press.

—— (1985), *The Evolution of Law*, Oxford: Basil Blackwell.

Williamson, OE (1985), *The Economic Institutions of Capitalism*, New York: The Free Press.

Wolf, C (2000), *Effective International Joint Venture Management*, New York: ME Sharpe.

Wolf, J (2007), 'Standards Delay May Hit SME Investment', *Financial Times*, October 1.

Woolcock, S. (1996), 'Competition among Rules in the Single European Market', in WW Bratton, JA McCahery, S Picciotto, and C Scott (eds), *International Regulatory Competition and Coordination: Perspectives on Economic Regulation in Europe and the United States*, Oxford: Clarendon Press, 289–321.

World Bank (2004), *Doing Business in 2004, Understanding Regulation*, Washington, D.C.: World Bank.

Wymeersch, E (2007), 'Is a Directive of Corporate Mobility Needed? ', *European Business Organization Law Review* 8': 161–9.

# Index